Lost Ships

The Discovery and Exploration of the Ocean's Sunken Treasure

Mensun Bound

SIMON &
SCHUSTER
EDITIONS

SIMON & SCHUSTER EDITIONS
1230 Avenue of the Americas
New York, NY 10020

SIMON & SCHUSTER EDITIONS is a trademark of Simon & Schuster Inc.

LOST SHIPS is a trademark of Zev Guber Productions Inc. and is used by permission.

Produced by The Prospect Group, Washington, D.C.
Designed by Toolbox Graphic Design, Washington, D.C.

Library of Congress Cataloging-in-Publication Data

Bound, Mensun.
    Lost ships : [the discovery and exploration of the ocean's sunken treasures] / Mensun Bound.
        1. Shipwrecks. 2. Treasure-trove. I. Title.
    G525.B763 1998
    910.4'52—dc21   98-36551
                                                                                      CIP

1 3 5 7 9 10 8 6 4 2

Manufactured in Canada

ISBN 0-684-85251-9

To Fethi Chelbi in Tunisia,

Peter Winterstein in Germany,

and Hector Bado, Sergio Pronczuk,

and Carlos Coirolo in Uruguay.

Without them, the work would not

have been possible.

ACKNOWLEDGMENTS

In writing this book and making the accompanying documentary films, I have become indebted to a number of people. In particular, it is a pleasure to acknowledge the help and inspiration I received from Matthew Wortman, Zev Guber, and Walter Ludwig. It was Matthew who initiated it all, Zev who framed and finessed it, and Walter who made it all work. Without them, there would be no *Lost Ships*, on film or on paper.

In the work on the Mahdia ship, one person stands out above all others; my friend and codirector, Fethi Chelbi, whose patience, wise counsel, and generosity of spirit made our time at Mahdia so enjoyable and archeologically rewarding. Others to whom I am grateful include Dr. Abdelaziz Daoulati and the officers of the Institut National de Patrimoine of Tunisia; Ben Younes Habib, the director of the Musée National du Bardo; the staff of the Département des Études d'Archéologie Sous-Marine; the director of the *bordj* at Mahdia; the tourist board of Mahdia; Peter Winterstein, Professor Christoph Börker, and the committee of DEGUWA; Dr. Gisela Hellenkemper-Sallies of the Rheinisches Landesmuseum, Bonn; Sumner Gerard and Kasref Sliem.

For the work in Uruguay, special thanks is owed to the divers who found the *Agamemnon* and *Salvador*, Hector Bado and Sergio Pronczuk and their associates Don Francisco von Kuhn, Carlos Coirolo, and Max Mainzer. Support for the work came from the Comisión del Patrimonio Histórico, Departamento de Arqueología (Jorje de Arteaga, Elianne Martinez, and Carmen Curbelo); the Ministry of Tourism (Benito Stern); the Ministry of the Interior (Washington Bado); and the University of Montevideo (Antonio Lezama Astigarraga). Essential help and technical aid came from the Uruguayan navy, in particular Captains Alberto Braeda, Ricardo Medina, Gerardo Cabot, and the Grupo de Buceo y Salvamento de la Armada, as well as the navy and prefectura at Punta del Este.

Other organizations and individuals to whom I am indebted include ANCAP, the Victoria Plaza Hotel, Scott Perry, Miguel Periera, Christine Anne Sarkis, Carlos Arielo, Pablo de la Fuente, and Omar Medina of the Malvin Maritime Museum.

Above all in Montevideo, I would of course like to express my thanks to the president of Uruguay, Julio Mario Sanguinetti, whose personal interest in the work led to its success.

It is impossible to thank all those who helped in the making of the three documentaries, but I cannot escape paying tribute to Heinz, Werner, and Ralph Bibo and Kurt Köhlbecker and their staff at Bibo TV in Germany. In the States I am deeply grateful for the advice and close assistance of Richard Wells and Gary Parker at The Learning Channel.

With regard to this book, it is a pleasure to record my gratitude to Alaister Rickets of St. Peter's College, Oxford, in whose library the book was largely written, as well as to the editors and designers who shaped its contents and appearance: Laura Foreman, Carl Posey, Marilyn Ludwig, Ellen Phillips, Becky Clark, John and Jean Yellowlees, and, from Toolbox Graphics DC, Brian Liu, Jason Faust, Greg Stadnyk, and J. Robbins. A special note of thanks is also due Bill Rosen and Sharon Gibbons at Simon & Schuster, primarily for their patience.

It is impossible to mention all of the team members by name, but I cannot overlook the contributions made by the chief divers and site supervisors: Habchi Abdessalam, Brian and Ann Smith, Tom Cockrell, Francis Pope, and Lorna Taylor. Others who also made important contributions include Heidi Guber, Mark Silk, Zena Holloway, Gary Kosak, Cay Hehner, Richard Marson, Tania Alexander, Jill Potterton, Yannis Costopoulos, Simon Stoddart, Christies of London, Klein Associates, and Gull Diving UK.

Heartfelt appreciation is extended to the veterans of the Battle of the River Plate who answered my questions with unfailing courtesy and patience: Kurt Diggins, Federico Rasenack, Günther Schroeder, Hans Ghann, and Rudolfo Dxierxawa of *Graf Spee*; George Deacon (whose photographs are featured prominently in the last chapter of this book), Eric Smith, and Ron Clover of the *Ajax*.

My final thanks go to the management committee of Oxford University MARE, in particular the chairman, Professor Sir John Boardman, and to the Master of St. Peter's College, Oxford, Dr. John Barron.

But above all I thank my wife, Joanna, who helped and encouraged me in my work on these wrecks just as she has on every wreck we have surveyed or excavated together over the past two decades.

—*Mensun Bound, June 1998*

Lost Ships

The Discovery and Exploration of the Ocean's Sunken Treasures

Mensun Bound

Introduction

Introduction 7

Galley of the Gods

I. Galley of the Gods 10

The story of one of the most important archeological sites in the world—
full of priceless treasure from Sulla's sack of Athens 2,000 years ago.
The Mahdia wreck was explored twice before Mensun Bound's
expeditions—once by Jacques Cousteau—but both times lost.

Ghost of Trafalgar

II. Ghost of Trafalgar 56

Mensun and his team explore *Agamemnon*, Admiral Horatio Nelson's first ship of the
line. Nelson was the greatest naval commander in history, "the embodiment
of sea power" in the wars against Napoleonic France, and this
ship was his favorite, alongside him at Trafalgar.

Dive for the Graf Spee

III. Dive for the Graf Spee 110

The exploration of this wreck by Mensun Bound and his team completes the
story of one of Nazi Germany's most successful warships. The "pocket
battleship" *Graf Spee* was one of Hitler's secret weapons,
captained by one of Germany's most honorable men.

The seas that surround us hide an infinity of human secrets. In those vast deeps, a thousand generations of sailors lie dead with their ships, their vanishing bones surrounded by the accoutrements of war, the treasures of trade, the gear and tackle and trim of life twenty centuries ago, or ten, or five, or three. Herman Melville, a sailor himself, called the rolling waters a potter's field, a graveyard for the unknown, where millions of shades and shadows lie dreaming, rocked in the sea currents like slumberers in their beds.

From time to time over the millennia, the sea gave up hints of its secrets, reluctantly surrendering to fishermen's nets a waterlogged timber, a coral-encrusted sculpture, or a tall amphora that had held the wine of the ancients. Only in the last fifty years, however, have archeologists been able to approach lost ships as they would approach tombs or towns, examining, mapping, dating, and retrieving objects to piece together an image of life long gone. Underwater archeology is a new branch of the science.

It is a discipline with distinctive appeal and value. A drowned ship provides a

INTRODUCTION

different picture of the past than does the ordered paraphernalia of a tomb or the layered detritus of a long-lived-in town. The ship is like those rare land sites—Pompeii being the most famous example—where everyday life in all its complexity suddenly and catastrophically ended. Its artifacts are the motley that people kept around them as a matter of course: tools and equipment; articles for trade, for cooking, for worship, for entertainment; even keepsakes of no more than sentimental significance. If the archeologist can understand them, he has a good chance of building a vivid picture of life as people lived it at a certain moment— the moment when the ship went down.

From the perspective of adulthood, my interest in maritime archeology now seems inevitable—almost not of my choosing. I spent my childhood in the Falkland Islands, best known for the brief war they occasioned between Britain and Argentina in 1982.

In the 1950s, however, the Falklands were among the most remote frontiers of the waning British Empire, two large islands and hundreds of islets huddled together in the South Atlantic. The islands were primarily rolling tundra—the windy climate discouraged trees—inhabited by two thousand people and many thousand sheep. All around and in between, the cold sea roared and slammed the shore.

Bleak or not, it was a boy's paradise, filled with adventure. Like most islanders, we half lived on the water. I sailed with my far-from-reputable Uncle Cracks, the most notorious seaman in the islands and probably the last true pirate. He used his schooner for the appropriation of sheep, fencing, or whatever else took his fancy. I went along, learned to sail—this was important because I was sometimes the only sober or even conscious person on board—and I learned to respect the sea.

The islands lie 500 miles downwind of Cape Horn, and the skeletons of the square riggers wrecked in the Cape's famous storms loomed on our beaches, their huge ribs and spars preserved by the chill, unchanging climate. These phantoms from the Great Age of Sail captured my imagination. I could see one of them from my bedroom window—she was called the *Charles Cooper*.

The sea and its ghosts pervaded those islands at the end of the world. There was, after all, little else. Rare Antarctic expeditions used the Falklands as a staging post; once a month a mailboat arrived from Uruguay. Four times a year, a cargo ship brought supplies from England.

Among the supplies were books. Falklanders, hungry for news of abroad, were voracious readers. My parents, for instance, belonged to several book clubs, so our house was always full of reading matter. Among the books we had was one published in 1953, Jacques Cousteau's *The Silent World*.

It opened up another world for me. Even its chapter titles spoke of strange adventures: "Menfish," "The Drowned Museum," "Monsters We Have Met." Cousteau, the pioneer of underwater exploration, wrote about warmer, clearer seas than ours, and older ships—pre-Christian ships, ships of the classical world. "The argosy was a museum of classic sculpture," Cousteau wrote of one. "The divers found marble statuary and bronze figures scattered across the floor as though they had been deck cargo, strewn as the ship side-slipped down like a falling leaf."

He was writing about the Mahdia ship, sunk off the coast of Tunisia in the first century B.C. I was ten when I read his book, and I read with electric attention. What were the bronze figures? Whose ship was it? Where was she going? How did she sink? As you will read in the first section of this book, I am one of the lucky few men whose childhood fascinations were fulfilled in adulthood. But, before that could happen, there was much preparation.

Cousteau's vivid images stayed with me for years. The Falklands idyll ended when I was eleven and my parents sent me to the British International School, an antipodean version of England's public schools in Montevideo. I left in 1969 with a good record but without a diploma and certainly without any money. Not that this worried me: I signed on as an ordinary seaman on the tramp steamer *Darwin*, working the South Atlantic routes. When the *Darwin* was sold, in 1971, I jumped ship. To my parents' horror, I then hitchhiked from the southern tip of South America to New York City, where I spent my first night in Central Park.

It was time to get serious. I had a good school record and eventually I was provided a term-by-term scholarship to Fairleigh Dickinson University: all I had to do was perform.

Because I was studying ancient history—shades of Cousteau—this wasn't too difficult. The classical world enthralled me. I went on to graduate study in classical archeology and ancient art at Rutgers, and then to Oxford. In between, I had a research assistantship in Greek pottery at the Metropolitan Museum of Art.

Odd jobs paid for graduate school. I loaded freight in New Jersey and drove a cab in New York City, work that, as it turned out, taught me skills—forklift operation and aggressive driving—useful in archeology. By the late 1970s, I was at Oxford and directing excavations in the Mediterranean.

꒰ꙩ꒱

Tolstoy once wrote, "There are only two stories in all of literature—a man takes a journey, a stranger comes to town." Like nothing else I can imagine, searching for and exploring shipwrecks—lost ships—embodies both these stories. For me, the beauty of maritime archeology lies not only in the artifacts, whether ancient Greek statues at Mahdia or the powerful engines of war that we retrieved from the *Agamemnon* and *Graf Spee*, but in the lives and stories of those on board. Here again, the unique "snapshot" nature of maritime archeology makes the task of extracting the stories easier.

When I begin an exploration, each ship—no matter how storied—is a stranger. Her captains and men, no matter how celebrated in history books, become truly known, truly *real*, only when I can come near to seeing what they saw and can place my hands where theirs once were.

Man's curiosity and desire to experience the adventure and danger of the past, together with our need to know the truth of history—all of these are good reasons for us to explore lost ships.

—MENSUN BOUND, JUNE 1998

Filming the columns.
Inset: Statue of a seated youth whose head, legs, and one hand have been badly eroded by worm action.

Opposite: Fethi Chelbi.

The Mediterranean is a body of water like no other. It is the world's largest inland sea; its shores have seen more empires come and go, and more civilizations rise and fall, than any other on earth. Two thousand years ago, it was the center of the Roman world, "Mare Nostrum"—our sea—and upon its waters galleys carried the cargo of empire. The sea would claim many of those vessels for itself. This is the story of one of them, a ship of Rome that went down with the glories of Greece.

Her original name was lost in antiquity; she is now known simply by the name of the town on the bit of land nearest to her submerged bones: Mahdia, on Tunisia's Cap d'Afrique—the old Barbary Coast. Since I first read of her as a boy, I have been fascinated by the Mahdia ship and the fabulous cargo she carried with her to the grave, over a hundred feet deep.

GALLEY OF THE GODS

"Whoever

touches this

wreck becomes

part of it."

—Fethi Chelbi

My involvement in the Mahdia legend began in February 1993, when I received an urgent phone call from my friend Peter Winterstein in Germany. He needed to see me soon, on a mysterious matter that he would only discuss in person. We agreed to meet at Manchester University, where I was scheduled to lecture in a few days. I wondered what all the secrecy was about.

I had met Peter a couple of years earlier at an archeological conference I had organized in London. During a break, he told me about two wrecks that he had found while on holiday in the Mediterranean. Unlike many amateur maritime archeologists, he had documented his find with drawings, photographs, and videos, and was eager to see the project pursued at a professional level. I promised to contact the archeological authorities in the country concerned, and, whether or not my intervention helped, those authorities went on to survey and partially excavate one of the sites. Sadly typical for such situations, Peter was not invited to join the project, which was all he had ever

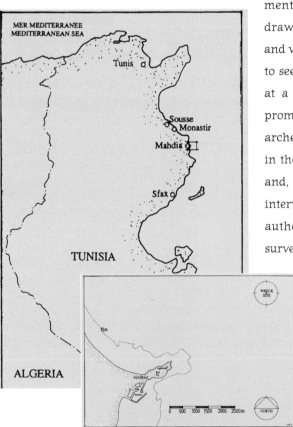

MER MEDITERRANEE
MEDITERRANEAN SEA

Tunis

Sousse
Monastir

Mahdia

Sfax

TUNISIA

ALGERIA

asked in return. Somewhat disenchanted, he decided to start a maritime archeological society in Germany, the German acronym for which was DEGUWA.

When we met in Manchester, Peter explained that the National Museum of Tunisia, the Bardo, and the Rheinisches Landesmuseum in Bonn were collaborating to preserve the Mahdia's treasures, which were deteriorating because there were no adequate conservation techniques available at the time of their recovery. In the course of the program, it had been decided that the wreck should be relocated and properly surveyed with a view toward establishing what was left of the famous ship and her precious cargo.

There was a maritime diving unit in the Tunisian archeological service, but it was not at that time fully functional, and could not undertake the task by itself. They asked DEGUWA, but Peter felt that his organization lacked the experience needed to take on a project of such complexity. Peter was doing me the honor of asking me to direct the mission.

I had never in my life been offered anything that I wanted more.

As a boy born and brought up in the Falkland Islands, forgotten dots of empire at the very bottom of the world to the east of Cape Horn, I had unknowingly been preparing for what would become my life's work. My interests centered on three things: the sea, ships, and books.

I can remember from the age of nine or so, going out with my Uncle Cracks Davis on his schooner. He was the most notorious sailor in the Falklands, and certainly the Islands' last true pirate. From my earliest days, I was fascinated by the schooners and the hulks of the great 19th-century square-riggers —"Cape Horners"—that dotted the Falklands' shores. The latter were all ships that had been hammered upon the anvil of Cape Horn. Limping before the wind, they headed for the Falklands, where many were abandoned as unseaworthy.

When I wasn't sailing or roaming the shores, I read. Everyone read; our remote location provided little else in the way of diversion. There was no television, and radio was available for just a few hours in the evening. I was the bookish child of bookish parents; I remember my father and mother reading nuggets from the *Oxford Book of Quotations* to each other over the dinner table.

My own particular literary favorites, not surprisingly, were about ships. Lord Nelson was one of my heroes; Jacques Cousteau was another. An English translation of Cousteau's masterpiece, *The Silent World*, had been published in 1953, the year I was born. It was a book I would return to again and again—I was fascinated by the great explorer of the deep, the coinventor of the aqualung, the man who gave us the freedom to see for ourselves the wonders of the world that covers most of the surface of our planet.

I was mesmerized by the stories and pictures of his adventures: the attempts to find out how deep he could go, the exotic fish he saw, the drowned caves and canyons he explored, his encounters with giant lobsters and sharks; there were even ghoulish photographs of drowned airmen still in their parachutes. And it was from Cousteau that I first learned about the wreck full of statues off a town on the coast of Tunisia with the wonderful name of Mahdia. I was never quite sure where Tunisia was, but it held for me all the spellbinding power of the Arabian Nights. I remember trying the town's name out loud. Where was the inflection? Was it a soft, labial *d* or was it a hard *d*? It was wonderful however you said it.

Using the new aqualung technology, Cousteau and his crew had visited the Mahdia wreck in 1948. Even though he was not an archeologist, Cousteau's work on the Mahdia ship contributed materially to the birth of the new discipline of maritime archeology. In fact, the Mahdia ship was the first wreck from antiquity to be explored and studied using the aqualung.

Upper left: Long before he was a television star, Jacques-Yves Cousteau, together with his friend Emile Gagnan, invented the aqualung. To demonstrate the potential importance of his new apparatus to underwater science, he went searching for the Mahdia ship.

Below: Cousteau's book *The Silent World* contains an account of his dive on the Mahdia site, which inspired my childhood interest in shipwrecks.

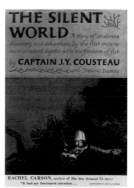

THE SILENT WORLD A story of undersea discovery and adventure, by the first men to roam at weird depths with the freedom of fish
by CAPTAIN J.Y. COUSTEAU with Frédéric Dumas

RACHEL CARSON, author of *The Sea Around Us* says:
"It had my fascinated attention…"

Above: Excavations beside the *Bordj* have proven that, even before the Romans, the Phoenicians were at Mahdia. This harbor, hewn from the bedrock, is typical of Phoenician construction.
Right, top: Greek sponge divers of today are outfitted much as they would have been in Merlin's time, in a Siebe-type suit and heavy boots.
Bottom: Fishermen repairing nets at Mahdia. In some respects, not much has changed since Merlin's day.

Opposite: This 1882 engraving depicts a hard-hat dive suit of the type worn by Greek sponge divers.
Inset: Alfred Merlin (1876-1965) the French archeologist behind the Mahdia recoveries. He first learned of the wreck in 1907, then, in 1908, 1909, 1910, 1911 and 1913, led expeditions to the site.

But Cousteau was not the first man of our century to see the Mahdia ship with his own eyes, as she lay in her 2,000-year-old grave on the ocean bed. That man was not an archeologist either, nor a professional explorer, nor a scientist of any kind: he was a simple Greek diver from a tiny island in the Dodecanese archipelago who had ventured along the Barbary Coast in a small wooden sailing boat locally known as a *caique*. He and his shipmates were in search of sponges.

THE SPONGE DIVERS

The Mediterranean sponge industry is now all but dead, but at the turn of the 20th century, entire fleets would set out in their *caiques* for the sponge harvest.

Before the Industrial Revolution, a diver would go down naked, holding his breath for up to three minutes while he groped around for sponges. Around the mid-19th century, though, Augustus Siebe's revolutionary "hard-hat" diving gear reached the Greek islands, and a "gold rush" for sponges began. Whole families were involved; waterfront houses were converted into warehouses; villages grew wealthy. But sponge-diving was

perhaps the most dangerous occupation in the world.

By modern standards, divers' equipment was primitive. The suit was made from tanned twill and rubber, with vulcanized rubber cuffs and collar to make it watertight at the wrists and neck. A metal corselet, or breastplate, went on over the shoulders, and it was to this that the great round 35-pound tinned-copper helmet was attached. Thick plate-glass windows with lead seals allowed the diver to see where he was going and what he was doing. Heavy boots and 40-pound weights on the chest and back helped keep him upright and stable.

To breathe, a diver relied on air from a hand-operated pump on the surface. Air entered his helmet through a non-return inlet valve; an outlet valve allowed the diver to control the amount of air in his suit and, thus, its buoyancy. A lifeline, used to haul the diver up, also provided a means of communication via a prearranged code of pulls and jerks: one pull for "How are you doing?"; one pull back for "OK." Two pulls to the surface signified "More air," and repeated jerks meant "Get me up fast!"

Divers had no knowledge of decompression sickness—the bends. They dived deep and stayed down long. One in three was dead or crippled before reaching marriageable age. Even years later, when I was on the Dodecanese as a student, it was still not uncommon in the waterfront cafes to see men who had been crippled or paralyzed as a result of the bends. Once, during a festival, I saw an unusual dance—more a shuffle really—I was told it was the "bent diver's dance."

But those who survived might return to the surface with more than just sponges. In 1900, a Symiot diver off the tiny Aegean island of Antikythera saw what he thought were human bodies emerging from the sand. The terrified man surfaced at once, gibbering about human forms with their flesh eaten away. Unperturbed, his captain, Dimitris

Kondos, suited up and went down to see for himself.

In a few moments, he too was back, but with a life-sized arm made of bronze. More discoveries followed. It is unclear whether Kondos's crew tried to sell their finds or reported them to the authorities, but soon Kondos and his boat were back at Antikythera, along with high-level officials and staff from the University of Athens. Their finds included a number of bronzes, marble pieces—many badly damaged by marine borers—a gold brooch depicting the god Eros, pottery, amphorae, and tiles.

Within the decade, an even more remarkable salvage would take place, this time off the Tunisian coast of North Africa, directly out to sea from the ancient town of Mahdia.

MERLIN

The likelihood that the cargo of a vessel like that of the Mahdia ship, once found, should ever have been saved for posterity was remote—but saved it was. Over a half dozen summers, enough works of art were recovered to fill five rooms of the Bardo Museum in Tunis. And it was all thanks to a Frenchman named Alfred Merlin.

Born in Orleans in 1876, young Merlin brought to his explorations a solid foundation in academic study. With degrees in history and geography behind him, he had gone on to specialize in ancient numismatics and epigraphy (coinage and inscriptions) before completing a doctorate.

While in his early 20s, he joined an archeological mission to the French protectorate of Tunisia. There, he conducted excavations at Dougga, one of the nation's most famous Roman sites, a great inland city of honey-colored stone on the rim of a great valley with breathtaking views. In a few years, he would become the country's director of antiquities, with responsibility for the Bardo Museum. In addition, he authored several volumes of scholarly research. At a relatively young age, Alfred Merlin enjoyed an enviable reputation as a learned aesthete, an outstanding scholar, and an able field archeologist.

The tale concerning Merlin's first encounter with the Mahdia wreck is hazy, and his own account is vague (I suspect deliberately so). I have heard various versions of the story from people who were privy to the internal politics surrounding it, including Cousteau and his friend and diving comrade Frederic Dumas. Did someone tell Merlin of the sponge divers' find, and perhaps show him a statuette? Or did he by chance spot one the items in the famous *souks*, or bazaars, of Tunis? If indeed Merlin did spot something in a market stall, there can be no doubt that he possessed the level of knowledge and critical

judgment necessary to recognize it for what it was, as well as to appreciate its potential significance to archeology.

When I met Jacques Cousteau in the late 1980s, we spoke at some length about Mahdia. He admitted that there had been some tension between him and Merlin over Cousteau's work at Mahdia, and that cordial relations between the two were not reestablished until the late 1950s (which may explain why Cousteau was not overly generous to Merlin in his writings).

Despite what he had written in *The Silent World*, Cousteau did state that Merlin himself had told him that his first knowledge of the wreck came from spotting some of the artifacts in the *souks*. As I say, there were many stories. Nevertheless, in the full knowledge that I may be perpetuating a myth, let me tell the story as it came to me:

It all began one day in 1907 when Merlin, strolling through the *souks* of Tunis on his way to work, happened to notice in one of the stalls a small bronze statue partially covered with marine deposits.

It isn't difficult to imagine the scene; the great *souks* of Tunis are not so different now from what they were in Merlin's day, or indeed from what they were several hundred years before that. As you leave the traffic-congested avenues of the modern city and pass through the grand Bab el-Bahar (bazaar gate), you enter another world—that of the ancient *medina*, or market. It's a world of narrow, barrel-vaulted flagstone alleys, side lanes, curved archways, and mysterious, ornately decorated wooden doorways.

Once beyond the Bab, you are in a world that in spirit and appearance is almost medieval—cars, Western suits, and modern technology do not penetrate. The bazaars are full of exotic fruits, spices, sweetmeats, cut glass, leather goods, carpets, and caftans. Individual stalls are also known as "souks," and each *souk* has its own specialty: the gold and silver *souks* offer bracelets, brooches, and rings; what was once the slave *souk* now markets small, colored vials of scent. There are also, of course, the tourist stalls selling pottery, crystallized desert stones, hand-hammered metalwork, and all manner of trinkets.

Everywhere there are coffee shops where old men in long cotton *djellabas* sit, talk, smoke water pipes, and play cards or dominoes. As you leave the bustle of the main corridors and enter the even narrower passageways and back alleys where the children play, you get a glimpse through open doorways of the simple life behind the walls. It reminds you that the *souks* are not there for the delectation of tourists; they are a vital part of the city and a way of life that goes back for centuries.

Now, imagine the 31-year-old Alfred Merlin strolling into that raucous, fragrant warren of narrow stony alleys. His eye falls on the ancient little statue; he recognizes it as an original, from the late Hellenistic period.

Anxious not to betray his excitement, he lets his eyes roam around the stall; he touches one object, then another; he takes his time. At last he reaches for the little figure.

It is not only its age that has him transfixed. Antiquities are for sale almost anywhere in the *souks*—illegally, but the laws are not energetically enforced. It is the outstanding technical and artistic merit of the piece, and its extreme rarity, that mesmerize him.

Feigning indifference, he commences a casual conversation with an old man—we are told his name was Ibrahim—seated on a stool in the doorway. "Where did the statue come from?" Merlin asks. Whether through coercion and threats or the promise of a reward, he extracts the information he wants: The statue came from a shipwreck, found by Greek sponge divers just off the coast at Mahdia.

That very same day, Merlin set off for Mahdia on a mule to try to find the divers.

THE MERLIN CAMPAIGNS

At that time, the town of Mahdia was little more than a fishing village situated on a tiny finger of land in the Gulf of Gabes. It lies roughly between the cities of Sousse and Sfax, about a hundred miles from Tunis. It is a town with little to recommend it

Below, top and bottom: There are conflicting stories of how Merlin came to be aware of the treasures at Mahdia. The most common one was re-created for the documentary film.

Opposite: In the *souks* of Tunis—"a world that in spirit and appearance is almost medieval—cars, Western suits, and modern technology do not penetrate."

Tunis, 1907

apart from a good harbor, an imposing Bab, and a small and rather nondescript *medina*. The houses were whitewashed cube-like constructions, with colored doors. If not for the mosques and the dress of its inhabitants, it might have passed for a Greek island village.

But this impression would be deceptive. Mahdia was a town with a big history.

In the 10th century, it had been the center of the Fatimid Empire, named after a descendant of Fatima, daughter of the prophet Mohammed. The town itself took its name from El Mahdi (He Who Is Directed by God). The Mahdi aimed to take control of the entire Islamic world, and very nearly succeeded. At their peak, the Fatimids would control not only most of North Africa, the Red Sea coast, and part of Syria; they also struck into the margins of Europe.

For several hundred years, Mahdia would remain one of the Mediterranean's most formidable strongholds, guarded by high walls, now in ruins, and a great citadel called the Bordj el Kebir.

During its period of greatness, Mahdia withstood numerous sieges by European Christians, crusaders who were intent on converting or destroying the infidels. Later, as a pirate stronghold, it reached a colorful peak in the 16th century, when the famous pirate Dragut made it the headquarters from which he and his ships ranged all over the Christian north, ravaging islands and coastal communities. In 1550, Spain took the town, withdrawing four years later after demolishing its great walls. After this, apart from occasional raids by Spain or the Knights of Malta, Mahdia became nothing more ferocious than a peaceful fishing port.

Surely Merlin, who had a taste for the more recondite corners of Mediterranean history, would have been familiar with these events, and, as an archeologist, he must have reflected on them as he rode into Mahdia that summer day in 1907, and saw the great Bordj and the remnants of those once-massive defensive walls.

He was in luck; the divers who had discovered his statue were there. I have not been able to determine whether the fleet was in the area now occupied by the modern fishing port, or the small Fatimid port below the

Bordj. I suspect it was the latter, in which case Merlin would have ridden beneath the citadel walls and down along the paths through the cemetery at the end of the promontory.

The Greeks would have been quiet and suspicious at first, as divers are to this day when talking about their wrecks. But a combination of threats of prosecution and promises of reward must have loosened their tongues, and soon they were telling Merlin how, in June, they had found the wreck.

The bare-bones account of the events at Mahdia is not very different from that of the earlier discovery at Antikythera: A diver returning to the surface had seen a tightly packed group of cylindrical shapes, which he at first took to be great cannons lying on the sand. The next man, sent to investigate, had returned with a bronze statuette in his arms. Although the record is not clear, it is likely that it was a satyr or Priapus figure, and that this was the item that Merlin had first seen in the *souks* in Tunis. The diver who had retrieved it breathlessly reported that between and around the great cylinders (which were of stone and therefore could not be gun barrels) were more statues, some near life size.

But, the captain told Merlin, there was nothing left; the divers had taken them all.

Merlin immediately realized the significance of what he had heard. A cargo of statues by ancient masters! One of the greatest archeological finds of all time! He must have been in a fever of excitement; this, by far, was the biggest event in his professional life.

He was a good archeologist and he knew it. Still a young man, he was already in charge of the Tunisian Antiquities Service. He had some safe, if rather uninspired, publications to his credit, and he had earned the respect of those colleagues whom he respected. After a few more years in the colonies, he could look forward to the directorship of one of France's better regional museums, or an appointment to the faculty of a prestigious university; perhaps he might even head one of his country's great institutes at Rome, Athens, or in the Near East.

Now he had blundered into something that might, for better or worse, dramatically alter his professional fortunes. He could hold on to what he had, or he could gamble on this site. If the latter, then he would have to mobilize a lot of equipment, people, and,

Above: **The Sidi Jabar lighthouse and the cemetery that today sprawls across the tip of Cap d'Afrique in beautiful disorder. The ruins in the foreground are all that remain of the great defenses demolished by Charles V in the 1550s.**

Opposite: **The Bordj el Kabir, Mahdia. The precise origins of the Bordj, or hilltop citadel, are unclear, but a plaque above the inner door is inscribed: "This blessed fort was completed with the help of God—may his name be praised—by the endeavors of his servant Abu Abdallah Mohammed Pasha—may God give him triumph—on 6.IX.1595."**

above all, money. If the captain was correct and there was nothing left, Merlin would be left looking stupid, very stupid—and then, just as now, archeologists have long and cruel memories.

Back in Tunis, he made up his mind. Taking the bull by the horns, he telegraphed the internationally esteemed French Academy in Paris, describing in glowing terms some of the fabulous works brought to the surface by the Greek sponge divers. In particular, he waxed enthusiastic about two of the finds: a head of Dionysus, the Greek god of wine, and the statue of an "adolescent" whom he would later identify as Eros.

The head of Dionysus topped a long oblong shaft with square bosses instead of arms. The curious form was known as a herm, after earlier models that usually bore the head of Hermes, the messenger god who was also the protector of travelers and homes. Herms, originally used to mark crossroads and land sacred to Hermes, were later commonplace at street corners, sanctuaries, and public places and were used to mark boundaries and guard doors and gateways.

The most exciting aspect of the Mahdia herm was that it bore an inscription identifying it as the work of an artist known as Boethos of Chalcedon, who had been mentioned in the writings of Pliny and others, but from whom no other undisputed works had come down. For an archeologist, it was rather like knowing of Tintoretto or Velasquez by name and reputation only, and then sud-

denly finding one of their signed paintings by accident.

Later, Merlin would describe the Eros statue as "Cupid victorious after an archery contest. He has just alighted and his wings are outspread; his right hand . . . indicates the newly-won crown [and] in his left he holds his bow, now broken." In its balance, harmony and realism, the Mahdia Eros represents a level of perfection in the representation of the human form that would not be seen again until the High Renaissance.

Among other objects raised by the Greek sponge divers were two large bronze cornice pieces displaying busts of Ariadne and

Above: **Bronze herm of Dionysus. The insets from the eyes have been lost. It dates to the middle of the second century B.C. and was one of a number of "antiques" that the Mahdia ship was carrying.**

the young Dionysus, believed to have come from a votive offering in the form of a ship's prow.

In a report to the French Academy, Merlin deliberately sought to tantalize his colleagues: "One would love to know . . . why these works of art, these columns, and these fragments of marble are crammed together pell-mell . . . on a 40-meter-deep seabed more than seven kilometers from the coast. Are we in the presence of a submerged town or a sunken ship?"

The Academy was sufficiently intrigued to take the bait, and the next year, 1908, found Merlin and a colleague, Louis Poinssot, in Mahdia, preparing for the first season of official recovery work. Merlin had received Academy support, government funds, and a grant from a French archeological foundation. For a team, he had some navy divers as well as a number of Greek sponge divers, and for boats he had use of the navy tug *Cyclops*, two torpedo boats, and the *caiques* belonging to the sponge divers.

To an inexperienced sailor, that sponge boat must have been an instrument of torture. At a conference in Tunis three years later, Merlin gave a vivid account of a trip to the site:

Leaving port we go along the shore of the promontory; we leave the town far behind, passing first the imposing rocky mass of the Casbah and then the lighthouse. With a good wind we still have a further hour of navigation; without a breeze, which is not very often, it would take two or three hours. . . . Any calm that reigns soon generates a nasty surprise from a sea that Sallust described as "terrible," and which well merits that name. The voyage is most certainly not to be recommended to anybody without sea-legs, especially on a boat like a *caique*, which is extremely unstable. On days of bad weather it is pointless to put out, for as you leave the shelter of the coast the gusts seize you, and you cannot fight it.

The first problem was finding the wreck site. Not understanding ships or the sea, Merlin had thought it would be easy. "The Greeks," he wrote, "had simply said that the antiquities had been discovered approximately seven kilometers north-east of Mahdia." They had assured him that they could find it again. But, after several days, the captain of the

Opposite, right: **Bronze of Eros (or Agon), recovered by Merlin, at the Bardo Museum, Tunis. An incorrect reconstruction of the statue's hip by early restorers led to many arguments in the art world.**

Below: **Here, one of Merlin's divers returns to the surface. Another diver, his lead-booted foot slung over the bow, is ready to go down next.**

Below, top and middle: Merlin's divers faced immense hazards during his five campaigns on the wreck; some died in agony from the bends, others were left paralyzed.
Bottom: The caiques were unable to lift the columns, so Merlin brought in larger vessels with heavy-lifting capability.

sponge divers was forced to admit that he did not actually know where the wreck was—all he could remember was that it was well out to sea from the citadel.

Merlin went apoplectic with rage and stormed about the deck like the Queen of Hearts. He had reason for concern: his whole career was on the line. He had badgered many important people, including government ministers, admirals, and academicians; he had accepted considerable sums of money, most of which had now been spent on accommodations, equipment, salaries, and boats. He had no choice but to continue.

He sought help from some local residents, including the Abbé de Smet, a priest who had been with the Greeks when they recovered the treasures the previous year. Finally, after scouring the area for eleven days, one of the divers came up to report that he had seen something like "a series of large cannon regularly laid out and partially buried in the sand." The "cannon" were coral-encrusted marble columns; the site, of course, was the Mahdia wreck.

Merlin was much concerned about losing the ship again. One of the captains explained to him the age-old system of taking visual transits; that is to say, siting points by locating them relative to two or more pairs of landmarks on the shore. To find the spot again, one simply relocates the exact place where the lines of sight cross. When the landmarks are well defined, the angles wide and the site is close to land, the system is remarkably precise. But the Mahdia wreck is a long way out to sea, and from it the coast is nothing but a narrow ribbon of land shrouded in mist. The landmarks are tiny and unclear, and the angles between the transits are narrow. Taking visual transits is not an accurate system for locating sites such as the Mahdia wreck.

Nevertheless, Merlin attempted to do so. One segment of the ruined city walls is a distinctively shaped pile of rubble that Merlin called "the broken tooth." The tooth, aligned with a corner of the Bordj, would serve as one of his transits. He took two more—one a windmill aligned with an olive grove; the other a lone tree aligned with a small hill.

Merlin never really comprehended the navigational complexities of locating, and later relocating, an underwater site so far from land. Even after several years, his descriptions were confusing and sometimes contradictory.

But locating the Mahdia ship was only the first of Merlin's problems. His notes and reports told a dismal tale of rough seas, night storms, lost marker buoys, and the dangers and hardships faced by the team.

Yet despite the problems, he would follow the 1908 campaign with further explorations in 1909, 1910, 1911, and 1913 (due to a lack of funding, no campaign was mounted in 1912). By 1914, the clouds of war were gathering over Europe, and there was little enthusiasm and less money for such diversions as shipwrecks and excavations. Merlin's involvement with the Mahdia ship was, for all intents and purposes, over. But, thanks to him, the Bardo Museum, and indeed our knowledge and understanding of the ancient art world, was infinitely richer.

THE MYSTERY OF THE MAHDIA TREASURE

When one attempts a critical assessment of Merlin's work at the Mahdia site, it is necessary to remember certain facts about the man and his times.

First, he was an "objects" person; he was always more interested in the items the ship carried rather than the ship itself, its construction, and the lives and society of those on board. But this is typical of the period, and we must remember also that, in Merlin's case, he had to please his benefactors with glamorous finds if he was to keep their imaginations alive and their purse strings loosened.

It is also important to remember that underwater exploration was then in its infancy. There were few professional divers, except for a handful of naval men, salvage experts,

and, of course, sponge fishermen such as those who discovered the Mahdia wreck. For a nondiver such as Merlin, it was almost impossible to conceive of what the undersea world was like. Then as now, even divers had problems. No two of them ever see anything the same way; the nature of the environment, coupled with the druglike effects of depth on the mind, prevents them from seeing or remembering with clarity. The deep-water seabed is a world of shadows and bent realities, not unlike a hall of mirrors. Water is not our environment, and our senses are not designed for immersion.

Merlin, with no understanding of the constraints under which divers must labor, would, without realizing it, have been trying to make sense of a complex site from inherently defective secondhand infomation. This, together with the workings of his own imagination, would inevitably have produced something in his

Below: **Mensun beside the "broken tooth" in a clip from the film.**

Above, top and middle: The columns recovered by Merlin were brought into Mahdia suspended from the bow; they were then transferred to a small harbor-barge for transport ashore. *Bottom:* Lifting one of the three columns Merlin's team recovered, two of which are in the Bardo. (The other serves as a humble bus stop in Mahdia—see page 44.)

Opposite: Bronze statuette of Hermes the messenger god (c. 100 B.C.).

mind that was far from the reality. In projects of this nature, the only thing that works, and which you must have before all else, is a clear, scientifically prepared site plan—and this Merlin did not have.

The unsung hero of the Mahdia campaigns was Merlin's lifelong friend and collaborator, Louis Poinssot, who was often left in charge when Merlin had to go to Tunis. It was during one of those absences that Poinssot, working with one of the Greek divers, produced a map of the site—which Merlin would later dismiss as "a thoroughly curious document." Thanks to Poinssot's son Claude, also an archeologist, I have seen the map. It had been carefully prepared, and although obviously more primitive than the results we can achieve today, it is plausible. However, it did not accord well with Merlin's descriptions—was Merlin perhaps so dismissive of it because he feared that it might reflect badly on what he had previously written? And, if so, that it might have an adverse effect on his sponsors, who were wondering if the site justified their continued support?

Whatever their shortcomings, Merlin's expeditions produced a wealth of artifacts—and a multitude of questions. The most obvious objects were columns, bases and capitals of mismatched sizes and styles. The marble had come from quarries in the Attica region—around Athens—but the mixture of styles and sizes remained a puzzle.

But also, of course, there were the works of art. The bronze and marble statues of maenads, satyrs, gods, and goddesses included wonderfully contrasting busts of a warlike Athena and a dreamy, flirtatious Aphrodite, the goddess of love and beauty. With respect to the latter, Merlin noted that, oddly, the right side of her upper body had been purposely cut away. There were androgynous figures, or hermaphrodites, that reflected the Greco-Roman fascination with beings who feature the primary and secondary sexual characteristics of both genders. Then there were grotesque portrayals of dwarves, dancers, musicians, and actors.

Merlin's final campaign took place in 1913. Funding by then was neither plentiful nor easy to obtain; one reason was that he was finding fewer works of art, another was the increasing political tension in Europe. It was during this two-month season that Merlin raised the two great columns that can be seen today in the Bardo. Merlin made no secret that he resented the time and money that was spent in their recovery, for he was desperate for more statues. He ordered the divers back to one of the richest and earliest-explored areas of the site and immediately began finding more ships' fittings and accoutrements as well as more art. His most famous find from this season was a foot-high figure of Hermes, the messenger god, portrayed as an orator, on a bronze pedestal and wearing only winged boots and a cloak over the left shoulder.

By this time, Merlin's financial situation was serious. In desperation, he decided to make one last appeal to the French Academy.

Using the statue as his hook, he sent a telegram to its "Secretaire Perpetual"—

6 June 1913—Mahdia—8.25 hours. Superb statuette of Hermes in bronze, height 32 cm found at Mahdia—but funds having been exhausted excavation will cease definitively next Sunday—would be very grateful if the Academy would permit the prolongation by finding, for example, another 500 francs—respects—Merlin.

Merlin evidently found the additional funding (although not from the Academy) and was able to complete his campaign. Within a year, the world was at war, and, afterward, Merlin returned to France, reconciled to the fact that he would probably never again direct excavations on the wreck—which he was convinced still contained many wonderful things waiting to be discovered.

Despite minor flaws, Merlin's work was an archeological triumph. The work on the Antikythera wreck some years before had not been done under proper archeological supervision, and, more important, there was no proper scientific publication of the findings. The fact that Merlin did not dive cannot be held against him; few men did in his time. He was an astute, perceptive, and highly learned professional who published his findings accurately and promptly. The standards he set for maritime archeology would not be equaled for nearly half a century.

From the outset, Merlin had been asking himself a number of vital questions:

Where was the ship coming from? Where was she headed? Why and when did she sink? And what was the explanation behind its enormously rich, but at the same time very mixed and complicated, cargo?

As he gathered the evidence from the seabed, partial answers to these questions began to form. In the 90 years since he began,

Mahdia, 1913

archeological scholarship has broadened and deepened dramatically, and remarkable new scientific and technical advances have been made. All this has been brought to bear on the Mahdia wreck—and Merlin's views have emerged largely intact.

⇜⇝

During the second campaign, Merlin's divers brought up three broken marble tablets, or stelae, that were inscribed in Greek. The words were eroded and difficult to read; long hours of effort went into deciphering them. One of the texts pointed to where the goods were first loaded. It was a decree by an Attic cult that worshiped the hero Paralos, son of Poseidon, whose only known shrine was in the Piraeus, the great port of Athens. The Piraeus was one of the largest, most impressive, and most professionally run ports of the ancient Mediterranean, and from it, ships were sent all over the then-civilized Western world. That the stelae came from here is supported by the facts that the marble came from the same area, and that the artists were also from the Greek world.

Questions have arisen as to why the stelae were on board in the first place. It has been suggested that they were functioning as ballast, but with such a deadweight of stone columns already in the hold, this was obviously not a ship that needed ballast. A more plausible explanation is that they were used as wedges to help jam the cargo into place;

one of the greatest fears at sea is that a cargo might shift its weight and destabilize the vessel. Perhaps, too, the intention was to erase the inscriptions so that the blocks could be recycled as veneering, for this was a time when Rome was desperate for marble. It had no established marble trade of its own, so even minor pieces would have had value.

Equally interesting was the question of the ship's destination. Given its location, Merlin's mind naturally first turned to North Africa. Possibly, this cargo had been ordered by some minor North African potentate to embellish his palace—but the cargo did not seem right for an ordered consignment. Besides, ever since the destruction of Carthage in 146 B.C., there had been no market for Greek luxury goods along this section of the lower Med-

iterranean coast. But there was at this time an insatiable appetite for Greek marble and works of art among the *nouveaux riches* of Rome and the Bay of Naples. An empire awash at its top end with money, full of rapid urbanization, ambitious public-works programs, corrupt politicians and wealthy generals—all with villas to decorate—helped create an environment hungry for Greek finery.

Further proof of the ship's intended Italian destination came from elements of its cargo. There were on board a number of rather baroque-looking marble candelabra and monumental stone craters, objects that were mass-produced in Athens just for the Italian market. No Greek would ever have tolerated such garish items in his home or public places. In addition, the only parallels for these pieces have all come from Italy—none have ever been found in Greece.

The more Merlin thought about it, the more convinced he became that the Mahdia vessel's destination was Rome, or, more precisely, Ostia, its port at the mouth of the Tiber.

If this was true (and few have ever argued it), then what was the ship doing off North Africa? To be sure, piracy was rife at the time, but the more obvious and compelling explanation was that while on her way from Peloponnesus, perhaps while crossing the lower Ionian Sea, but certainly somewhere on her way toward the Straits of Messina and home, she got caught in a savage northeasterly storm.

In her overloaded state, she would have ridden low in the water and handled like a dog. Unable to tack with any facility, unable to claw her way northward, and in water too deep to anchor, the safest solution was simply to run before the storm on minimum sail. Having left Europe, the next stop was Africa. Possible final scenarios are many: perhaps her strained hull simply opened at the seams; maybe she was swamped from behind by a large wave; maybe she was driven broadside to the sea by a rogue wave, in which position she was just shoved over on her beam-ends and taken in one gulp. The possibilities are many, and all are equally plausible to anybody who has ever been caught under sail in the central Mediterranean during an end-of-summer storm.

We now come to the most delicate of Merlin's questions: chronology. Given the state of ancient-art historical learning during the first decade of the 20th century, it is small wonder that Merlin was reluctant to date the wreck on the basis of the artistic styles alone. Besides, the artistic styles were in themselves confusing; some of the pieces appeared to be much older than others. What he was hoping for was coins, for on that subject he was an expert, but what he got was a small terra-cotta lamp that was charred at the nozzle and still contained its wick. This lamp, which obviously belonged to the ship, could be dated to the first century B.C. by analogy with finds from excavations on land. It was a starting point.

Opposite, left: **One of the fine marble candelabra.** *Inset:* **Detail from another crater decorated in relief with a Dionysiac scene.** *Bottom right:* **The Mahdia ship was also carrying a number of monumental marble craters, mostly not intact.**

Below: **The final scenarios are many: perhaps her strained hull simply opened at the seams; maybe she was swamped from over the stern; perhaps she was driven broadside to the sea by a rogue wave, shoved over on her beam-ends, then swallowed whole. (Animation is from the documentary of the last moments of the Mahdia ship).**

The lamp focused the problem. Boethos of Chalcedon was generally thought to have worked around the middle years of the second century B.C., but if the lamp dated to the first century, then this meant that the ship was carrying antiques! This was strange, for then as now, ships usually only carried contemporary products.

This brings us to Merlin's final question, the enigma of the Mahdia ship's cargo. In broad terms, it consisted of architectural pieces and works of fine art in bronze and marble. Some of it was new, some of it was being recycled, and a number of pieces appeared to be antiques.

The architectural items were mainly columns, drums of columns, capitals, bases, and some other pieces that may have been from the entablature (the blocks that go across the tops of the columns). It has been suggested (although most would agree today that this was based on some very shaky thinking) that the majority of Mahdia pieces were intended to be part of a specific construction or complex in Italy. Especially now that I have seen the site for myself, I have considerable difficulty with this theory.

First, there is the mixture of sizes. Surely in a single consignment, or even two, one might expect to find a certain uniformity in the dimensions and proportions of the pieces. Merlin's crew brought up only three columns, of which two went to the Bardo. The third now serves as a pylon at a bus stop in downtown Mahdia, and this latter is very different from the other two, and so are most of the other pieces still on the seabed.

The styles are likewise mixed. Greek temples and public buildings used three types of columns: Doric, Ionic, and Corinthian. Versions of all three—some of them rather crude and some with unusual variations—are represented in the capitals (the decorative blocks that sit at the top of the shafts) and other column components.

Much has been made of the fact that at least some of the columns are unfluted—they lack the vertical grooves seen on columns from temples such as the Parthenon on the Acropolis. It is true that columns were often left in a crude, unfluted state when they were intended for export, because if they were finished, their delicate edges would have been vulnerable to damage while in transit. But we do not know whether all the Mahdia columns are unfluted; those on the seabed have been so eroded by borers and are so covered by sponges and other marine growths that it is impossible to tell.

Also, small columns like those on the Mahdia ship were often used in the interiors of temples or shrines, or in domestic constructions; such columns were often left unfluted.

In their range of subjects, chronology, and style, the art objects from the Mahdia cargo are even more confusing. There are, as already noted, the antiques, such as the herm of Dionysus with its "archaizing" features, but also found on board were some votive plaques that can be dated to the fourth century B.C. And then there are the "classicizing" pieces, such as Eros and the heads of Aphrodite and Niobe, which hark back to the Golden Age of Athens and which certainly date to before the first century B.C., the date suggested for the wreck by the lamp.

To contrast with these there are the more resolutely Hellenistic pieces, such as the lamp bearers and some of the satyrs. They all reflect the new realism of the third or second century B.C. Against these, however, we have the caricature-like art of the grotesques and the sugary-cute kithara player. I can picture them in any tourist shop of the day, were there such things. They are kitsch, the Greco-Roman equivalent of poster reproductions of Van Gogh sunflowers or huge-eyed circus clowns painted on black-velvet backgrounds.

But what to make of it? Why these wildly differing styles from very different periods of history? Why so much sacred art, why the plaques from the sanctuary of the Paraloi at the Piraeus? Then, as now, no place of worship would ever voluntarily let go of its holy images or written records. Merlin was the first to whisper the word "plunder."

If, then, it was plunder from some massively destructive sacrilegious event in the first century B.C., could that event be linked to some known upheaval in the ancient histories? It was a distinguished classicist and ancient historian named Salomon Reinach who first suggested, in 1910, that the Mahdia cargo might be plunder from Sulla's sack of Athens in 86 B.C., one of the most brutal acts of violence and desecration ever committed by Rome.

Reinach had been reading *Zeuxis and Antiochus,* by Lucian, that wonderful old wit, raconteur, and compulsive scribbler of the second century A.D. In it, Lucian mentions how a painting by Zeuxis, one of the most famous painters of his age, was "put on a ship bound for Italy with the rest of Sulla's art treasures, and was lost with them by the sinking of the ship, off Cape Malea, I think it was."

Reinach wondered whether perhaps the Mahdia ship could be Sulla's lost plunder galley, and even whether it could be the very ship that carried Zeuxis's painting. The idea was not as farfetched as it seems. Cape Malea, at the tip of the eastern peninsula of the Peloponnesus, was as notorious a ship-killer in ancient times as, say, Cape Horn was in the days of the great square-riggers. In the 19th century, any ship that disappeared without a trace on an interoceanic voyage was simply assumed to have been lost off Cape Horn. In antiquity, any ship that never came back from a voyage around Greece was assumed to have been lost off Cape Malea. But for all anybody

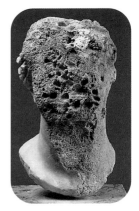

Above, top: **The teredo, a bivalve mollusk, is well known for the damage it can do to wooden hulls, but the animal also attacks marble and limestone. Any marble left exposed on the seabed was left looking like a sponge.**
Bottom: **Small bronze bust of Artemis, a decorative appliqué from one of the couches carried as cargo on the Mahdia ship.**

knew, the ship might just as easily have been lost off Cap d'Afrique.

Merlin at first was silent on whether the Mahdia wreck could have been one of Sulla's treasure ships; no doubt he was wisely waiting until he had as much information as possible before making any pronouncement on the matter. Finally, in 1913, he came out in general favor of the idea, and, before long, it had found general acceptance.

But who, then, was Sulla? And how did it happen that his history seems to be inextricably entwined with that of the Mahdia ship?

SULLA

Lucius Cornelius Sulla was one of the most ruthless, contradictory, and remarkable figures of the Roman world. As a student of history, I myself have struggled with his character and deeds, and, like others before me, I have been left confused and torn between revulsion and a rather begrudging admiration. As a soldier and politician, he was unquestionably a great man, but he was also a vindictive one who seems to have taken pleasure in cruelty. A genuine believer in the republican ideal, he nevertheless hastened the end of the Roman Republic.

Born in 138 B.C., Sulla began his rise to power in the North Africa War, in which he secured the capture and eventual execution of the Numidian king, Jugurtha. After serving with distinction in a later war against Germanic tribes that were threatening to invade Italy, he returned to Rome and a profligate life, mingling with circus gladiators, actors, and prostitutes.

Turning eventually to political office, Sulla improved his public standing by importing a large number of lions so that the plebians could, for the first time, enjoy the blood spectacle of man versus lion.

Meanwhile, though, the Republic was disintegrating and Rome was losing control over its territories. One of those territories was Athens, which revolted in support of Mithradates, king of Pontus. Their defiance was short-lived: in 87 B.C., Sulla arrived with five legions, determined to return Athens to the Roman fold and mete out cruel punishment to the rebels. The historians Appian and Plutarch have left us vivid descriptions of the events that took place; it is from their chronicles that I have constructed my account.

Today, Athens and the port of Piraeus are one continuous city, but in antiquity, they were two distinct entities. Athens was some eight kilometers back from the sea, its houses crowded around the ancient hill of the Acropolis, crowned by the world's most famous building, the Parthenon. The Piraeus, to the southwest, served as Athens's port, and had done so for hundreds of years.

Sulla divided his legions into two groups. One would lay siege to Athens; the other to the Piraeus. Equipped only with siege ladders, their first assault on the Piraeus was rebuffed, and Sulla retreated to the sacred center of Eleusis to plan a fresh assault. He needed siege engines of all kinds: rams, catapults, towers, tunneling equipment.

He also needed the materials to build them, so he ruthlessly chopped down the sacred trees of the Academy—the world's first university—in whose shade Plato had once strolled, and with the timber built his engines of war. He used the remains of the long walls that had once enclosed the two cities, making them effectively one. When all was ready, he resumed his attacks.

Appian tells of how, at this stage, Sulla began receiving help from slaves within the city, who were either loyal to the Romans or anxious to save their own skins. They inscribed intelligence reports on lead balls and lobbed them to the Romans with slings.

As the siege dragged on, food began to run out and the besieged became desperate; all animals were killed and some of the residents even resorted to cannibalism. But Sulla's legions were also growing disgruntled and showing signs of mutiny. To pacify them, Sulla permitted the looting of the treasures at sacred shrines of Epidaurus, Delphi, and Olympia. Surely, he felt, the gods loved him enough to underwrite his activities!

Deciding that impending starvation would eventually win him the Piraeus, Sulla turned to Athens, specifically the area of the *cerameikos*. As its name implies, the *cerameikos* was the quarter where potters worked. Sulla's men had heard from those talking over the walls that it was poorly defended, and after confirming this for himself, Sulla ordered his men to storm and breach the wall.

All resistance collapsed, and a pitiless slaughter followed. Men, women, and children were massacred without mercy. According to Plutarch, blood streamed down the streets of the inner *cerameikos* and even into the suburbs. Perhaps 100,000 were butchered.

With the siege of Athens over, Sulla brought up rams and a range of projectiles and concentrated on finishing off the Piraeus. The commander of the besieged troops fled by sea, and Sulla's men enthusiastically set fires that would destroy much of the city. One of the great ironies of the incident is that these fires preserved several statues of outstanding merit, which were excavated in 1959 from the remains of a burned-out warehouse. When the warehouse collapsed, it buried the statues. Had Sulla known of their presence, they would have been on their way to Rome.

The siege ended, but a major question loomed: How was all of the treasure looted from the sacked cities to be transported to Rome, some 1,500 miles away? In those days, overland transportation consisted of ox-drawn carts; roads were few and the hills were precipitous and daunting. The plunder would have to be transported by sea.

After three more years of fighting, Sulla would return to Rome in triumph. But one of the ships containing tons of the greatest glories of Greece would not be there awaiting him: it lay on the bottom of the Mediterranean, a few miles off the coast of Africa.

Above: Recently excavated stones that had been hurled by Sulla's siege engines in the siege of Athens.

Opposite: The Temple of Olympian Zeus, completed by the emperor Hadrian in the second century A.D. According to ancient historians, Sulla looted some of the blocks from one of the earlier building phases of the enormous edifice.

Athens, 86 B.C.

Above: Cousteau's exploration of the wreck was the first using the aqualung, and was also well documented on film by Cousteau's team.

RICHES BEYOND GOLD: THE COUSTEAU EXPEDITION

As two world wars came and went, Merlin's wonderful discoveries made between 1907 and 1913 off the North African coast were almost forgotten. The world moved on, and so did undersea technology.

In 1943, Jacques-Yves Cousteau and Emile Gagnan invented the first automatic demand valve for breathing underwater. Now, if a man wanted to go beneath the surface, he no longer had to encase his head within a metal helmet and plod along in lead boots, dragging an umbilical with him. Now he was free; he could swoop, hover, and glide like a fish.

The essential (and patentable) principle behind the new invention was its two valves. The first supplied air to the diver, on demand and requiring only slight suction, while the second provided for exhalation, allowing carbon dioxide to exit the system. Inhalation and exhalation pressures were in balance, so that the diver could breathe almost normally through his mouth. This was the technological breakthrough behind the aqualung, or, to give it its American name, self-contained underwater breathing apparatus (SCUBA), which would open the oceans to scientists and recreational divers and which, over time, would alter the way we view the undersea world.

Cousteau was born in 1910, the year of Merlin's second expedition. In 1930 he entered the French naval school at Brest and served on warships until 1942, when he joined the Resistance and spied for the Allies from within Vichy France. All the time, he was experimenting with new diving techniques, equipment, and underwater filming. In 1944, at Toulon, he and his old friend Philippe Talliez formed the Groupe d'Études et Récherches Sous-Marine of the French navy.

Cousteau, of course, went on to become the world's most famous and best-loved underwater explorer. His 1953 book, *The Silent World*, which would lead to an Oscar-winning film of the same name, sold over 5 million copies in 20 languages and inspired many young people—myself included—to consider careers in marine science. Television films of his expeditions on the converted minesweeper *Calypso* enthralled millions more. Later generations, nurtured on a regular diet of underwater TV documentaries, must find it hard to appreciate his impact on the world of the 1950s and 1960s.

But Cousteau was not yet famous when, in June 1948, he and his friends Talliez and Frederic Dumas slipped out of Toulon on a rechristened German diving tender, the *Ingénieur-Elie-Monnier*. Their shipmates included a party of staff officers, members of the Group d'Études, and an odd Jesuit priest, Father Poidebard, who was well known in archeological circles for his work on the ancient Phoenician harbors of Sidon and Tyre.

Ostensibly, their mission was to train staff in diving techniques, take some soundings, and search for submerged constructions off the ancient Tunisian city of Carthage. When I met him years later, though, Cousteau told me candidly that he also wanted to demonstrate the possibilities of his aqualung to marine science and to showcase it in a way that might increase its commercial appeal. This he would do through a film—the first underwater film made in color.

Although he did not admit it to me, he had yet another secret agenda: to find the legendary Mahdia ship and film it.

The work at Carthage was a failure—no submerged features of any kind were found. By June 20, the ship was anchored off Mahdia. As it had been for Merlin, the first challenge was finding the wreck. Reestablishing Merlin's transits was impossible; key landmarks were either missing or unidentifiable—the only alignment that made sense was that of the "broken tooth" with a corner of the huge citadel, the Bordj. They decided to follow this transit out to sea, and, when they came to about the right distance and depth, conduct a series of underwater search patterns. The strategy was not immediately successful.

When all seemed hopeless, however, Tailliez surfaced, gesticulating madly and shouting, "A column! I've found a column!" It was one that Merlin's team had moved. More columns were sighted. Then, finally, a vague configuration of cylindrical forms came into focus. It was the galley itself, the Mahdia ship.

By 1948, the fundamentals of decompression sickness were understood, and divers were limited to no more than three dives a day of 15 minutes maximum duration, with staged decompression stops on the way back up. To mark off the time, a rifle was fired into the water every five minutes (not as dangerous as it sounds). Yet even with these precautions, Dumas came down with the bends and required two hours in the decompression chamber that the *Ingénieur* carried.

By the time Cousteau's expedition found the site, there were only five working days left. Total diver time on the wreck, including descents, ascents, and decompression stops, was only 11 hours. Water jets were used in an attempt to keep the work area clear, but the basic tool of exploration was the hand.

Although they found no statues, the divers did raise an amphora, an anchor stock, a millstone, some fishing weights, and some thick lengths of wood that still contained copper fastenings and wooden treenails, as well as two Ionic columns encrusted with marine life.

Cousteau's work on the Mahdia ship is significant, in that it marked the first time that wreck excavations were carried out using the aqualung. But it was not archeology. There was no proper archeological supervision and

Below: **Mahdia today. The Sidi Jabar lighthouse, one of the navigational landmarks used in our search for the wreck. In the foreground is the ancient harbor believed by many scholars to be of Phoenician origin.**

no proper recording or scientific publication of the results. Some artifacts, such as a column that was found riddled with holes, were even deliberately destroyed.

The downside of Cousteau's aqualung and his work at Mahdia was the interest it excited in shipwreck discovery. Within a few years, his aqualung would be commonplace all over the northern Mediterranean, and soon wrecks of all periods were being found. Above all, the divers wanted ancient wrecks; in particular, they wanted to find amphorae, the great earthenware storage jars of the Greco-Roman world. Because divers were so many and diving archeologists were so few, these wrecks were picked apart—an incalculable loss to historical understanding.

When Merlin had to stop work, he felt certain that the Mahdia wreck still held secrets and treasures waiting to be discovered. Thirty-five years later, Cousteau and his comrades felt the same way. Cousteau would write of his work, "If our hard-hatted predecessors had very carefully creamed off the wreck, they had made only a superficial dent in the cargo."

THE 1950s CAMPAIGNS

Although Cousteau's work on the Mahdia wreck lasted less than a week, it was enough—aqualung archeology was born. In the early 1950s, Cousteau and others began excavations on a variety of wrecks off the coasts of southern France and Italy, and in

1954, a group under the leadership of Guy de Frondeville decided to continue Cousteau's work on the Mahdia wreck. They had the personal support of Gilbert Picard, then the director of antiquities for Tunisia, and a buoy-maintenance vessel, *Finistere*, later supplemented by another ship, the *Petrel*.

Like the Merlin and Cousteau teams before them, de Frondeville's group encountered problems in finding the wreck, but eventually a diver found the landmark columns. The team's broad strategy was to move the columns and blocks away from the center of the site to create a space where they might begin excavation with an airlift, a device for sucking away the sediment. With the help of the ship's winch, they moved some 60 tons of marble from the site.

From an archeological point of view, this was a disaster. While the columns had been left undisturbed, their undersides were buried in mud and thus protected from marine borers that can, over several years, reduce a marble surface to something resembling Swiss cheese. When de Frondeville's divers moved the stones, they did not bother to lay them out as they had been: the sides that had been in the mud were now exposed to attack. In our dives, just four decades later, we found that most of the stones had been eaten away on all sides, which, of course, greatly reduces their archeological value.

One of the greatest dangers of amateur teams like those of Cousteau and de Frondeville is that they cannot usually interpret what they see, nor do they know what they should be looking for. Therefore, they cannot plan proper archeological strategies aimed at acquiring new knowledge, which is what field work is all about.

During their final campaign, in 1955, no more columns were displaced, but most of the ship's keel was exposed, and a portion of it was recovered and sent to the Bardo Museum. Several other sections of hull were also recovered, but in the 1950s, the conservation of waterlogged wood was a little-understood science, and these pieces soon shrank and decayed.

Although dogged by bad luck and technical problems, the 1955 efforts resulted in some success. In terms of new works of art, little was raised; the main achievements of the season were the successful recovery of that length of keel and a sketched map of the site, drawn by de Frondeville himself.

THE ART HISTORIANS' DETECTIVE WORK

The next event in the sprawling saga of the Mahdia ship did not occur in the field, but in the more sedate world of the library. In 1963, the archeological world was rocked by a scholarly *tour de force* from an internationally renowned ancient-art historian, Werner Fuchs. In a monograph entitled *Der Schiffsfund von Mahdia* (The Ship-find of Mahdia), he argued that apart from the late-classical pieces, all of the statues were not only more or

less contemporary, but they were mostly from the same workshop, and that they could be dated to the final quarter of the second century B.C.

The winged youth and the herm of Dionysus were key to his argument. Merlin and Poinssot had assumed the youth to be Eros, but, since the 1920s, it had been accepted that the two statues went together. Early restorers had given the youth a raised right foot, which, it was argued, must have been resting on the pedestal of the herm. Furthermore, the statue's right elbow was positioned to lean on the herm. The remains of a missing object in the statue's left hand were identified as a palm branch, the symbol of victory. It was a known combination from the classical world. So, rather than Eros, the statue must be Agon, the personification of the athletic contest.

Since the herm had been signed by Boethos of Chalcedon, it was logically assumed that both pieces must be his. Fuchs extended this thinking to include many of the other statues, and dated the wreck itself to

around 100 B.C.—by this theory, the cargo could not possibly be from Sulla's sack of Athens.

Fuchs's ideas were soon universally accepted. As a student in the 1970s, my text was Fuchs, and certainly his were the views of the Bardo Museum in 1987, when I went to Tunis to find out whether I myself might be given a permit to conduct a search and survey of the Mahdia wreck.

During this visit, I met with Tunisia's senior government archeologists and museum directors.

Below: Statuette of erotic dancer with an exposed right breast. A ring on her back indicates that she was intended for suspension.

While they were cordial, there was at the time no structure for maritime archeology within the country. If the project was to go forward, a lot of practical support would be needed, and Tunisia at that time could not provide it.

Nonetheless, I was allowed to see and study the material from the wreck; it had been withdrawn from exhibition because of its deterioration—corrosion on the bronze objects was particularly alarming. I could see that the Mahdia wreck was a complicated and

sensitive issue, and, very reluctantly, I returned to Oxford and to field work elsewhere.

During the same year, though, the Bardo and the Rheinisches Landesmuseum in Bonn reached an accord concerning the conservation and restoration of the Mahdia statues. This agreement became the basis of a fruitful relationship that set new standards in international intermuseum collaboration. Leaders on the project were Aicha Ben Abed, then director of the Bardo, and Dr. Gisela Hellenkemper-Sallies, a senior curator of the Landesmuseum. More than 80 archeologists, art historians, and scientists from all over the world were involved; throughout, science, conservation, and research went hand in hand. It was this agreement, too, that would lead, indirectly, to my telephone call from Peter Winterstein six years later, and to the events that followed.

One of the most important discoveries made in Bonn concerned the same herm of Dionysus and figure of Agon. A deconstruction and fresh study of the statue revealed that its hip had been wrongly restored and that, when properly put together, one leg could not possibly have been raised. With its new posture, it was difficult to see how the statues had been an ensemble. These doubts were confirmed by isotope analysis of the lead that had fixed them to their marble pedestals: this analysis demonstrated beyond doubt that the lead had come from different sources.

Clearly, they were not a pair, which meant that the winged youth was probably not the work of Boethos of Chalcedon, and that maybe he was not Agon. Taking a new look at the statue, the conservators and archeologists concluded that Merlin had been right —it *was* Eros, and the missing object from his left hand was a bow.

All this, of course, left the Fuchs monograph open to reevaluation. If some of his theories on the statuary were wrong, then maybe his views on the origins and chronology of the ship were also wrong. Could it be that his date of 100 B.C. for the wreck was incorrect, and that this was indeed one of Sulla's plunder ships?

So far, the only proven pieces of plunder were the inscriptions from the sanctuary of the Paraloi, the relief plaques, the herm, and the statue now shown to be Eros. Surely, if this was a plunder ship, there would be indications that more of the works of art were spoils of war? Hellenkemper-Sallies and her colleagues began searching for evidence.

Remember the "Aphrodite" head, one of seven life-sized marble busts, one that had puzzled Merlin because her right shoulder had been vertically cut away? Detailed examination showed that such statues were designed for mounted display against a wall, most likely within round niches known as *tondi*, which could explain why Aphrodite had lost her shoulder. Other busts were also found to have been wall-mounted. All were of deities and very likely had come from the same temple or sanctuary. Religious centers would not willingly give up the images of

their gods: those heads must also have been plunder.

Then there were the busts of Dionysus and Ariadne, which had presumably come from a ship's prow or rostrum similar to the marble prow under the Victory of Samothrace in the Louvre. Sure enough, detailed examination revealed nail holes. Those pieces had obviously also been mounted for an unspecified period before being taken, no doubt as plunder, for transport to Rome.

There were also a number of items in the wreck's cargo that were new at the time of the ship's departure, many of them apparently mass-produced for the Roman market. Stock favorites would have been in continuous production without waiting for specific orders, so in other words, there could have been a backlog of items in various stages of completion or in storage at the time of Sulla's attack. Perhaps production kept going even as the siege was in progress. Nobody expected the level of reprisal exacted by Sulla, and, whatever the outcome, the Roman appetite for Greek luxury goods would have remained undiminished. Thus, continuing manufacture during the siege made good business sense.

With Fuchs's chronology for the wreck in serious doubt, and with so much new information pointing to the plunder scenario, the scholars began searching for fresh evidence that might improve the dating of the wreck. A breakthrough came when they found parallels to some of the "contemporary" objects from the Mahdia ship on other Roman

Below: This statue of the winged youth was recovered by Merlin in a number of pieces over several seasons. To help understand the pose and its identity, the conservators made a copy to experiment with. Here the missing object from the left hand has been restored as a bow. The fully restored statue is below.

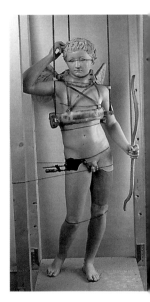

Bonn, 1987

wrecks whose dates were better established. Also, excavations on land since Merlin's day had produced a new body of evidence that could be applied to the Mahdia wreck. For instance, certain amphorae could now be dated to the eighth and ninth decades B.C. Interestingly, one of the amphora types had been given its earliest recorded date based on an example excavated from a well in the Athenian marketplace, in a layer of debris from Sulla's sack. Following the devastation of the city in 86 B.C., the residents who were left cleaned up by simply throwing the debris into the nearest well; it was easier than digging pits, and there were no longer any animals in the city to carry it away.

The wreck could now be dated to between 90 and 70 B.C., which fits perfectly with the sack of Athens and the Piraeus in 86 B.C., or the period of misrule and lawlessness that followed.

THE 1990s: REDISCOVERY OF THE MAHDIA WRECK

It was at one of a series of international colloquia hosted by the Landesmuseum that someone asked whether it would be possible to relocate the Mahdia wreck and conduct the first-ever proper archeological survey of the site. The idea was well received by everyone, including the Tunisian authorities, but who could do the work? It was decided to ask Peter Winterstein's new underwater-archeology organization, DEGUWA. Peter's re-

sponse, and his invitation to me to direct the project, are described at the beginning of this story.

Because of a number of survey commitments I had already made, and because of all the problems that previous investigators had encountered in finding the site, Peter suggested that he and a team go to Mahdia and try to locate it. If they were successful, I would lead a team to begin the survey later in the summer.

We moved on to talk about search methodologies. There had to be a precise system of navigation and position-fixing; otherwise the team would blunder about in hope of being lucky, as Cousteau had done.

A system I had used with much success involved establishing onshore two or more radio beacons that emitted a continuous signal, which could be picked up by a receiver on the ship's mast. It gave positions to within a meter. Search patterns were then plotted by computer onto a chart and interfaced with tracking data from magnetometers, sub-bottom profilers, and other remote sensing equipment deployed from the stern. The problem was that this system was very expensive.

The alternative was to use the Global Positioning System (GPS), which calculates position using satellite signals. Although slightly less accurate, it is much less expensive and infinitely easier to use.

I was not overly optimistic about Peter's chances of finding the wreck; never-

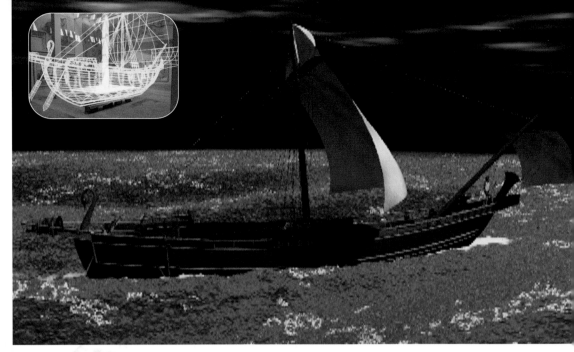

theless, my thoughts were all the time with him. Then, one day while I was on survey in the Channel Islands, I returned to my room to find a telephone message on my door. It contained three simple but compelling words: WRECK FOUND. PETER.

As soon as I could, I flew to Germany and went to the beautiful old university town of Erlangen, where I was met by Peter and Professor Christoph Börker, a distinguished scholar of ancient art and archeology who was also president of DEGUWA. Entering a locked auditorium, I was shown a video.

At first, there was nothing on the screen but dapples of light in water. Everything had a dissolved quality as the camera struggled to find something on which it could fix its automatic focus. I could hear deep, irregular breathing from the cameraman—either he was fighting the current or he was excited at the prospect of seeing the wreck. Bursts of bubbles came into focus and then were gone; clearly, he had a dive partner somewhere below him.

Then, from out of the dissolve emerged cigar-like forms. At first they were ill-defined, but as the camera moved closer, they drew into sharp distinction. Bathed in artificial light, they lit up in color. Flora, fauna, and rock forms became a dazzling

kaleidoscope of reds, greens, yellows, and purples, and fish darted in and out. This truly was Cousteau's "oasis," and I was totally enthralled.

I was aware of Peter watching me from across the room, waiting for my reaction. I smiled at him in silent congratulation.

Afterward, over *schnapps*, we talked until dawn. It was a familiar story: bad weather, currents, mixed visibility, impossible navigation points, and, in the end, sheer unadulterated luck. Typically, it had all come together at the last moment. They had managed to shoot the video and take a few slides, but that was all.

We had to make a quick decision as to when to begin the survey. It was June; my other projects would have me committed until

Above, top: Computer-animated re-creation of the galley, created for the film. *Inset:* Wire-frame used in building the re-creation, set on keel of actual wreck. *Bottom:* Frame from Peter Winterstein's first video of the site.

Background: Model of a Mahdia-era Roman galley.

mid-September, which is very late for the central Mediterranean. Fethi Chelbi, the head of Tunisia's underwater-archeological unit, also had other commitments. As for Peter, the timing was impossible.

I suggested postponing the project until the following spring, but one problem with doing so was that two volumes of scholarship on the Mahdia wreck were due to go to press in a few months. Gisela Hellenkemper-Sallies was the editor, and she was anxious to include new information on the site. Because we owed her so much, Peter and I wanted to oblige, but we would be taking a big gamble. We spoke to Fethi, who was firm in his conviction that it was bad timing. Yet while doing everything to dissuade us, he also said that he would support us in whatever schedule we determined. We decided to take a chance and go operational in September.

It was a bad decision. I had been directing surveys and excavations every year since 1981, but I had never known the kind of frustration we would experience that season in Mahdia. I hope never to do so again.

THE 1993 SURVEY

As the plane approached Tunisia that fall, the "arms" of the Bay of Tunis seemed to reach out in greeting. The midday sun cut deep, narrow shadows and created sharp contrasts between the russet cliffs crowded with villas and the turquoise waters of the Mediterranean. I could see the rooftops of the *medina*, and, in the heart of the *souks*, the minaret of the great Mosque of the Olive Tree—one of Islam's finest monuments. Founded in the eighth century, it has been a center for the study of Koranic law and philosophy for as long as anyone can remember. As my eyes lingered on it, I was struck by the notion that, as a university of sorts, it was even older than my own much-loved Oxford.

I took a taxi to Sidi Bou Said, where I was to spend the night with an archeologist friend from my student days. Sidi Bou Said is unlike anywhere else I know of on the Mediterranean littoral: it is native Tunisian mixed with Arab, Andalusian, a little French Riviera, and a hint of the Aegean.

Below, top: Fethi Chelbi.
Bottom: Looking out towards the site from our headquarters at the Bordj. It was like a little boy's fantasy having this entire medieval castle all to ourselves.

Whitewashed houses splashed with magenta bougainvillea tumble down a steep promontory into the Bay of Tunis. As you climb and wind along the narrow streets and alleys, you find a surprise around every corner: recessed verandas, secret courtyards, long terraces from which you can look across the bay to Cap Bon, a great thumb of land hooking up toward Europe.

That evening, we wandered down to the port, where a stout elderly man sidled up and, in a rather conspiratorial manner, began to produce Roman lamps from his pockets. Then, with frequent furtive glances left and right, he unfolded a handkerchief to show us some coins—good fakes, but still fakes. "The heads," he assured us, "were of the great Carthaginian general, Hannibal."

"No, they weren't," I said.

Later, I confided in my friend that I was very worried about the upcoming project. First, it was late in the season, but more important, I was concerned about the team and whether they would accept me. They were all German; I was British. It was an extremely raw team, for DEGUWA was a new organization and there had been no opportunity for them to gain experience. A few had done some reading and one or two had taken a course, but except for Ulrich Muller, who had worked with me in Gibraltar, there was nobody with a practical knowledge of underwater archeology and shipwrecks.

As a rule, I never go into the field without what I call 60 percent continuity—that is, 60 percent of the team having been with me on a previous project. That way, I can usually be certain that everything will be up and running by the second day and that by the third we will have settled into the rhythm that is so important in this kind of work.

Three of my own veterans would be part of the crew, but they would not be arriving for several days. Meanwhile, I would have to give a few talks and demonstrations on basic procedures, something I had not done in years.

One other item was worrying me. I would be working closely with Fethi Chelbi, and, although I had met him once at a conference, we did not really know each other. It was vital that we be able to function as friends as well as colleagues. I felt certain that he would feel the same way.

The next day, I took the bus to Mahdia, arriving in the early afternoon. I was not sure where the members of our team were staying, though I did know that, thanks to Fethi, the authorities had given us the use of the famous citadel, the great Bordj el Kabir, as our headquarters. Furthermore, a large green van was to have arrived the day before by ferry from Marseilles; it contained our compressors, boats and other heavy equipment. By this time it should be unloading.

The Bordj totally dominated the peninsula. As my taxi snaked up the dirt road, I looked around for the van. Not only could I not see a van; I could not see any sign of life except for a couple of dogs sleeping in the

Mahdia, 1993

shade of an old iron cannon. The taxi drove off, leaving me standing in its cloud of dust. Apart from a massive, very old-looking wooden door, the entrance to the citadel was remarkably understated. I moved up to the door and slowly pulled it open. From the battlements somewhere above, someone shouted down in awkward French, "What do you want, monsieur? We're closed."

In equally clumsy French, I explained who I was, and the face of a second custodian appeared at the doorway; clearly he had been sleeping off the noonday sun. Yes, he said, there had been some young Germans there that morning, asking about "*un gros camion vert*"—a big green van. They were at the Corniche, an old beachfront hotel on the western side of Cap d'Afrique.

I was shown the rooms that had been refurbished for our campaign. They were perfect, with all the space we could ever wish for: literally, a castle to ourselves.

Wandering around the battlements, I could see the Sidi Jabar lighthouse, a name I had first read as a boy in the Falklands and something I never expected to see. To the east was a small harbor; it was probably here that the Greek sponge fleet had put in for shelter and where Merlin had first met with them.

The sea, a deep boundless azure, appeared calm, but there were frequent little smudges of white that told me otherwise. Whitecaps were never a good sign; usually they meant that the sea was too boisterous for work. It left me feeling uneasy.

The coastline was marked by several rather abstract-looking piles of collapsed masonry and building blocks. My eyes focused on one that was somewhat squarish, but lopsided. It resembled—A BROKEN TOOTH! Our clue to finding the wreck! Somewhere out there, drowned on the horizon, was the spot where the ship was situated. But if our calculations were just a shade off course, we would find nothing but the empty wastes of the Mediterranean bottomlands.

I set out to find the team at the Hotel Corniche. Since then, the hotel has been refurbished and professionalized, but at that time, it was what you might call, if you were feeling kind, "quaint and disarming," when what you really had in mind was "dirty and disgusting." Down at one end, it had a seedy little bar that I was told had a certain reputation in Mahdia. I made a mental note to spend as many nights as possible in the Bordj.

Markus and Ulrich were sitting outside the bar, looking, I thought, a bit glum. The van, they said, had been impounded by customs in Tunis; Fethi was doing everything he could, but there was no immediate prospect of its release. All of our equipment was in the van, and without it we were able to do nothing.

Our campaign was due to begin the following morning. When, after several days the van cleared customs, it took twelve hours to reach Mahdia and another half day to offload, motorize the boats, and set up our compressor stations and labs.

Then the winds came. With everyone poised to go, we could do nothing but sit in the waterfront bars watching the sea send up sheets of lacelike spray over the breakwater. We discussed archeological procedures and the survey techniques we would use, and then, when everything had been talked to death, we held competitions to see whose spoon would stand up longest in the sludge left at the bottom of a cup of the local coffee.

It was at such a point that Fethi arrived, and my concerns about how we would get along evaporated. Looking with mock horror at the coffee I had been drinking, he ordered mint tea topped with pine kernels—"a real Tunisian drink"—and we began discussing how the work should proceed. In the process, we established, in the words of that other North African epic, "the start of a beautiful friendship."

By the time we set out for the site, I had learned that the boat we had chartered, the *Bessam*, was a tub that, at the first sign of a swell, went into a long, slow roll that soon had half the team seasick. Her only asset was her very capable captain, Boutaoui Ben Mrad.

Once out at sea, I truly understood the complexity of finding the wreck. I could make out the Bordj, but the broken tooth was lost in the mist. With a cheap sextant, I tried to take an angle off the lighthouse, but it wouldn't stay still, and, even when I thought that I had it, the *Bessam* could not hold course.

We had a GPS fix, but it had been taken in haste somewhat off the site on the

last day of the previous search. Soon, we were blundering around in circles, hoping for a glimpse of the broken tooth. With half the team flat on the deck, sick as dogs, morale was slipping away.

In desperation, we decided to dive the GPS coordinates even though we knew the depth wasn't quite right. Markus and Ulrich went over the side. Three-quarters of an hour later they were back. As Markus grabbed the ladder, he tore off his mask and spat out the mouthpiece: "*Nicht gefunden*" was all he said. In other words, no luck—words I would hear again and again in the days to come.

The mood became increasingly subdued as the reality of our situation sank in. All day we hunted the elusive wreck. We sailed, we searched, we dived, we tracked, we dived, we sounded, we dived. Nothing but sand and eel grass.

Finally, toward the end of another fruitless day, when we were talking about heading back, the sonar chimed 39 meters, Cousteau's depth reading for the wreck. The angle on the Sidi Jabar lighthouse wasn't far out; the broken tooth transit looked about right. We had two divers left and just enough air. Chris Fitton and Tim Sharpe went down. Thirty-five minutes later, they were back with a report of an isolated column: the wreck was tantalizingly close. We marked the spot with a buoy and began the hour-long trip back to port, spirits soaring.

That night, however, the winds came again. I lay awake listening to the sea break-

Above: The season over, *Milbrook* noses into the ancient harbor of La Goulette, in Tunis.

Opposite: Detail from a mosaic of a galley at the Bardo.

Above: For reasons (↻) unknown, one of the columns raised by Merlin is not in the Bardo, but serves as a marker at this Mahdia bus stop.

ing on the rocks. The next morning, with the wind gone and the sea subsiding, we spent an hour searching for our buoy before accepting the fact that it had been carried away in the storm. We were back where we had started. The same thing had happened to the Merlin team, and later to Guy de Frondeville.

By the middle of our campaign, I had to face the reality of our situation: we had already failed. Even if the weather was perfect on every remaining day, we could, at best, hope for no more than a partial site plan.

But the weather was not perfect. For three days, a sirocco blasted in from off the Sahara. With it came the sand that made eyes burn and deposited a film of dust on everything. I finally accepted defeat.

There were a few small compensations. Toward the end of the port, I located one of Merlin's columns. Stationed upright, it was serving as a marker at a bus stop. I looked for evidence of tool marks. Was it a finished column, or had it been merely roughed out for transport? There were plenty of marks, but nothing inconsistent with a slab of stone that had been subjected to wear and tear for eight decades in downtown Mahdia, and to the dep-

redations of the seabed for nearly two millennia before that.

Although we did succeed in locating the wreck, our time on it was very brief indeed. All we managed was to map one small corner of the site. I only got down twice; on the first dive, I felt something pull at my wrist as I went into the water. It was my watch. During my second dive, I went looking for it but found only a small modern-looking cylindrical object, covered in marine deposits. Low on air and time, I slipped it into my pocket. On the way back to Mahdia, I chipped away at it with my nail until I revealed a greenish bronze rifle shell. Curiosity satisfied, I tossed it over the side. As it went *plop*, I realized too late what it was: a cartridge from one of the shots Cousteau had fired into the sea as a time signal to his divers. I had just thrown away a little part of the Mahdia legend.

THE 1996 CAMPAIGN

The 1993 season had been an archeological failure. We had been beaten by the weather. In all my years of leading underwater surveys and excavations, it was one of my lowest moments.

On August 6, 1996, I returned to Tunis with a full team. Fethi and I were going to try again. I went first to Place de la Victoire, where the great gate of Tunis, the Bab el-Bahar (the Sea Gate) stands; sadly, it is all that is left of the walls that once protected the *medina*. It would have been easier to go around, but I made a point of going through it before plunging into the *souks* and letting myself be carried by the human flow along rue Jamma ez Zitouna, the main artery in this ancient labyrinth, to the Great Mosque.

I was on my way to Fethi's office in the Casbah on the other side of the *medina*. As I wandered through the maze, I wondered which was the route Merlin had taken on the day in 1907 when he first spotted the bronze statuettes that would so completely change his life, and, some 90 years later, my own.

The Casbah was as quiet and empty as the bazaars were noisy and crowded. Although the alleys were just as tortuous, the tranquillity gave the impression of more space as well as the opportunity to catch your breath and enjoy the architecture. Nowhere is the Islamic love of architecture more evident then in the *medina* of Tunis, with its arches, cupolas, chipped and worn wall tiles, and, above all, the wooden doors with their metal-studded patterns and knockers in the form of the lucky "hand of Fatima." Some are varnished, others blue or mustard, and a few are of a color that can best be likened to an old Madeira. The windows can be equally beautiful; most are louvered, but some still carry the wrought-iron *mashrabia*, the opening through which, in less enlightened times, cloistered wives could see and not be seen.

It was behind one such facade that the Institut National du Patrimoine (INP) had its central offices. The INP is the government agency responsible for all archaeological activities in Tunisia. I walked across an elaborately tiled courtyard, knocked on the door, and asked for *le chef de Département des Études d'Archéologie Sous-Marine*, Monsieur Fethi Chelbi.

Since 1993, Fethi's maritime archeological unit had grown to become one of the largest and best in the Mediterranean. Now, in 1996, we had to be operational in three days, so we did not have much time. We sat down immediately to finalize some of the outstanding details of the campaign. In broad terms, our aim was simply to map the site and record everything that was showing above the seabed. As before, we would use the Bordj as our headquarters and billet most of the team in a hotel in the center of town. The main change to the program was that we would no longer be using the Hotel Corniche, which had gone upmarket and become too expensive. Nor would we be chartering the *Bessam*; this time we would be using an ex–Royal Navy supply vessel called the *Milbrook*, owned by an old friend of mine, Sumner Gerard, who had fitted her out for maritime research work. She was stable, fast, well equipped, had good working space on deck,

The *Milbrook* at sunset.

Above, top: Milbrook owner
Sumner Gerard and mate
Andy Bell. On first meeting,
it would be easy to typecast
Sumner as a crusty, grumpy
skipper, but he is, in fact,
a war hero and former
diplomat. *Bottom:* Joanna
Yellowlees-Bound aboard
Milbrook.

That day, an emergency missing-ship bulletin was issued from Gibraltar. That night, I slept once again beneath the stars on the battlements of the Bordj. The next day I was awakened at five by the muezzin's call to prayer and an accompanying dawn chorus of roosters, dogs, and an occasional donkey. I scanned the horizon. Lots of whitecaps, but no *Milbrook.*

I walked into town to see if I could hire a fishing boat for three weeks. It was Friday, market day. The stalls were already up, and men dressed against the chill were laying out their wares. Beautiful olive-wood bowls and metal kitchenware vied for space with figs, dates, raisins, and all manner of other fruits, spices, and exotic foodstuffs. Killims, camel bags, leather goods, and velvet circumcision suits hung from rails, and along the pavement, to entice the tourists, were sponges, crystallized desert rocks, and the ornate birdcages for which Tunisia is famous. Even at this early hour, the shoppers were circling; most were elderly women in *sifsaris*; some were veiled, all were anxious to complete their purchases before the sun rose any higher.

The dock was on the other side of the market. As I pushed my way through, the first thing I saw was *Milbrook.* With her high-swung bow and broad bridge, she looked very self-important among all the simple wooden fishing boats. She had come in overnight.

As I climbed on board, the heavy aroma of bacon and eggs wafted up from her galley. In the mess, I passed five of her crew

and could sleep 20. The only problem was that she had disappeared.

I had visited her during her refit in England and had linked up with her again just a couple of weeks prior to my arrival in Tunis, while we were working in Gibraltar. She had left Spain for Tunisia a week ago and nobody had seen or heard of her since. What was particularly worrisome was that during the week, the western Mediterranean had been whipped by two severe storms.

We had all arrived in Mahdia by August 8. The team numbered 30; eight were from the INP, thirteen were DEGUWA members from either Germany or Switzerland, and the remainder were either from Oxford University MARE or from the film crew that had come along to make a documentary for television. At our briefing, we broke the news about the missing *Milbrook*—it was not well received.

shoveling in a full-cooked English breakfast. I passed on down to the wardroom, and, sure enough, sitting alone and eating toast, was Sumner.

Although I had known Sumner for a long time, this was to be the first occasion on which we had ever worked together, mainly because he was based in Florida and the Caribbean. At first meeting, Sumner was no more than a typical crusty, old, hard-as-leather, spit-in-your-eye, no-nonsense ship's skipper; but to those of us privileged enough to be taken into his confidence, he was a very layered personality. Although American to his core, he had read history at Trinity College, Cambridge, and considered England his second home. A promising career in academia had been cut short by World War II, during which he served with distinction in the Middle East, China, Burma, and India. He rose from a private in the Army to a lieutenant in the Navy and ended his service as a captain in the Marine Corps. After the war, he devoted himself to ranching and state politics in Montana, serving in the legislature and eventually becoming minority leader in the state House of Representatives and then in the Senate. In the 1970s, he was appointed am-

bassador to Jamaica by President Nixon.

In addition to ships and the sea, Sumner and I shared another love: Tunisia. For Sumner, it came from having lived in the country in the 1970s, during which time he was director of the U.S. International Development Mission. His work earned him the rank of Commander of the Order of the Republic, awarded by Tunisia's first president, Habib Bourguiba.

Now, down in the wardroom, he explained his delayed arrival. In order "not to end up like the Mahdia ship," he had put in at Majorca to await better weather. But, as he didn't hesitate to point out, there he was on the opening day of the campaign and ready to begin work first thing in the morning.

Despite that, there was no start to the work that day. Nor the next. In fact, it was not until August 12 that the weather subsided and we were at last able to get underway.

The mood that morning was not terribly upbeat. We had just learned that two men working for the company which was

Above: Back on the surface, the expedition doctor examined the divers for any trace of nitrogen bubbles in their blood. If there was any doubt, the divers were immediately put on oxygen.
Below: Weather, mechanical, and supply problems had me wondering at one point whether it would be a repeat of the 1993 debacle.

providing our decompression chamber had been killed—while testing the chamber under pressure, it had exploded. People were talking of the curse of the Mahdia wreck. The slaughter by Sulla of the innocents in Athens; the men who had drowned on the ship; the divers who were killed or paralyzed during the Merlin and de Frondeville campaigns; now this. Although I didn't like all the talk of curses, there was no doubt that it was a wreck steeped in sorrow.

As we nosed out of port, our bow wave set the fishing boats nodding and made the masts of the yachts swing like metronomes. Everybody stopped to watch us—a vessel like the *Milbrook* was an unusual sight in Mahdia.

We hugged Cap d'Afrique until we reached its farthest point and then swung for the horizon. As we moved from the shelter of the coast, we picked up the wind, and soon the broad buoyant bows of the *Milbrook* began to lift and plunge. Within an hour we had half the team sprawled seasick on the deck. I have always thought of seasickness as the great leveler: whatever your

race, creed, sex, or color of skin; whatever your station, whether you are a doctor from Heidelberg, an archeology student from Tunis, or a cabbie from London—even the great Lord Nelson himself suffered from it all his life—when you are seasick, you are no more than a pathetic lump of suffering humanity. There is no scope for pride, ambition, or any of the other vanities when all you can think about is vomiting.

All day we tracked, boxed, and circled. Fethi, Peter Winterstein, and I scanned the horizon with binoculars; Sumner watched the depth and sonar; the chief diver Habchi Abdessalam (known as Salam) watched the GPS while mate Andy Bell held the wheel.

We had improved our position-fixing since 1993, but not by much. We had the transit of the broken tooth and the corner of the Bordj, we had an angle on the Sidi Jabar lighthouse, we had two GPS readings, we had a distance from shore, we had latitude and longitude, and we had depth. At the point where they all converged we should have been directly over the wreck. The trouble was we couldn't bring them into convergence, or anything like convergence. Some were clearly inaccurate—but which?

The coast was just a ribbon on the horizon separating sea from sky. The broken tooth and the lighthouse swam in mist. I stared at the coast through my binoculars until my

Below: **We had a tool to pinpoint the wreck site that Merlin and Cousteau would have envied: the Global Positioning System, or GPS. Once we found her, she would never be lost again.**

eyes burned. Sometimes we were on transit, but then the waves or wind would push us off. Sometimes we were suddenly at the right depth, only to be out of it a few seconds later.

In the end, Fethi and I jumped a few of the divers just to break the tension and get them in the water. I dived last and soon realized we had another problem: visibility. Because of the storm, the water was carrying a lot of suspended matter, and visibility was less than five meters. If we were going to find the wreck in this murk, we would have to put the divers right on top of it.

That evening, we headed back to Mahdia feeling a little despondent—we could see this going on for days, as in 1993. We debriefed in the wardroom. I opened proceedings with a pointed critique of our navigation. When the talking was over, Fethi produced an idea that clearly had merit.

He had been doing his homework in the archive in Tunis and had found a scribbled notation in the margin of one of the Merlin documents. It seemed to be a sextant angle on the Sidi Jabar lighthouse that varied slightly from the one we were using. It was not in Merlin's handwriting, so it was probably by one of the senior officers on one of his boats, and, therefore, argued Fethi, was perhaps more reliable. We decided to give it a try.

The next day, all memory of the storm had gone. There was not a breath upon the water, not a cloud in the sky. It was a morning of unimpeachable calm and serenity—a perfect day to put Fethi's new bearing to the

Left: Computer-animated rendition of Cousteau's lines of sight.
Below: The team aboard *Milbrook.*

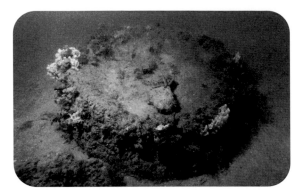

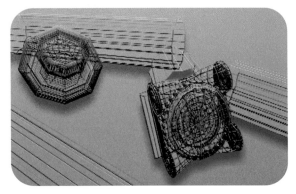

Above: **Underwater and computer-generated columns and capitals.**

test. We anchored and, in search patterns around the ship, deployed pairs of divers from an inflatable. Underwater, the visibility was good, but one after another the divers came back with nothing to report; just empty prairies, patches of sand, and endless fields of eel grass bending in the current. During the afternoon, the wind began to build, as usual. Most of us were taking it easy in the shade of the awning that we had put up over the foredeck—we had just eaten and were all feeling a bit languid.

I remember hearing the timekeeper announce that the divers were up, and the outboard ruining the peace as it roared to life. And then the radio crackled with the words Fethi and I longed to hear: "We have found the wreck. We have found the wreck."

In an instant, everybody was on their feet cheering. A bottle of something appeared, and, against all the rules, we each took a mouthful and Fethi poured a libation over the side to the gods of the deep.

The wreck had been found by Nizar Lassoued, a short, stocky diver with an infectious smile. Nizar had only seen one column at first, but as he and his partner moved in closer, they could see another, and then another, until at last they came to the wreck.

Nizar was the man of the hour. He was a popular person on the team and everybody shared his delight. Even Sumner, not a man who smiled easily, was grinning all over, that day. Sumner had been involved in maritime archeology for many years and he knew that this was a moment to cherish.

All I had seen in 1993 was an outlying column that had been dumped there by one of the earlier teams. At last, I was to see the wreck. Spread-eagled and face down, we let ourselves fall through the water. My eyes strained for their first glimpse of the Roman plunder ship.

It wasn't until I reached 25 meters that the first phantomlike shadows began to appear from out of the dissolve. A few meters more and I was looking down on a logjam of columns. The first thing that struck me was the richness of the marine life over the site. Hundreds of tiny wrasse and corvina fussed around us, and every now and again, small schools of bream and red mullet sliced by. The columns themselves were hardly recognizable as such, for, over two millennia, they had been nibbled, gnawed, and bored and were covered in a range of corals and several types of sponge. One of the divers who was with me turned on his camera lights, and all at once, the columns were illuminated in a crescendo of color that surprised even the fish.

Between the columns were the hunched forms of capitals and column bases; some of the narrower forms suggested components from the entablature that went over the columns. At two places in the sand, I saw wood from the ship's hull protruding.

The next day we were all up at 4:30 A.M., anxious to cram in a full day of diving before the afternoon winds came. Bryan Smith was with me. He was a former oil-rig diver and retired ship's captain who had first joined one of my wreck projects in 1983, when we were working off the Tuscan Islands. Every year since, he and his wife Ann had worked with me on sites all over the world. As far as I was concerned, there was nobody better or more experienced at wreck survey than Bryan. Fethi and I decided to give him the responsibility of mapping the site.

The next day, Bryan briefed the team on what was required, and they began the task of laying a baseline and establishing datum points. By the end of the day, everything was in place and ready to begin mapping. That afternoon Fethi, Sumner, Bryan, and I were sitting in the wardroom when Andy the mate appeared at the doorway. From his somber expression, I knew it was not good news

Below: Documenting the columns on video and for the site plan. *Inset:* After days of mounting despair, Nizar Lassoued (in the middle at the stern) proved the man of the hour. One of Fethi's divers, Nizar was already a favorite of the crew, but after finding the wreck, he even got Sumner Gerard grinning.

Above: Bryan Smith and his wife, Ann, have been a mainstay of Oxford University MARE field operations since 1982. Bryan had the responsibility of establishing the survey points and mapping the site.
Below: Surveying the area with a metal detector.

even before he handed us the slip of paper with the next day's weather forecast on it. Two words said it all: Force 5.

It was a sirocco, coming in off the Sahara, a hot wind, dry rather than sultry, so dry that it sucked the moisture from your very marrow. It made you feel as if your tongue had been dipped in talcum powder. Waiting it out, we drank a lot—we had to. Most of my time during this period was spent in the *medina* in the tiny and unspoiled Place du Caire, which one of the team's guide books described as "the most perfect little square in all Tunisia." There we would sit all day under the trees reading, writing, and drinking coffee. Sometimes we would order hookahs, or water pipes, and sit around in a listless state that reminded me of the caterpillar on the mushroom in *Alice in Wonderland*.

For over a week, we sat waiting for the weather to improve. We ventured out twice, but on both occasions had to return to port. Once again, Fethi and I knew that we had been beaten by the weather. In the time we had left, we could not possibly complete the map. To Bryan and me, this was a source

of great vexation, but the men from INP accepted it with an equanimity that was foreign to us. It was from them that I learned my first word of Arabic, *maktub*. All is *maktub*, "written," preordained.

Serious diving began again on August 24. Although we could not finish, we were determined to do as much as we could. I dived with my wife, Joanna. The storm had scoured away some of the sand, exposing more timbers. Joanna spotted some amphora fragments and the base of a cup. Clearly, there were more things under the sands, including the many arms and heads and other bits that were missing from the artworks raised by Merlin.

Slowly, over the next four days, the measurements and angles began to come in from the site, and, bit by bit, Bryan and Fethi's draftsmen produced a faithful plan of just over half the wreck. "Another three days of good diving and we can finish it," said Bryan hopefully. But it could not be; the following day the *Milbrook* had to leave for Tunis, where a press conference had been arranged.

That evening, I was in a cafeteria beside the great *bab* of Mahdia, the Skifa el-Kahla (Dark Gate), all that is now left of the massive fortification wall built across the headland to protect the town from attack. I was sitting in a round-backed wicker chair under a ceiling fan, feeling a bit like Sydney Greenstreet, when in came Amat, an acquaintance from my days at the Corniche. He proceeded to remind me of something that I had

almost managed to forget. Now it had come back, but with a twist.

One night during the 1993 expedition, a member of the team got drunk and bought himself a camel. The next morning, horrorstruck by what he had done, he came to me to sort it out. Anxious to avoid an international incident, I had gone to see the vendor, an old rogue (let's call him Daud) whom I knew in a passing way from the bar of the Corniche. He refused to take back the animal, insisting all the time that it had very fine teeth. In the end, I had to pay him the same amount to be rid of the cantankerous-looking brute as our team member had paid to acquire it.

It turned out that Daud had been telling the story to anybody who would listen for the last three years, and Amat wanted to know if it was true. Reluctantly, I admitted it was.

"And did you know that the camel wasn't his?" he asked. I guess the expression on my face must have answered the question,

Above, top: One of the Ionic capitals recently returned from the conservators in Germany. Mensun noted that the decoration was not perfectly symmetrical. But when it was in place at the top of a column, who from twenty feet below would ever notice?
Bottom: An unrestored capital in the Bardo Museum.

for without waiting, he went on to explain that Daud himself hadn't seen the animal before that night. Evidently it was just some old beast that had spent its life going around in circles, blindfolded, drawing water from a well.

"You Europeans," Amat said, "you are all so . . . how do you say, *crédule*?"

"Gullible?" I volunteered.

"Yes," he replied.

"Quite," I said.

The next day, the *Milbrook* left for Tunis. As much as I would have enjoyed a trip up the Sahel coast and around Cap Bon, I was anxious to arrive as soon as possible in Tunis, where arrangements had been made for me to see the Mahdia material that was in storage at the Bardo.

The Bardo Museum, at one time the palace of the Beys, or rulers, of Tunis (one of whom plays a small role in the next chapter),

Above, top and opposite: This piece of the ship's keel was cut from the wreck by the de Frondeville expedition in the 1950s. Although shrunken and much deteriorated, it nonetheless gave us key information on the vessel's construction. *Above, bottom:* Habib Ben Younes, director of the Bardo (right), shows Mensun some of the architectural pieces from the wreck.

is the finest museum in North Africa outside of Cairo, and it boasts the best collection of mosaics in the world. They are all over the walls and floors, each a snapshot of life under Roman rule.

I was met with great warmth by Habib Ben Younes and Dr. Sliem Khosrof, the museum's director and the chief conservator, respectively. Together they took me through all the closed rooms where Mahdia material was temporarily stored. Much of it was still in boxes, having just been returned from the exhibition in Bonn. Bits of statue, crates, capitals, items covered in canvas, it all reminded me of the warehouse scene in *Citizen Kane*.

But what I really wanted to see was arranged on boxes in a room all by itself: the section of keel raised by de Frondeville in 1955. Because there had been no adequate conservation methods available for timbers of this size at the time, it had shrunk, shriveled, and contorted. The technical information, however, was all still there, and I could see that, as I suspected, the Mahdia ship was a well-made vessel, using all the best materials and techniques of her day.

On September 5, we held a press conference on board the *Milbrook* in La Goulette (the Gullet), the deep-water port on the Bay of Tunis. The next day, the story of our work was carried in all the Arabic and French newspapers. One paper summarized it best when it said, "for the first time in its long and convoluted history, the Mahdia ship has been studied by archaeologists."

The following day I went to Fethi's office to say goodbye. We talked for a while, about the dive and the work still to be done, and then I suggested that we take a last coffee together in the *souks*. I had just enough time before having to leave for the airport. He thought about it for a moment and then said, "I have something I want you to see before you go." Instead of heading toward the main door and into rue du Chateau as I expected, he led me up a series of old staircases until at last we came out on the roof.

It was beautiful. We could see out over the city in all directions. It was early evening and the sun, turning crimson from the dust that was coming in from the Sahara, was low over the Jebel Ammar. The colors were now soft and the shadows long. We could see Lac du Tunis and follow its dikes to La Goulette, where *Milbrook* was riding at anchor. I looked at my watch; Sumner would now be eating in the wardroom, his only companion a book.

We talked a little about the Mahdia wreck and then for a while said nothing as we studied the cupolas and minarets of the *medina*. Fethi looked at me to speak; from the pause that followed I knew he was trying to shape a fairly complex thought from Arabic into simple English. "You know, Mensun, we are now part of the Mahdia wreck. . . . Whoever touches this wreck becomes a part of it." It was a strange thing to say; but I knew what he meant. I knew exactly what he meant. ❑

On the deck of HMS *Rose*, a replica Nelsonian ship that resembles the *Agamemnon* in many respects.

Six thousand miles from home, the great wooden fighting ship lay on her starboard side, mortally wounded. For three days her crew had picked her decrepit old carcass clean, salvaging stores and sails and rigging, anything that might be of use to ships still afloat, for this one would never sail again. Her sailors had mourned her, tired tears mingling with chill rain as they said goodbye. But they were gone now, and her last living denizens, the rats, had left too, gibbering and squealing as they fled the rising water within her and made for land.

She was alone, deserted on a mud bank beside a desolate little rock of an island off the coast of South America that was now her gravesite. In the gathering dusk of the austral winter, the wind wailed a dirge as the enfolding sea flowed through her timbers. Slowly, His Majesty's Ship Agamemnon*, once the pride of the British fleet, settled deeper into the sand—eventually to break apart.*

The sea would cover her soon enough, but it would never efface her history; the Agamemnon *was part of a legend. On her decks was forged the fame of Horatio*

GHOST OF TRAFALGAR

Nelson, Britain's most beloved hero and the greatest admiral ever to sail the ocean. She had been his first ship-of-the-line command, and even after he left her, she remained his "favorite"—fierce, fast, and agile, a ship with a heart that beat for battle, just as his did. She would outlive him; he would die gloriously and she pitiably. But they would both be entwined in immortality just the same.

Below: **Portrait of Nelson by Lemuel Abbot in 1798–99. The decorations on his left breast include the Turkish Order of the Crescent, the Neapolitan Order of St. Ferdinand and of Merit, and, at bottom, the Order of the Bath featured on the seal recovered from the** *Agamemnon.*

"I'm thinking about sponsoring some wreck excavations off Uruguay," he said, adding that he had heard that I did evaluations and consulted on historic wrecks. He wanted me to go to Uruguay for him, survey the sites, and report back.

The timing was bad. A big summer of wreck excavation was looming, and I was thin on personnel and equipment. I was not inclined to accept the job, despite Scott's inducement that I could take my family and any team members that might be required.

"Tell me about the wrecks," I said at last, expecting the usual mix of fantasy and fishermen's stories.

"They've found three wrecks, all in Maldonado Bay beside Punta del Este," he told me. Speculation was that the first was a slave ship called the *Seahorse*, the second a Spanish troopship called the *Salvador*. Interesting, but hardly compelling.

The third, he said, was believed to be a Royal Navy ship of the Napoleonic era, the *Agamemnon*.

I didn't need to hear more. At that instant I knew I had to go.

YOUNG HORACE

It was the legend that had drawn me here, to the chocolate-dark waters of Maldonado Bay at the yawning mouth of the Rio de la Plata. As a schoolboy, I had learned as though it were a catechism the story of Vice Admiral Lord Horatio Viscount Nelson, of his exploits at the Battles of the Nile and of Copenhagen and—greatest of all—Trafalgar, where his genius foreshadowed the doom of Napoleon. I remember how as a youngster I would watch the ceremonies on the anniversary of Trafalgar, when naval officers would lift their glasses and solemnly toast: "To the immortal memory." I could not have imagined then that one day I would, in a sense, meet the shade of Nelson, almost face to face.

The adventure began unremarkably enough. I was in Greece on an expedition in 1993 when I received a phone call at my hotel from Scott Perry, an old schoolmate from my days in Montevideo. He was still in South America, in the shipping business, and I had not heard from him in 20 years. But he had some news he thought might interest me.

That I felt a link with Nelson was hardly unusual—in all parts of what was once the British Empire, almost every boy aspired to such kinship at one time or another, for no man has ever been more venerated by Britons. This was true even in the remote Falkland Islands of my childhood, where we boasted a special bond: had it not been for the Falkland Islands, Nelson might never have gone to sea.

Those with a penchant for the more obscure corners of history may remember that in 1770, the Falklands took Britain, Spain, and France to the brink of war. A Spanish force had attacked and occupied the British settlement of Port Egmont on the tiny island of Saunders in the West Falklands. Since the Treaty of Paris in 1763, Britain had been the world's dominant power, and this impertinence by Spain was not to be endured. Matters rapidly deteriorated after Britain demanded immediate restitution of the islands, for instead of complying, Spain's King Charles III sought an alliance with France. Britain girded herself for war.

Ships that had been decommissioned and mothballed at the end of the Seven Years' War were recommissioned. One of these was the warship *Raisonnable*, captured from the French after a fierce struggle 12 years earlier. To mobilize the new fleet, naval officers that had been pensioned on half pay were recalled to duty. The man recalled to command the *Raisonnable* was Captain Maurice Suckling, uncle of Horatio Nelson.

Notice of the appointment appeared in a local paper in Norfolk, where it was seen by the father of "Young Horace," as Nelson was known to his family. As one of eight surviving children of a well-bred but impecunious rural parson, Young Horace's prospects were doubtful, the more so because the boy was consitutionally frail. Probably with these limitations in mind, young Horace urged his father, the Reverend Edmund Nelson, to write to Uncle Suckling seeking a position for him on the *Raisonnable*.

"What has poor Horace done, who is so weak, that he above all the rest should be sent to rough it out at sea?" Suckling jocularly inquired. "But let him come; and the first time we go into action, a cannonball may knock off his head, and provide for him at once."

So it was that because of the Falklands, Young Horace Nelson arrived in Chatham in 1771 to report for duty as a midshipman on board HMS *Raisonnable*. He was 12 years old.

As he looked around Chatham that day, Horace's eyes might well have lingered on the great form of the 102-gun *Victory*, ordered in the year of his birth. He could not have known, of course, what part that huge she-elephant of a ship would play in his future. Although she had been launched in 1765, she would not be commissioned until seven years later, and her time of glory as part of Nelson's legend was still decades away.

Opposite, top to bottom: Punta del Este, where the team's boats were berthed; "souvenir" cross, and a barnacle-encrusted wine-glass from *Salvador*, a wreck close to *Agamemnon*.

Below: Horatio, Viscount Nelson, Duke of Brontë, by John Hoppner. The painting was commissioned by the Prince of Wales, and Nelson sat for it in 1802. The naval battle in the background of the original was Copenhagen, but in copies made after Nelson's death, it was altered to Trafalgar.

Norfolk, 1771

So was Nelson's glory, as things turned out, for his first venture at sea was brief and uneventful. France's King Louis XV had no desire for another war with Britain and declined Spanish invitations for an alliance. Spain returned the Falklands to Britain. Honor satisfied, war fever quickly subsided and the *Raisonnable* was again decommissioned. Nelson had been aboard a mere five months.

At 14, Nelson would resume his midshipman's training and thereafter rise quickly through the ranks, partly because he was a competent officer and partly because his Uncle Maurice, who was eventually named comptroller of the navy, did his best for his favorite nephew. (Such nepotism was in no way viewed askance in those days; for those lucky enough to have family influence, using it was

expected and accepted.) Nelson was made a captain when he was only 20 and was subsequently given larger and larger ships.

After attaining captaincy, however, several of his next 14 years were spent in peacetime duty. To his restless dismay, Nelson saw no action in major sea battles and never commanded a fighting ship. No glory was to be had in peacetime patrols of England's colonies, and this tortured him, for he was in the grip of a vision.

On one of his earliest missions—duty aboard a frigate in the East Indies—the teenaged Nelson had contracted "a malignant disorder," probably a fever of some kind, and been sent home. Skeletal and delirious, he spent much of the voyage back to England in a near-suicidal depression, fantasizing about

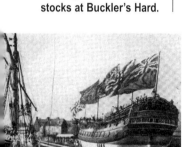

Top to bottom: Launching of the *Agamemnon*; model of the *Agamemnon* on the stocks at Buckler's Hard.

his future, apparently beset by occasional hallucinations. In one, he saw a "radiant orb" beckoning to him. "After a long and gloomy reverie, in which I almost wished myself overboard, a sudden glow of patriotism was kindled within me, and presented my King and Country as my patron," he later wrote. "My mind exulted the idea. Well then, I exclaimed, I will be a hero, and confiding in Providence I will brave every danger."

Young Horace would grow into a small man—sickly, unimpressive, and prone to melancholy. But his faith in that youthful epiphany would never waver. Years before his countrymen would call him "The Hero," he believed himself destined to be exactly that.

THE BIRTH OF A FIGHTING SHIP

About a year before young Horatio Nelson attained the rank of captain, the vessel that would carry him toward his destiny was beginning to take shape.

Considering her future renown, the *Agamemnon*'s beginnings were humble. She was born not in one of Britain's great ship-building centers or ports, but at Buckler's Hard, a rural shipbuilding community on the Beaulieu River, which flows into the Solent Channel by way of the New Forest area of Hampshire, one of the lovelier corners of southern England.

The townsfolk of Buckler's Hard (a "hard" is an area of shoreline or riverbank suitable for landing) had been building ships since the 17th century, and it was there that master builder Henry Adams laid down the *Agamemnon*'s keel in 1777.

Adams, whose house still survives beside the shipyard and whose portrait hangs in a little local museum, had arrived at Buckler's Hard in 1740 to oversee the construction of ships for the Royal Navy. It is a measure of the regard in which he was held by the admiralty that no fewer than 27 naval vessels were built by him, three of which were among the 33 ships of the line that fought at Trafalgar.

Much of Adams's value lay in his knowledge of mathematics; while most ship-builders worked from models, he was able to follow a designer's plans. *Agamemnon* was the third in a series of seven ships of the *Ardent* class designed by Sir Thomas Slade, a notable naval architect who had also drawn the plans for the *Victory*. (A "class" was named after the first ship in the series.) Slade had a unique feel for balance and proportion, and his ships were notable for being responsive and fast.

The great wooden sailing ships of those days grew from the spine outward and upward. The *Agamemnon*'s spine was an elm keel nearly 132 feet long, laid out on blocks in a bay cut into the embankment on the main foreshore of the yard at Buckler's Hard. From the keel rose oak ribs, or frames, of different lengths, their curves and countercurves pointing skyward,

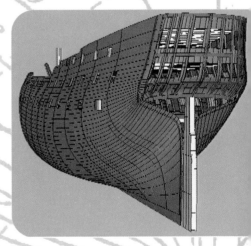

Below: Part of a computer-animated re-creation of *Agamemnon* made for the documentary film.

Background: Schematic of the *Ardent* class.

some punctuated with breaks that would become gunports.

Bracing the frames were her clamp, waterway, and beam timbers, which marked out what would become her various deck levels. Her bow would be broad, while at the stern there would be a deep tuck below a wide transom—the area for the captain's gallery, a balcony from which he could hail the men on the poop deck above.

Once the ship's skeleton was in place, she was clad inboard and out with thick planks of English oak. Forty acres of hundred-year-old oaks went into the making of the *Agamemnon*. One hundred tons of wrought iron and about 35 tons of copper nails and bolts helped hold her together. Her figurehead was a fierce-looking, black-bearded rendering of Agamemnon, legendary king of Mycenae, the ill-starred ruler who led the Greeks to victory in the Trojan War, only to be murdered at his homecoming by his own wife. He held a sword in one hand and a gold-painted helmet rested on his head.

The cost of the *Agamemnon*'s basic construction was £20,579, about $25 million in today's money. (A comparable modern warship may cost as much as $500 million.)

The hull was completed on March 28, 1781, and on April 10 she was launched in the presence of a small crowd that included Navy Board surveyors and visiting lords and commissioners of the Admiralty.

It rained torrentially that day—supposedly an ill omen—but *Agamemnon* was beautiful nonetheless. Her polished oak and fittings gleamed in the gray light, and huge flags flew from temporary spars rigged to her still-mastless decks. After speeches by dignitaries and a band's rendering of some patriotic tunes, the chocks were knocked away from the freshly greased main rails of the slipway, and *Agamemnon* began her stately slide into the Beaulieu River. Among the onlookers was her first captain, Benjamin Caldwell, who pronounced himself well pleased with her.

The following day, she was towed by oared open boats out into the Solent and then on to Portsmouth, where she arrived six days after her launch. There she was moored alongside a vessel fitted with "sheer-legs," a kind of derrick used to guide her oaken lower masts into position. Afterward, the upper masts were fidded into place. At the same time, shipwrights and riggers labored to complete her timberwork, rigging, and fittings. The *Agamemnon* carried no less than 20 miles of rigging, controlled by 1,000 pulleys, with which to manage an acre of sail.

Finally, when almost ready for sea, she was dry-docked to have her hull below the waterline felted, pitched, and coppered for swiftness and durability. The patchwork copper sheathing retarded marine growth that would have compromised her speed, and more important, protected her from voracious marine borers, worms that can turn a wooden hull into a maze of tunnels the thickness of one's little finger.

On July 6, the *Agamemnon* was fitted out with her real reason for existence: her guns. British naval ships of the day were rated according to the armament they carried, their size being commensurate with the cannons they bore. A third rater—not among the biggest of the men-of-war—the *Agamemnon* bore 64 cannon: twenty-six 24-pounders on her gun deck, twenty-six 18-pounders on her upper deck, ten 9-pounders on the quarter deck, and two 9-pounders on the forecastle. The cannons' designations represented the weight of the ammunition each delivered in a salvo.

Now fully armed, she sailed out of Portsmouth on July 9 for her maiden voyage. Her first stop was Spithead, where she arrived later the same day and waited five weeks at anchor while she took on her full complement of nearly 500 officers and men, as well as 141 marines.

On August 19, she departed on a five-day shakedown cruise prior to joining the Channel fleet. Captain Caldwell was well pleased with her performance: *Agamemnon* responded well at the stern, held the wind easily, rode well at anchor, and, above all, she was *fast*: with all her sails bellied out before the wind, she could manage 10½ knots without straining. She would soon earn a reputation as one of the swiftest ships in the Royal Navy.

PERILOUS DAYS

The *Agamemnon* was sailing into dangerous times. The European political scene was a chessboard of shifting aims and alliances, with the great powers jockeying for supremacy on the Continent and fighting to maintain, expand, and exploit their colonies abroad, including those in the New World. Indeed, the vessel had come into being during a frenzy of shipbuilding as England strove—futilely, it turned out—to quell a rebellion by some upstart North American colonies that had taken to calling themselves the United States of America.

When the *Agamemnon* was launched in 1781, the insurrection—which the eventual victors were later able to call the Revolutionary War—had been in progress for six years. Although the colonists were no threat to British naval dominance, their allies the French—Britain's perennial enemies—were. France had entered the fray as a pretext for attacking the British at a time when the Royal Navy was stretched thin. The English fleet had all but annihilated the French navy in the Seven Years' War, but Louis XVI had authorized massive rebuilding, so that France's 74 ships of the line, plus another 60 fighting vessels from allied Spain, solidly outnumbered those of the British fleet.

Below: Longitudinal section of the *Agamemnon.*

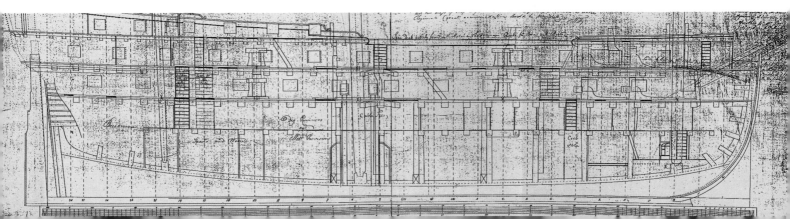

The French fleet in the Americas depended on a supply train across the Atlantic, which the British thus targeted. On December 12, 1781, the *Agamemnon* was one of 12 warships under Rear Admiral Richard Kempenfeldt that devastated a French convoy, including an escort of 19 fighting ships, off the coast of Brittany, about 150 miles southwest of Ushant. The British took 15 merchant ships, each full of badly needed military supplies.

Tactically, Kempenfeldt's battle had been fought in formal 18th-century fashion: The ships of one side formed a line, and the opposing ships formed another line. As the two lines drew parallel—generally with ships carrying similar firepower matched up against each other—they began blazing away with cannons. The side that shot fastest and truest, as the experienced and well-trained British usually did, was apt to win.

The line-to-line battle had become so traditional—it had not varied in a century or more—that its configuration had given its name to fighting ships: "ships of the line." Since the tactic usually worked well for England, it had become enshrined in the Royal Navy's manual of fighting instructions.

But times were changing, and these great formal engagements were becoming less and less effective. Gun technology had not advanced much since the days of the Spanish Armada, but shipbuilding had; although a single broadside could deliver half a ton of solid shot, at a distance this was no longer always lethal against a generation of heavily wooded fighting ships. In close, where a 32-pound ball could smash a head-sized hole through two feet of solid oak, such openings were easily plugged by good carpenters long before a ship's seaworthiness would be affected.

Indeed, such was the progress in shipbuilding and repair that in one of the 18th-century wars against France, not a single British ship was lost to enemy action. By the time of the American Revolution, it was obvious to all but the most myopic that line battles did not win wars anymore. About a year after her launch, the *Agamemnon* was on hand when new tactics were introduced.

In February 1782, the *Agamemnon* had sailed for the Caribbean in a squadron of 12 ships under Admiral Sir George Rodney, there to link up with the British West Indies fleet under Rear Admiral Lord Samuel Hood. In April, the British fleet of 36 ships encountered 33 French ships near a group of little islands called The Saintes, between Guadeloupe and Dominica. The usual lines were formed, and the two fleets converged on opposite tacks—but then something remarkable happened.

Two ships astern of the *Agamemnon*, Admiral Rodney turned his flagship *Formidable* into an opening in the French line, firing broadsides as she went. Seeing this, the cap-

Below: HMS *Victory* was a first-rate, 100-gun three-decker, floated at Chatham in 1765. These guns could deliver over a half ton of shot in a single broadside. She was designed by Sir Thomas Slade, the same man who conceived *Agamemnon*. *Victory* is open to the public at Portsmouth.

tain of the *Duke*, just ahead of the *Formidable*, also turned his ship. Between them they sandwiched four enemy vessels and mauled them badly. As other ships of the French line went through the time-consuming process of coming about to aid their threatened sister ships, they too became easy prey. The battle dissolved into a free-for-all, and the British, with superior seamanship and gunnery, were the clear victors, capturing five French ships.

Two years later, off Ushant in what became known as the Battle of the Glorious First of June, Admiral Richard Howe ordered his ships to again break the French line; the result was another significant British victory.

These two unorthodox battles did not revolutionize naval warfare overnight, but their impact was felt—not least by young Captain Horatio Nelson, who was moving ever closer to the *Agamemnon* and his destiny.

URUGUAY, 1993

Destiny seemed to be whispering to me, too, though perhaps not in so grand a way as it had to Nelson. Coming back to Uruguay in November 1993 after being away for 21 years, I felt that one great circle in my life was closing, another opening.

With me was my wife, Joanna, our three-year-old son, Cody, and some members of my crew, including Gianluigi Saco (affectionately known by all on my team as Gigi), a longtime colleague from Italy.

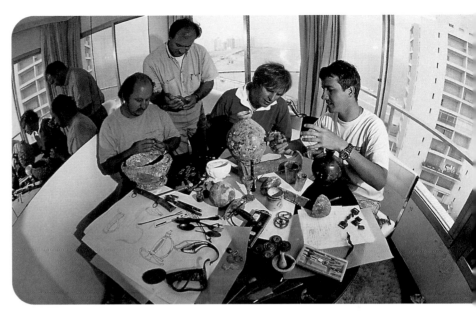

I watched from the window of the plane as the jungles of Brazil gave way to the grassy savannas and rolling pampas of Uruguay. As we began our descent, we circled over a huge quilt of brown water that was instantly familiar to me as the Rio de la Plata—the River Plate, as the British have always called it. It is the widest estuary in the world, reaching more than 100 miles from one side of its mouth, in Uruguay, to the other, in Argentina. Its tenebrous waters look serene enough from the air, but I knew this to be deceptive. The Plate's vast, mutating mud banks, furious currents, and notorious southwesterly storms —the *pamperos*—had swallowed more fine ships than had even the infamous Goodwin Sands of the English Channel.

As we drove through Montevideo toward our downtown hotel, I thought that the old city had not changed all that much despite big shopping centers in the suburbs

Above, top: Sergio Pronczuk, Ugo Pintos, Mensun, and Hector Bado examine and clean some of the artifacts from *Agamemnon* and *Salvador*. Punta del Este can be seen outside the window.
Above, bottom: The search for the *Agamemnon* was complicated by the wreck of a Spanish ship, *Salvador*, of the same period that went down nearby. This leering skull is one of many remains near the wreck.

Uruguay, 1993

drawing people away from the city center, and the main street, avenida 18 de Julio, looking a bit faded from my schoolboy days (although, perhaps, this was no more than the inevitable effect of passing time). To the outsider, Montevideo may have little in the way of imposing buildings, museums, or monuments that mark great cities, but it has its own exotic charm. To me, simply, it is the finest city in the world. I loved seeing it again.

After checking into the hotel, I went to meet the two divers who had first found the wreck believed to be the *Agamemnon*, Hector Bado and Sergio Pronczuk.

Hector and Sergio are about as different from each other as two people can be. Hector, of Italian origin, is full of flair, imagination, and impulsive drive. Sergio, of Polish extraction, is phlegmatic, dependable, cautious, and untiring. But for all their contrasts, they—and I—shared a common bond: a passion for ships, shipwrecks, and the sea. From our first meeting, we all got on well. They flattered me by knowing much about my previous work. For my part, I was enormously impressed by the quality and extent of their archive research and the results of their searches in the River Plate. It seemed to me that if these men were convinced that they had found Nelson's ship,

then based on the work they showed me, they were probably right.

Our search for the *Agamemnon* and the other two wrecks that I had agreed to evaluate began with a drive to Punta del Este, a two-hour tour along the coast toward the Brazilian border. Punta del Este is the most expensive and exclusive resort in all of South America: anybody who is anybody, particularly from Brazil, Argentina, and Uruguay, spends at least part of the summer (November to March, south of the equator) at Punta. Once summer ends, the place empties as the great villas are boarded up and the restaurants and nightclubs close until the next season. We would be there in the off-season, and the town would be devoid of tourists.

Scott Perry had arranged a large apartment for us just off the main street, overlooking Maldonado Bay. The view was much as I remembered—miles of beach and dunes. A mile or so across the water lay the long, flat form of Gorriti Island, the desolate spot where the *Agamemnon* had run aground. In her day, it had been overgrown with wild asparagus and inhabited only by rabbits. Pine trees grew there now, but it still looked quite bleak and forlorn.

Maldonado Bay had been important to the old sailing ships because on its shores was the town of San Fernando de Maldonado, whose attraction was a stream of pure, limpid water. Unless a ship wanted to risk going up the Plate estuary, with its partly charted channels, deadly currents, and glutinous sands, this was the best watering hole for hundreds of miles north or south.

For a diver, the Plate is difficult and dangerous; the currents are treacherous and the visibility near zero—*at* zero when the slightest wind ruffles the water to disturb its ever-present load of silt. During our first few days in Punta del Este, the bay was undivable. But just as the frustration was becoming unbearable and I was phoning Oxford to see if I could stay a week longer, the wind dropped, and within a few hours the sea began to settle.

Even so, our diving boat was pitching hard as we made our way out of the marina and helmed starboard into the bay. Our first mission was to explore the wreck believed to be the Spanish merchant ship *Salvador*, which lay only 300 meters offshore. The dive turned out to be one of the most memorable of my career, worthy of a book on its own. But it was not what I had come for: less than a mile away across these murky waters probably lay the remains of *Agamemnon*.

AGAMEMNON UNDER NELSON

When destiny at last united Horatio Nelson and his first fighting ship, Britain and her navy were facing certain war. For a man of Nelson's nature, things could not have been better.

In the wake of the French Revolution, Europe was in turmoil. Having beheaded Louis XVI and Marie Antoinette—and

countless others—France was determined to export its bloody brand of republicanism to the rest of Europe; England was just as determined to protect the principle of monarchy. On January 30, 1793, an overjoyed Nelson received his commission to command the *Agamemnon*. Twelve days later, France declared war on England.

Britain's navy was ill prepared, but so too was that of the French. Almost a quarter of its experienced officers had either been guillotined or fled the country.

The Royal Navy set about organizing itself into two fleets. The first, under Lord Richard Howe, would be responsible for the Atlantic and home waters; the second, under Lord Samuel Hood, with his flag in the *Victory*, would take the Mediterranean station. Not only did

Opposite: Hilts from dead soldiers' swords were found on the wreck of *Salvador*.

Below: Human bones are rife among the many wrecks in the Plate; this one was caught in the flukes of our anchor.
Bottom: The replica of HMS *Rose* was used in the filming of the documentary.

Britain have vital interests in this area, but France was really a Mediterranean power, and there was no use blockading its Atlantic coast if the ports along its great southern underbelly were ignored.

Nelson was anxious that his crew should be the best—no resentful press-ganged sailors or dregs of the fleet from other ships. With the agreement of the Admiralty, no bills requesting men for the *Agamemnon* were posted around London until Nelson's own appointment was announced. In the meantime, he advertised for recruits in his home county of Norfolk and adjoining Suffolk, where his name was already known. Soon his muster lists began to fill with volunteers. It was the custom to refer to crewmen collectively after the name of their ship, so these recruits would become, then and forever, "Agamemnons."

From the start, Nelson was well pleased with the "Eggs and Bacon," as his crewmen—evidently not ardent classicists—affectionately called the *Agamemnon*. As he wrote to his wife, Fanny, "I have the pleasure in telling you that my ship is without exception the finest 64 in the service." From fighting in the Americas, she already had a reputation as a fast ship and a good sailor. "*Agamemnon* sails admirably," he wrote. "We think her better than any ship in the fleet."

Nelson's quarters were well appointed and comparatively spacious. His cabin was paneled, and around its sides were bookshelves, pictures, and a desk, table, and other items of furniture of his own choosing. A wide expanse of curtained windows gave him a good view of the sea and ensured that by day his cabin was well lit. To one side of the windows was a rack for his swords and pistols. A charcoal brazier provided heat. The cabin did have a low ceiling, but this would not have troubled Nelson, who was barely five-foot-six. Along one wall was his cot, and, in the center of the room, sat a large dining table where he could entertain guests who ate off the captain's own service with his own silver. In addition, Nelson had with him his devoted valet and his cook, who worked from the captain's private galley.

Although he clearly enjoyed the comforts of his office, Nelson was always attentive to the well-being of his men, anxious that they should be well dressed and well fed, and their quarters well ventilated. Doubtless the crew appreciated such concern, it being rare coin in the Royal Navy. On most ships, the food was terrible, the crew wasting from scurvy, the living quarters cramped and rife with vermin. Discipline could be brutal and even lethal, and in wartime, death in battle was not at all unlikely. For men who enlisted voluntarily, naval service was a last-resort sort of job. There was little honor in it—not, at least, until Nelson.

On April 24, 1793, the *Agamemnon* sailed for Sicily, where she and five other warships made rendezvous with Hood's squadron. By the beginning of June, she was on her way to Gibraltar by way of Cádiz, soon to be part of the epic Mediterranean campaign.

The fleet, now comprising 15 men-of-war, sailed from Gibraltar for Toulon on April 27, arriving there in mid-July to enforce a blockade. Aboard the *Agamemnon*, Nelson pondered a problem that had long troubled the Royal Navy: how to make the French come out and fight when they did not want to.

As it turned out, there was no need to draw out the reluctant enemy at Toulon. France's revolution was in its most horrific phase, the Reign of Terror, and the nation was in upheaval. There was even talk that Provence would proclaim itself an independent republic and seek the protection of Britain. At the end of August, Toulon turned royalist, so Hood entered the city and began preparing to defend it. In December, however, Toulon fell to the republican army. The successful French assault was planned and mounted by an upstart 24-year-old artillery officer who acted in defiance of his superiors' orders. His name was Napoleon Bonaparte.

Hood burned most of the shipping in the harbor and withdrew with 1,500 refugees. Even with that effort, around 6,000 men, women, and children who were left on the quays were mercilessly slaughtered by the French republicans. It was not Britain's finest hour.

Before these dire events, the *Agamemnon*, as the fastest sailor in the fleet, had been dispatched to Naples to seek troops from King Ferdinand to help reinforce Toulon. It was Nelson's first independent mission in the Mediterranean.

His ship arrived in the Bay of Naples on September 11 and remained at anchor there for four days, during which time Ferdinand himself dined on board, delighting at the British success at Toulon and promising Nelson 6,000 troops. It was also during this visit that—fatefully—Nelson met for the first time the 63-year-old British ambassador to Naples, Sir William Hamilton, and his beautiful 28-year-old wife, Emma.

Nelson spent his time in Naples with the Hamiltons, with whom he evidently struck up an immediate and genuine friendship. Although there is nothing to suggest that Emma instantly became the grand passion of his life, he seemed to find her enchanting, as most men did. On the third day of his stay, he wrote to his wife, with understandable restraint, that Lady Hamilton was "a young woman of amiable manners, and who does honour to the station to which she is raised."

That same afternoon Nelson left Naples rather hurriedly in pursuit of a ru-

Above, top to bottom: During 1793–94, *Agamemnon* was involved in the blockade and occupation of Toulon, the main naval base along the southern coast of France. It was during this phase of the Mediterranean campaign that Nelson first met Lady Emma Hamilton. On July 22, 1805, in a prelude to Trafalgar, *Agamemnon* was one of 15 ships of the line that took on 20 French and Spanish ships about 100 miles west of Cape Finisterre. *Agamemnon* was fifth in the line. She lost one of her yards and her mizzen topmast.

mored French frigate. He would not return until after his great victory at the Nile five years later.

Nelson next received orders from Hood to join Commodore Robert Linzee's squadron in Sardinia. One night on the way down the Sardinian coast, *Agamemnon*'s lookout spotted a French squadron of four frigates and a brig. By piling on every inch of canvas, the *Agamemnon* was able to catch up with the French and engage the rearmost frigate, the *Melpomène*. She proved an agile foe under competent command, and she was able to deliver broadsides at Nelson's ship, which could only reply with its bow guns. At the end of a three-hour fight, the *Agamemnon* had suffered major damage to her masts and rigging. One man was killed and six were wounded. But the *Melpomène* had been so badly mauled that had the other frigates not gone to her rescue, she might have been lost.

Before breaking off the action, Nelson sought advice from his officers on whether the *Agamemnon* was fit to continue fighting. All agreed that she needed immediate repair. With that, Nelson's first sea battle, a comparative success, was over. In his report to Hood, the captain paid tribute to his Agamemnons, who "conducted themselves entirely to my satisfaction."

Clearly, Nelson's high regard for his company was reciprocated. In a letter to his father, 12-year-old midshipman William Hoste related that "Captain Nelson is acknowledged to be one of the finest characters in the service, and is universally beloved by his men and officers." Those men and officers had learned one thing about their captain in the *Melpomène* engagement: he loved to fight.

Shortly after being repaired, the *Agamemnon* sailed with Linzee's squadron to North Africa to remonstrate with the Bey of Tunis over his tolerance, and even support, of the French, who at times tucked in a fleet beneath the city's artillery. On meeting with the Bey at his palace in the Casbah, Linzee was under Hood's orders to dissuade him from aiding the monarch-murdering French. When Linzee delivered the message, the Bey dryly replied that he shared a distaste for killing sovereigns, but had not the British committed such an act themselves? Nelson, well aware that the British had indeed beheaded Charles I in 1649, could do no more than grit his teeth. He was not a diplomat.

Unexpectedly, orders arrived from Hood at that point directing Nelson to leave Linzee for a command of his own. Delighted, Nelson wrote that Hood, "certainly the best officer I ever saw," had ordered him "to command a Squadron of Frigates off Corsica, and the Coast of Italy, to protect our trade and that of our new Ally, the Grand Duke of Tuscany, and to prevent any Ship or Vessel, of whatever Nation, from going into the port of Genoa."

Nelson considered the command "a very high compliment," since there were five captains in the fleet older than he. But before undertaking the new mission, Nelson was ordered to take the *Agamemnon* to Leghorn (modern-day Livorno) on the Tuscan coast for a refit. It was there, in December, that he learned of Toulon's fall to the French republicans.

With the collapse of Toulon, Hood had moved his base to Corsica, which was in revolt against French garrisons there. The royalists looked to Britain for support, and the British were happy to help: if the French could be ousted from Corsica, the Royal Navy would gain a valuable stronghold from which to mount operations in the Mediterranean.

Hood sent several ships, including Nelson's, to prevent the resupply of the beleaguered French. The *Agamemnon* left Leghorn at the end of January 1794, and ran into what Nelson described as "the hardest gale of wind almost ever remembered here. The *Agamemnon* did well but lost every sail in her. Lord Hood had joined me off Corsica the day before and would have landed the troops but the gale has dispersed them over the face of the waters. The *Victory* was very near lost. . . ."

Soon, rebounding from the gale, Nelson was harrying the French wherever he could. Twelve vessels loaded with wine were set on fire, and, at L'Avisena, a fort was attacked and taken. The *Agamemnon* struck all along the Corsican coast; part of her strategy was to confuse the French about the British fleet's main objective. In fact, Hood was after the town of San Fiorenzo, which he attacked on February 7 and took after several days. Now that he had a secure base, the admiral's eyes turned to Bastia.

However, to Hood's annoyance and Nelson's rage, Major-General David Dundas, commander of the British troops, refused to move against Bastia without reinforcements from Gibraltar. Nelson had urged the attack—earning disapproval from some senior officers who thought that so junior a captain had no business meddling in strategy—but in the end Hood allowed him to blockade the port town on his own and probe its defenses. On February 23, with the *Agamemnon* and two frigates under his command, Nelson engaged the shore batteries at short range. Afterward, a party was dispatched to look for suitable landing beaches and artillery emplacements, and Nelson sent a request to Naples for artillery and other ordnance.

By the second half of March, the *Agamemnon* had been at sea for three months and was without supplies—without fuel for the galley, "wine, beef, pork, flour, and almost without water," Nelson wrote to Hood, "not a rope, canvas, twine, or nail in the ship. The ship is so light she cannot hold her side to the wind. . . . We are certainly in a bad plight at present, not a man has slept dry for many months." Yet, he wrote, he was eager to stay. As was his way, Nelson found the prospect of missing a battle insupportable.

On March 18, Hood recalled Nelson to San Fiorenzo. Dundas had quit his command following bitter arguments with Hood over the feasibility of taking Bastia, and Hood needed Nelson's support to convince the admiralty of the practicality of the plan. Nelson was ada-

Below: **Nelson and his crew dragged *Agamemnon*'s cannons up these hills at Calvi to besiege the French fort and, not least, stick a finger in Napoleon's eye.**

mant that the town could be taken and outlined his proposal for a combined assault by land and sea. Still, the army refused.

Exasperated, Hood and Nelson determined to act alone; 1,248 soldiers—listed as marines, over whom Hood had authority—were embarked. On the night of April 3, the men were landed just north of Bastia.

By midday the troops and eight of the *Agamemnon*'s 24-pounders were ashore, together with eight 13-inch mortars sent from Naples. The men cut a makeshift path up the craggy mountainside. The cannons were tied onto sledges; then, anchoring the ship's biggest pulleys and tackle to boulders, the Agamemnons hauled the guns up the slopes. Sail canvas was sent ashore to make tents; sandbags were filled and carried up the hillsides and installed around the batteries.

Eight days after the landing, when the *Agamemnon* was ready to commence her bombardment, Hood sent a message from the *Victory* to the French commander offering terms. The Frenchman bravely replied, "I have hot shot for your ships, and bayonets for your men." Hood then raised a red flag from his main mast to signal Nelson to begin the action. In response, Nelson raised the British colors from his camp ashore and ordered the batteries to fire.

Day after day the siege went on, with the French returning as good as they got. "We are in high health and spirits," Nelson wrote. "We are few but of the right sort . . . I am very busy, yet own I am in all my glory." Five of the

Agamemnon crew were killed and Nelson himself sustained a wound in the back.

In early May, Nelson wrote to Fanny, "As a secret, Bastia will be ours between the 20th and 24th of this month, if succours do not get in." On May 21, after 37 days of staunch resistance, the citadel indeed capitulated. At 6 P.M. on May 23, the British rushed into Bastia, with Nelson's stepson, Josiah, at the head. It marked the end of the most difficult and protracted battle that the captain had ever known.

When Hood's dispatches on the fall of Bastia were published, Nelson was disappointed that his name had not been given the prominence he felt that it deserved. "The whole operation of the siege was carried on through Lord Hood's letters to me," he wrote. "I was the mover of it—I was the cause of its success."

Nelson invariably commanded the love of his men; they knew that he never asked more of them than he himself was willing to give, never subjected them to danger that he did not face. But his relationship with his superiors was often uneasy: hungry for glory, he was sensitive to slights and impatient with the caution of men less daring than he—which meant almost everybody. Nevertheless, the rift between him and Hood was shallow and soon healed, and after Bastia, Nelson and the *Agamemnon* were sent to prepare the siege of Calvi, another Corsican town. Nelson was again in charge of the naval forces.

On this campaign, the British had to endure wild weather, pestilence, and spirited defiance from the French, but, by August 12, Calvi was theirs, and with it a firm toehold in Corsica—at least for the time being. The victory had been costly: many had died, and, under the merciless Mediterranean sun, half of the surviving 2,000 British troops had fallen ill, most with malaria. Nelson himself was sick and wounded—Calvi had cost him the sight in his right eye. On the morning of July 10, an enemy shell had hit the parapet of the advance battery he was standing beside, spraying him with stones, sand, and splinters. One of the splinters hit his eye, which soon went blind.

It was a nasty, painful wound, but characteristically, Nelson made light of it. "I got a little hurt this morning," he wrote to Hood, "not much as you may judge from my writing." The injury never kept him out of action, and his name was not included on the official casualty lists. Later he lamented the loss of his sight, but noted wryly that the splinter had been "within a hair's breadth of taking off my head."

On October 11, 1794, Hood left for England in the *Victory*, and Vice Admiral Sir William Hotham succeeded him as commander in chief. Nelson was much saddened to see his friend leave. He was also homesick, even dreaming in his letters to Fanny of "some little cottage" in England. Yet when Hood gave him the opportunity to stay with the fleet, Nelson remained—with the fleet and with the *Agamemnon*. Hood had offered him a bigger command, a 74-gun ship, but Nelson could not bring himself to part with old Eggs and Bacon, or with "the ship's company with

whom I have gone through such a series of hard service as has never before, I believe, fallen to the lot of any ship."

Toward the end of November, Nelson put into Leghorn for a much-needed refit. There his ship remained until late in December to be dismantled and stripped down. It was not a happy period. "Lying in port is misery to me," he wrote. "My heart is almost broke to find the *Agamemnon* lying here, little better than a wreck." And beyond that tender sentiment was the overriding fear that the enemy might put out and that he would miss the action: "I am uneasy enough for fear they will fight, and the *Agamemnon* not present—it will almost break my heart."

He did well to worry. It was midwinter by the time the *Agamemnon* was operational again, and by then France was preparing for action. In a letter to his wife from Leghorn, dated March 2, 1795, Nelson stated that the French were assembling troops and transports, obviously planning an amphibious assault somewhere. On March 8, Admiral Hotham got word that 15 French ships of the line, along with assorted smaller vessels, had put out from Toulon and were heading for

Above: On July 10, 1796, during the siege of Calvi, Nelson lost the sight of his right eye when he was hit in the face and chest by splinters thrown up by an enemy shell. Despite the pain, he wrote to Lord Hood simply that "I got a little hurt this morning."

Corsica. The next morning, Hotham's fleet of 14 warships and one Neapolitan 74-gunner set out to intercept. They first sighted the French on March 10 and set out in pursuit. The fleets converged in long, drawn-out, uneven lines. This was to be Nelson's first line battle, and, being the fastest British fighting ship, his *Agamemnon* was out in front of the British charge.

On the morning of March 11, the *Ça Ira* (named after a French revolutionary song), third from the rear of the French line, collided with the vessel ahead of her and lost her fore and main topmasts. Her motive power much reduced, the great 80-gun Frenchman immediately dropped astern of the fleet, where she was set upon by the slippery little 36-gun frigate *Inconstant*. The *Inconstant* delivered two broadsides before being mauled by the *Ça Ira* and the *Vestale*, a French 36-gunner that had moved in to take the *Ça Ira* in tow. By that time, though, *Agamemnon* was bearing down.

Nelson's ship could not afford to get caught in an artillery duel with the *Ça Ira*, which was, Nelson wrote, "absolutely large enough to have taken the *Agamemnon* in her hold." Nelson's plan was to take his bow almost up to the stern of the *Ça Ira*, then to come

Ça Ira, despite being "absolutely large enough to have taken *Agamemnon* in her hold," was dismasted during a two-and-a-half-hour battle in which she suffered over a hundred casualties.

about and deliver a broadside along her full length. But "so true did she fire," he wrote later of his ship, "that not a shot missed some part of the ship, and latterly the masts were struck every shot, which obliged me to open fire a few minutes sooner than I intended. . . ."

Wasplike, the *Agamemnon* harried the *Ça Ira* from behind for two and a half hours, tacking back and forth across her stern, firing, losing seaway and regaining it, firing again, always avoiding the Frenchman's big side guns. By the time Admiral Hotham hoisted the recall signal, the *Ça Ira* had taken severe punishment, and about a hundred of her crew were dead or wounded. The *Agamemnon* had only seven wounded.

To Nelson's amazement and profound contempt, Hotham did not order a general chase. Later, when the *Agamemnon* fell into line behind the flagship *Britannia*, Nelson went on board the latter and on the quarter-deck urged Hotham to continue the pursuit. Hotham, however, declared himself content. Livid with scorn, Nelson wrote to Fanny that had he been in command, "either the whole French fleet would have graced my triumph, or I should have been in a confounded scrape."

Nelson's next important encounter with the enemy came in July at Hyères, off the Côte d'Azur, where again the British fleet gave chase to the French. With smoke hanging thick upon the windless ocean, the British pressed in to attack, but the ever-cautious Admiral Hotham, still about eight miles to the rear of the action, hoisted the signal to withdraw.

"That has ended our second meeting with these gentry," a furious Nelson wrote to the Duke of Clarence. "In the forenoon we had every prospect of taking every Ship in the Fleet, and at noon it was almost certain we should have had the six rear Ships."

Letting the French fleet escape again was a mistake that, in time, would have dire consequences: the British would lose hard-won Corsica and abandon the Mediterranean entirely, and Spain, fleetingly England's ally, would align herself with France—a France which by then was led by Napoleon Bonaparte.

❧

In December 1795, the *Agamemnon* once more put into Leghorn for refit and repair, or in Nelson's words, to make her "as fit for sea as a rotten ship can be." She had been in service now for almost fifteen years, and she was sorely weatherbeaten and war-battered. Her captain was feeling much the same. He had been aboard her for nearly three years, he was tired, the war on land was going France's way, and he longed for home. But at Leghorn he got news that revived his spirits: Hotham had returned to England because of ill health, and his replacement as commander of the British Mediterranean fleet was Sir John Jervis.

At 63, Jervis merited his reputation as a hard man and a disciplinarian. But he was also the most esteemed and accomplished officer in the Royal Navy. As a man of action and an outstanding strategist and leader, it was natural that he should appreciate these same

qualities in another, and at once he began to treat Nelson (as Nelson later put it) "more as an associate than a subordinate."

Nelson met Jervis for the first time in January 1796. In the great after-cabin of the *Victory*, Jervis offered him a bigger ship—the *St. George* of 98 guns, or the *Zealous* of 74. He politely declined—although Nelson could now, at times, be quite disparaging of her, he was nevertheless still wedded to the *Agamemnon*. Three months later, however, Nelson was honored to accept from Jervis the news that his promotion had come through and that he might hoist a commodore's broad pennant. Nelson now commanded a squadron of two ships of the line and four frigates.

On June 11, 1796, the *Agamemnon* was ordered back to England for yet another refit. She needed it; she was by then reduced to what Nelson called "a tub floating on water." He could have gone home with her, but as much as he missed England, he still thirsted for action and wanted very much to remain under Jervis. So on June 13, Nelson transferred his pennant to the 74-gun *Captain*, and along with him went most of the *Agamemnon*'s officers. Old Eggs and Bacon wallowed her way back to England, her time in the spotlight not yet done, but Horatio Nelson's time on her over.

One of Nelson's greatest biographers, the American historian Alfred Mahan, summarized Nelson's *Agamemnon* years this way:

> With the exception of the *Victory* . . .
> no ship has such intimate association
> with the career and name of Nelson

as has the *Agamemnon*. And this is but natural, for to her he was the captain, solely, simply, and entirely; identified with her alone, glorying in her excellences and in her achievements, one in purpose and in spirit with her officers and seamen; sharing their hopes, their dangers, and their triumphs; quickening them with his own ardor, molding them into his own image.

If the *Agamemnon* years were not the era of Nelson's greatest fame, they were surely the time of his greatest joy. "To the fullness of his glorious course," Mahan wrote, "these three years were what the days of early manhood are to ripened age; and they are marked by the same elasticity, hopefulness, and sanguine looking to the future that characterize youth, before illusions vanish and even success is found to disappoint."

DISCOVERY

By the time we had finished our dive on the ghostly *Salvador*, the sun was low and the sea was getting choppy. My mind moved across Maldonado Bay toward the little island where the *Agamemnon* had foundered some two centuries before. Could we find and dive the fabled ship before the sun set or the chop worsened? Truly, another day could hardly make a difference, but it did to me. I was obsessed with the need to find her. Hector, watching me, smiled.

"Let's go for the *Agamemnon*," he said, and without waiting for reply he gunned the engine and the boat came alive, the front lifted and slammed into the first wave.

Fifteen minutes later, we geared down and began moving back and forth in slow parallels, watching the echo sounder for any irregularity that might be the reflected presence of a sunken ship. Hector had only a rough idea of its position. The water was so dark and fast that we had to be right over the site before we could dive. It was Sergio who first noticed a slight anomaly on the echo-sounder that suggested a wreck.

Hector and I were already in our dive suits. We buckled on our weight belts and slid into the harnesses bearing our tanks. In seconds, we were in the water and striking out for the seabed. We landed on coarse sand. Visibility was minimal; I could see no more than a foot ahead. Hector put his hand in front of my mask and pointed me in the direction he wanted to go. Shoulder to shoulder, we finned into the current. It was hard work, and I was soon gulping my air.

Suddenly, we were in a pile of amorphous lumps. They were ballast blocks—it was a wreck. Hector pointed to the surface and waved goodbye. We had planned that if we found the wreck, he would go up and have the others buoy the spot so that they could join us.

Alone in the darkness, I began feeling my way around the wreck. I had a small spotlight attached to my mask, but the water was nearly impenetrable. Slowly I felt my way up a mound that was matted in mussels, probing its deep chinks and crannies with my light, seeking something, anything, to confirm the vessel's identity. Something that said Britain; something that said Royal Navy.

In one hole, there was an eerie disturbance. Something large was writhing about. I recognized the smooth, patterned skin of a conger eel. Further on, my light caught the body of another, then its slash-like mouth and small, cold snake eyes. The ballast mound was full of congers.

It was difficult in the darkness to judge how far I had moved; probably no more than 12 meters, but all at once I was in a forest of narrow uprights, each about 30 inches high. I scraped away the mussels from one of them. The way it gleamed in the light told me that it was made of a copper alloy—a keel bolt, the kind used to bond a ship's frames to her long spine. I felt around for bottom timbers, but found nothing but sand. I was certain this was the *Agamemnon*, but there was still no proof. Shortly, I returned to the surface.

Below, top: The piece of double-headed bar shot (third down) told the team that this was not the *Agamemnon,* but a ship of likely Spanish origin; an identical piece of bar shot was fired into the *Victory* by the *Santissima Trinidad* at Trafalgar, killing eight men. *Bottom:* From out of the gloom appeared a row of verticals covered in mussel shells—they proved to be copper-alloy keel bolts.

The next day the sea looked good, and by 10 A.M. we were back over the wreck. Gigi and Jo dived first, to try to take photographs before our fins further muddied the water. Hector, Sergio, and I waited half an hour and then followed them down. I soon met up with Jo and Gigi, who took me to look at an area of timbers. As I ran my hands over them, I thought of Henry Adams; almost certainly it was his men who had so expertly assembled and fashioned them two centuries ago at Buckler's Hard. The timbers, with planking on the outside, appeared to be from the ship's frame.

I then joined Hector, and we came across a twisted piece of copper sheathing from the exterior of the hull. As Hector turned it over in his hands, I ran the beam of my light over it. I was not particularly looking for marks, but there was one—it was less than a centimeter long, and we both thought that we recognized it. Hector rubbed his thumb over it to remove the marine deposits. Now there was

no doubt about what it was, and no doubt that this was the *Agamemnon*: the mark was the so-called broad arrow, with which all British government property, especially military property, was stamped. No other Royal Navy ship had been lost in this area.

With the identity of the wreck confirmed, I was jubilant. But more was to come. Toward the end of the dive, Hector, Sergio, Joanna, and I moved away from the wreck mound to explore the immediate surrounding area. Here, Hector and Sergio blundered into one of the ship's 24-pound iron cannons. We knew that most of the cannons had been salvaged shortly after the ship was lost, but some of the guns on the port side had been impossible to reach. The full importance of the find began to dawn on me: this was quite possibly the only surviving gun to have been fired at Trafalgar.

AFTER THE *AGAMEMNON*

Honed and hardened by more than three action-filled years aboard the *Agamemnon*, Nelson continued his rise in the Royal Navy; his nation was much in need of him. The same year, 1796, that the commodore left his first fighting ship, Napoleon led a ragged, hungry band of soldiers over the Alps and into northern Italy, winning victory after victory, driving the Austrians out, and closing Italian ports to British ships. By the autumn of 1796, Spain and Holland were allied with France against England, and, by the year's end, Corsica was back in French hands, and Britain had given up all its Mediterranean possessions except Gibraltar.

Against this backdrop, Nelson's daring in action against the Spanish on February 14, 1797, would establish his fame among his compatriots. In a successful engagement off Cape St. Vincent in southwest Portugal, he took two of the four Spanish ships captured that day, storming one—the *San Nicolas*—with his crew and using it as a bridge to seize the second, the *San Josef*. These heroics earned him a knighthood and promotion to rear admiral, and won an earldom for Admiral Jervis. In July, however, Nelson suffered a painful defeat. In pursuit of a Spanish treasure ship, he mounted an amphibious assault on Santa Cruz de Tenerife in the Canary Islands. The attack on the Spanish possession was repulsed, and cost many British casualties.

While ashore at Santa Cruz, Nelson himself took a shot that shattered his right arm at the elbow, leaving the lower part of the limb dangling on a few strings of flesh and tendon. As he returned to ship, he reportedly ordered that the surgeon "make haste and get his instruments. I know I must lose my right arm, so the sooner it is off the better." He endured the excruciating amputation with his customary stoicism, recalling later "the coldness of the knife" as it made the initial circular cut just below his shoulder. If the wound and the surgery were not bad enough, the ligature applied by the surgeon during the operation to limit arterial bleeding got stuck in

Below, top: Nelson receives the swords of the defeated Spanish officers on the *San Josef. Bottom: The Battle of Cape St. Vincent,* by Sir William Allen (1782– 1850). Allen's painting of the battle of February 14, 1797. Nelson in the *Captain* (left) boards and takes the *San Nicolas* (center), from which he goes on to take the *San Josef* (right).

the flap of raw flesh that had been stretched over the arm's stump. Nelson was in agony until the rotted skin and stitch finally fell off.

Convalescing in England, he put in for a pension, citing his four fleet engagements, three actions with frigates, six exchanges with ground batteries, 10 cutting-out operations, a four-month siege, and that he had lost his right eye and right arm. Despite such a deserving record, his government had no intention of wasting him in retirement, and as 1797 drew to a close Nelson was given command of the 74-gun *Vanguard*, captained by Edward Berry.

Before Nelson left England, however, there was the matter of his investiture as a Knight of the Bath, which took place at St. James Palace with King George III himself bestowing the star. Along with Lady Nelson, Berry was also there. When the king first approached Nelson, he noted solicitously, "You have lost your right arm."

"But not my right hand," Nelson graciously replied, "as I have the honor of presenting Captain Berry to Your Majesty."

Berry, whose career was long entwined with Nelson's, was a dashing figure; he was lean, with chiseled features and fair, swept-back hair. Not a great strategist or technician, he was a courageous and relentless fighter. Few would see as many of the great sea duels of the period as Berry, who had served aboard the *Agamemnon* under Nelson and had gone with him to the *Captain*. Berry would eventually be back aboard the *Agamemnon*, captaining her in her greatest battle.

On April 10, 1798, Nelson sailed to rejoin Jervis, now Earl St. Vincent, off Cádiz. St. Vincent at once put him in command of a large detachment: trouble was coming.

The British had known for some time that in Toulon and Genoa, Napoleon was assembling a great flotilla of fighting ships and transports. In addition, there were 35,000 men waiting to embark. Clearly, Napoleon had invasion in mind, but where? Sicily? Corfu? Portugal? Some even speculated Ireland. Few suspected Egypt—but Nelson did. His mission was to seek out and attack French armament wherever he found it, and the British fleet raced for Alexandria under full sail.

Finding no sign of the enemy there, Nelson concluded that Sicily had been the real invasion site after all, and he turned back. But off Sicily, he again saw no sign of the foe and he retraced his route to Alexandria. This time, he found the Egyptian harbor full of empty French transports, and he encountered their escort of 13 fighting ships under the French Admiral François Paul de Brueys along the coast near the Rosetta mouth of the Nile at Aboukir Bay.

The French were lined up at anchor, forming an impregnable wall with its back against the shallows. De Brueys expected that Nelson would either wait for him to come, attempt a blockade, or fight him in a traditional line-against-line action.

Meanwhile, Nelson had vowed to attack the moment that he saw the French, regardless of time of day or conditions. True to

Egypt, 1798

that word, the British swept in on the wind. It was 5:30 P.M., August 1, 1798. The fleets were evenly matched. Nelson planned to concentrate fire on the leading ships of the French line, wedging his own ships in to divide the enemy force. But the French were drawn up in a solid wall against the shoals: there appeared to be no way to penetrate the line or go behind it without running aground.

As Captain Thomas Foley, in the *Goliath* at the head of the British line, approached, he thought he saw another opportunity. Each of the French ships was on one anchor; obviously, sufficient room had been left between the ships and the shallows for even the largest vessel to swing on the wind. Therefore, if there was enough room for a 74 to swing around, then there was enough room for another 74 to come in behind. Foley led the British vanguard behind the French line, while Nelson and the rest of the fleet took up station on the seaward side. Sandwiched, the

French took heavy fire from both sides. They fought with great courage but no chance of success.

The Battle of the Nile was one of the most thorough and devastating naval victories of all time, certainly the greatest of the 18th century. De Brueys's flagship *L'Orient*, situated at the center of the line, caught fire and exploded in a blast that shook every ship in the bay, but not before the gallant de Brueys had been cut in two by a cannonball.

Nelson was hit in the forehead by a piece of shrapnel that opened a large cut. He fell into Berry's arms, convinced he was dying. "I am killed," Nelson said, "Remember me to my wife." By 9 P.M. however, he was back on deck and, like everyone else, awed by the conflagration the British had wrought. By morning, the French fleet had been virtually annihilated.

Only two of its ships of the line escaped, the *Généreux* and the *Guillaume Tell*, the latter commanded by Rear Admiral Pierre

Opposite, inset: Captain Sir Edward Berry, by John Singleton Copley. Like Nelson, Berry (1768–1831) came from Norfolk. He was Nelson's first lieutenant on the *Agamemnon* and was with him on the *Captain* at the Battle of Cape St. Vincent. He was Nelson's flag-captain on the *Vanguard* at the Battle of the Nile and commanded the *Agamemnon* at Trafalgar.

Below: Battle of the Nile 1 August 1798, by George Arnald, depicting the destruction of the French flagship *L'Orient* at about 10 P.M. The noise of the explosion was heard 15 miles away at Alexandria. Both sides were so stunned by what happened that for several minutes all firing stopped. The ship in the center is the *Swiftsure*, another vessel built at Buckler's Hard.

Charles de Villeneuve. When he and Nelson next met, it would be at Trafalgar.

The Battle of the Nile left Napoleon and his army marooned in Egypt, as well as 5,000 French seamen dead. It also left Horatio Nelson "The Hero," acclaimed throughout Europe for his bravery and strategic genius. England's people gave him unstinting love and admiration; he had given them new heart in the long fight against France.

Among his most ardent admirers by this time was Lady Emma Hamilton, who wrote to him from Naples, "If I was King of England, I would make you the most noble present, Duke Nelson, Marquis Nile, Earl Aboukir, Viscount Pyramid, Baron Crocodile and Prince *Victory*, that positively might have you in all forms. Your statue ought to be made of pure gold and placed in the middle of London."

THE ADMIRAL AND THE LADY

Emy Lyon, as Emma Hamilton was born, was a poor country girl, a blacksmith's daughter from a dreary little village in Cheshire. When she was little more than a child, she went to London as a domestic servant. There she called herself Emma, a name she thought romantic. She had no advantage of birth, breeding, education, or money, but if she was plebian, she was also spirited and very beautiful. Violet eyes dominated her smooth, heart-shaped face, and she had the delicate nose and small, rosebud mouth so fashionable in her day. She was tall and statuesque, and her thick, auburn hair when unpinned cascaded down her back almost to her feet. She was a natural as an artists' model, which she soon became. Esteemed painters vied for her services, among them Romney, Reynolds, Lawrence, and Hoppner, and they conferred on her a certain celebrity.

Men loved Emma, and Emma loved men. In 1780, when she was only 15, she went to live in Sussex with a local aristocrat, Sir Harry Fetherstonehaugh. When she got pregnant, he threw her out. She then became the mistress of Charles Greville, who prevailed on her to give up her daughter, called Little Emma, for others to raise. Handsome but rather a cold fish, Greville found Emma's cleanliness pleasant and remarked that she was the only woman he had ever slept with who offended none of his senses. But she was a luxury. Mr. Greville, although he was son of an earl, was poor; he needed a wife with money.

Since Emma was an impediment to that aim, in the summer of 1784, he passed her along to his recently widowed uncle, Sir William Hamilton, the British ambassador to Naples. It was said by some the "gift" was made to settle debts. Hamilton at that time was 54, Emma just 19.

She could have done worse. The worldly Sir William was keenly intelligent, an avid sportsman, a patron of the arts, a lover of music and dance, a member of the Society of Antiquaries, and a collector with a particular passion for archeological relics. He was much esteemed within the courts of both England and Naples, and best of all, he was a kind man who treated Emma with generosity and affection. After all, he loved beautiful things.

There is little doubt, however, that Emma was in love with Greville and that he tricked her into the liaison with his uncle, sending her to Naples ostensibly to learn music and singing in the Italian manner. After tearful letters to her deceitful lover failed to rectify the situation, she vowed that if she were to stay with Hamilton, it would be as his wife, not his mistress. This ambition was lofty; in those days it was not the custom for gentlemen to marry their mistresses. But in 1791, Sir William did indeed marry her, and she always remained grateful to him. He had returned her, if not her innocence, at least her honor.

And she tried to do him proud. Though she never lost the crude, country accent that made upper-class English visitors to the Hamilton villa sneer, she quickly learned French and Italian, and she took to her role as the ambassador's lady with verve and zest. She enjoyed her star status at King Ferdinand's Naples court, where she was sought after both for her own endowments and for her close friendship with Queen Maria Carolina, the highly strung sister of poor Marie Antoinette.

Emma treasured the attention and courted it. She began to practice her soon-to-be-famous "attitudes," a series of graceful (and doubtless very sexy) mimes of classical and biblical figures.

Loving the limelight, Emma was also prone to love others who were in it. Whatever charms she found in little Horatio Nelson when he first appeared to her as an uncelebrated naval officer were surely greatly magnified when he reentered her life five years later as the man of the hour—hero of the Nile.

As for Nelson, he had been until that time more a fighter than a lover, though in his youth he had been prone to wild infatuations. Early in his career, on a voyage to the West Indies, the 22-year-old Nelson had married Frances "Fanny" Nesbit, the widow of a local country doctor and mother of a young son. Soon after, the Nelsons returned to England, living modestly for the next five peacetime years in the humble parsonage at Burnham Thorp in Norfolk with Nelson's father.

Below, top: **Monument to Nelson by John Flaxman in St. Paul's Cathedral. In the memorial, Britannia points out Nelson to two young sailors.** *Bottom, and opposite:* **Popular engravings from the Battle of Copenhagen.**

Thereafter, Nelson's career would allow the pair little time together. During his long absences from home, he enjoyed the odd dalliance with ladies in various ports; after all, what sailor did not? Still, correspondence between him and his wife indicates that they remained a devoted couple—affectionate and fond, if rather blandly so. Then came Lady Hamilton, and poor Fanny paled, a gray dove to Emma's bird of paradise.

Following the Nile triumph, Nelson headed to Naples to make repairs, and there he saw Emma again. "Oh God!" she cried. "Is it possible?" She swooned theatrically into his arms. They were passionately in love, then and for the rest of his life.

In Naples, Nelson reveled in his new renown and, with the full assent of her husband, the charms of Emma. Ever the sophisticate, Sir William had known when he married his spectacular and much younger bride that an affair was hardly out of the question, and he seemed quite content that the chosen lover should be a man he both liked and respected. So the *ménage à trois,* as it were, worked well for all involved: Hamilton had his wife's devotion, Nelson her passion, and the always generous Emma had two men she truly loved and admired.

If they were happy, the disapproving admiralty was not, but there were compelling military reasons for them not to cross Nelson and for him to stay in Naples, at least for a time. The French were threatening the city's Spanish Bourbon monarchy, and Nelson had to spirit away the royal family, along with their courtiers and the Hamiltons, from Naples to Sicily. In 1799, he helped recapture Naples and restore Ferdinand I to his throne.

But as the century turned, Nelson's romantic interlude was interrupted. In early 1800, the admiralty received intelligence that the French were preparing a small squadron to relieve their beleaguered garrison at Malta. It was rumored that the ships included the *Généreaux,* one of the two escapees from the Nile. Nelson put out to intercept, taking along with him the *Alexander,* three frigates, and a corvette.

When the *Généreaux* was sighted, Nelson, in the *Foudroyant,* raced ahead and

overtook his fellow ship *Northumberland*, declaring, "to my flagship she can alone surrender." The ensuing duel ended with the *Géné-reaux* lowering her flag under the combined assault of the *Foudroyant* and *Northumberland*. Nelson gave Berry the honor of going on board to accept the sword of the French Rear Admiral Pérée, who was dying of wounds, both his lower legs having been shot off by a cannonball.

Toward the summer of 1800, the aging Sir William Hamilton was recalled to England. At about the same time, Nelson himself asked permission to go home. He and the Hamiltons traveled overland to England, arriving on November 6. Nelson had been away for more than 18 months, and although Britain's military establishment and polite society had been scandalized by the Hamilton-Nelson *ménage*, the people were overjoyed at his return. Wherever he went, crowds turned out to cheer. His promotion to vice admiral in 1801 met with immense popular approval.

BATTLE OF COPENHAGEN

Despite Nelson's new rank, the admiralty appointed him only second in command under Sir Hyde Parker for an 1801 mission to the Baltic. The deranged Russian tsar, Paul I, had cast his lot with France and had pressured Denmark, Sweden, Norway, and Prussia to revive with him the Armed Neutrality of the North, a league that barred Britain from Baltic ports. The *Agamemnon* was part of the British

fleet that sailed northward to convince the Danes of their error.

Admiral Hyde Parker was somewhat daunted by the defenses in Copenhagen's harbor: Danish ships stood bow to stern before the city, their numbers interspersed with floating batteries. Never himself one to hesitate, however, Nelson said that he could engage and beat the enemy with only ten ships, and the sooner the better. Hyde Parker gave him a dozen. Nelson's plan was to evade the strong vanguard of the Danish line by sailing around the large shoal that dominates Copenhagen's harbor and going in behind, where the defenses were weaker. Once those ships were disabled, he would then take on the rest of the Danish fleet.

Navigating around the island was tricky, however, and three British ships, including *Agamemnon*, ran aground on a shoal.

Copenhagen, 1801

Nelson, aboard the *Elephant*, found himself beginning the fight minus a quarter of his squadron. And though the three grounded ships eventually joined in, they were too far from their targets to do much good. Nevertheless, the British persevered. In the ensuing battle, the Danes proved a resilient enemy and matched the British blow for blow.

Seeing the grim nature of the situation, Hyde Parker did the honorable thing and hoisted a signal to discontinue the action, reasoning (it is believed) that if the battle was not going well, then Nelson might appreciate an excuse to break off. Nelson's officers informed him of the order, and it was then that he famously lifted his telescope to his blind eye and declared that he saw no signal.

With Nelson continuing the fight, the British won that six-hour battle of April 1, 1801, though Nelson's heart was not entirely in the fight. He might have hated the French, but he considered the brave Danes to be brothers of the English, and he tendered reasonable terms, sealing the written offer with a signet bearing his personal coat of arms. Thereafter, with Hyde Parker's approval, he negotiated an armistice with Denmark's prince regent.

Victory in this case left a bitter aftertaste. Thousands of men had been killed, and for nothing: Unknown to the combatants, Tsar Paul I had been assassinated ten days before the battle, and his successor was not pro-French. The Armed Neutrality pact dissolved and friendly relations were restored between

Below: Battle of Trafalgar at 2:30 P.M., by William Lionel Wyllie, executed in 1905 by the famous marine painter to mark the centenary of the battle.

Opposite: Napoleon, with whom Nelson would contend for many years, from Toulon to Trafalgar.

its nations and Britain. Most of the British fleet went home, although Nelson, with a squadron that included his beloved *Agamemnon*, continued to sail the Baltic and the Gulf of Finland for a time, to show the flag. He was made a viscount in recognition of his latest heroism, but he was not especially pleased. He had expected an earldom.

TRAFALGAR

In April 1802, the Treaty of Amiens was signed, and Britain was, briefly and uneasily, at peace with France.

Nelson, who had separated from his wife the year before, retired with the Hamiltons to the trio's new country house, Merton, just outside London. There, in April 1803, Sir William died at the age of 72 with both Emma and Nelson at his bedside. Though Emma had by now borne Nelson a child, a daughter named Horatia, the admiral could not marry his cherished mistress: he was still married to Fanny, and divorce would have required an act of Parliament. Still, it seemed possible that he and Emma might have some protracted time to be happy together in the quiet serenity of Merton.

But peace did not last; Napoleon had never intended it to. He was amassing troops at Boulogne to invade England. On May 18, 1803, Britain declared war. Two days before the outbreak, Nelson was given command of the Mediterranean station, with his flag in the illustrious *Victory*.

For Napoleon to invade Britain, he had to control the English Channel. "Let us," he proclaimed, "be masters of the Straits for six hours, and we shall be masters of the world." If he could get a toehold, he could be in London within a couple of days. Fear spread throughout Britain. Londoners prepared for siege, the army was mobilized, and local militia were raised. On hilltops, semaphore stations by day and bonfires by night were prepared to relay the news of invasion.

Napoleon had prepared a flotilla of more than 2,000 flat-bottomed boats for the foray into Britain, and his troops, concentrated at Boulogne, stretched for nine miles, the soldiers poised with all their impedimenta to embark. But the French had no Channel port large enough for the rendezvous, so it would have to take place in the West Indies. The combined French fleets would then return to Europe, join with the allied Spanish fleet at Cádiz, and with greatly superior numbers, seize the Channel.

All that stood in the way of this tidy plan were winds, tides, and Horatio Nelson.

The man in command of the French, and, later, combined Franco-Spanish, fleet was Admiral Pierre Charles de Villeneuve, who had escaped from the Nile in the *Guillaume Tell*. Beginning in 1803, Nelson had kept Ville-

Trafalgar, 1805

of 20 fighting ships. They were 120 miles west of Cape Finisterre in heavy fog. Two French ships of the line were taken, but otherwise the battle was indecisive. Calder hesitated, and the French escaped, first to Vigo Bay and afterward to Cádiz, where they were joined by the Spanish fleet under Admiral Federico Carlos de Gravina.

Trafalgar, years in the making, was now imminent.

After a brief return to England, Nelson was at sea again by September 15, driving the *Victory* southward to rejoin Admiral Cuthbert Collingwood and the British fleet off Spain. There, he detailed his battle plan to his captains. It was bold, risky—typically Nelson. The British would divide the Franco-Spanish line by attacking its rear and middle in two perpendicular columns. While the ships at the front of the line (the van) went through the cumbersome task of turning back toward the action, a maneuver that could take two hours or more, the British would overwhelm and annihilate the Franco-Spanish middle and rear with superior gunnery and ship management. "It was new—it was singular—it was simple!" wrote Nelson, calling it "The Nelson Touch."

It was also terribly dangerous: as the two British columns attacked, they would have to endure many minutes of raking broadside fire without being able to reply. The heaviest and toughest ships would have to go at the head of each column. Collingwood in the *Royal Sovereign* would lead one, while Nelson in the *Victory* would lead the other.

Above and opposite: At Trafalgar, Nelson attacked the Franco-Spanish line in two columns. Nelson led one in the *Victory* and Collingwood the other in the *Royal Sovereign*. It was a dangerous plan, as during the approach the leading ships would be exposed to withering fire long before they could make effective reply. *Right:* Nelson briefs his captains on his plan of attack at Trafalgar. He later wrote, "When I came to explain to them the Nelson touch, it was like an electric shock. Some shed tears, all approved. it was new, it was singular, it was simple."

neuve's fleet bottled up in Toulon, but in March 1805, at Napoleon's orders, Villeneuve broke out during bad weather and headed for the West Indies.

Nelson followed de Villeneuve all the way across the Atlantic and then all the way back, but the French eluded engagement. As they headed back, Sir Robert Calder was directed to take up station west of Cape Finisterre off the Spanish coast. He had 15 warships, one of which was the *Agamemnon*, under the command of Captain John Harvey.

On July 22, just two days after Nelson reached Gibraltar, Calder met the French fleet

On September 17, Napoleon instructed Villeneuve to sail for Italy, and on October 20, Villeneuve and Gravina moved out of Cádiz with 18 French and 15 Spanish ships. They knew that Nelson would be waiting.

Nelson, at the time, was 50 miles to the west. The message "enemy coming out of port" was passed to him by a relay of frigates. Early the next morning of October 21, the Franco-Spanish fleet could be seen silhouetted by the sunrise against Cape Trafalgar. Both sides began to move into formation. The *Agamemnon* was number eight in Nelson's column.

At that time, Edward Berry had been the *Agamemnon*'s captain for about a month.

She had sailed to join Nelson early in October, and during a gale off Cape Finisterre, she ran into a French squadron of six liners and two frigates. The French gave chase and probably would have caught her if a convoy had not at that moment sailed into sight. The French sailed off in pursuit of the convoy, leaving the *Agamemnon* unscathed. It had been a close call.

On October 13, the *Agamemnon* joined the fleet off Cádiz. When Nelson saw her, he said in delight, "Here comes that damned fool Berry. Now we shall have a fight!"

The *Agamemnon* was instructed to cruise in shore of the main fleet as a scout. On

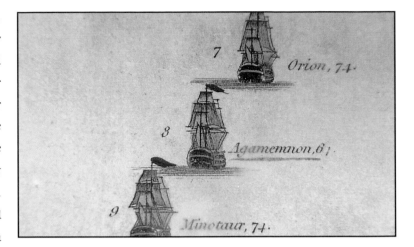

the day before the battle, Berry boarded a heavily laden merchant brig and took her as a prize. For reasons that are not clear (but presumably, because he could not yet see the ships), he started heading toward the enemy fleet. Captain Henry Blackwood of the *Euryalus* closed on the *Agamemnon* to warn her, and she quickly turned back. It had been her second narrow escape in just a few days.

The next morning, the weather was fine. There was little wind, and the great warships of Trafalgar moved ponderously with little push from the elements. At dawn, Nelson talked to his four frigate captains aboard the *Victory.* Blackwood stayed the longest, witnessing the admiral's famous will, requesting his country to look after Emma. (It would not; she would die neglected, penniless, and alcoholic in France.) The other witness was Nelson's flag captain on the *Victory,* Thomas Masterman Hardy. Hardy had served aboard the *Agamemnon* when she was first commissioned back in 1781 and was one of Nelson's most esteemed and trusted officers.

As Blackwood left the ship, he took Nelson's hand:

"I trust, my lord, that on my return to the *Victory,* which will be as soon as possible, I shall find your lordship well and in possession of twenty prizes."

"God bless you, Blackwood," Nelson answered directly, "I shall never speak to you again."

At 10 A.M., Nelson told his flag officer, John Pasco, that he would amuse the fleet with a message. He wanted to signal "England Confides That Every Man Will Do His Duty." Pasco asked if he could substitute "expects" for "confides," since "expects" would require only a single hoist, while "confides" would have to be spelled out. Nelson assented, and the signal was given.

Famous though it would become, at the time the message elicited some consternation. "What is Nelson signaling about?" grumbled Admiral Collingwood in the *Royal Sovereign.* "We all know what we have to do." The seamen's reaction was much the same: they knew their jobs. But they cheered anyway, mostly for love of Nelson, whose signal was followed hard upon by a second one: "Close Action."

The British battle lines, roughly 30 ships strong, moved forward.

The first shots were fired at noon. The *Victory*, her sails already rent by the long and dangerous approach, broke through the French line close to Villeneuve's flagship, the *Bucentaure*, firing broadsides that wrecked the French ship's stern and caused nearly 200 casualties. Nelson and Hardy then made for the *Redoubtable*, approaching her sideways and coming so close that the topmasts of the two ships locked like the antlers of great stags in combat. So joined, they pounded away at each other with their cannons.

❧

The ships' logs give little account of the battle. More remarkably, there are no fulsome first-hand descriptions of what it was like on the decks that day, but surely it was hellish. Thundering blasts, grape, solid shot, chain shot, splinters of wood and iron ripping through ships and people at point-blank range, grenades, the screams of the maimed and dying. Thick banks of acrid smoke hung in blankets upon the feeble breeze.

Through it all, Nelson strode the quarterdeck with Hardy. The admiral was unmistakable, wearing his Star of the Bath and three other large decorations. His ship's surgeon had asked him to change into a less conspicuous coat: he made too good a target. Nelson said there was no time.

Little is known of the *Agamemnon*'s precise activities at Trafalgar. Captain Edward Codrington on the *Orion* gives a glimpse of her "blazing away and wasting her ammuni-

tion." Her own log is typically terse: "engaging the enemy's ships as most convenient." As she came though the enemy line, she engaged the *Heros* to port, and then, together with the *Neptune* and *Conqueror*, took on the high four-decker *Santissima Trinidad*, the biggest and most powerful fighting ship in the world. At 2:30 they dismasted the *Trinidad* completely and carried on their unremitting fire for another ten minutes until the pride of the Spanish fleet, lying in ruin, at last surrendered. Sometime later, the *Agamemnon* took the French *Colossus* in tow.

Many hundreds died off the Spanish coast that day, but only two of them were from the *Agamemnon*. Physically, though, she had

Below: The four-deck *Santissima Trinidad*, then the largest fighting ship in the world. During Trafalgar she was harried and finally overwhelmed by a pack of smaller ships including *Agamemnon*. With all her masts shot away and her guns silent, the British thought that she had surrendered; an officer who was sent on board to take possession was told with great courtesy that she had not, and was escorted back to his own ship.

A print from J. M. W. Turner's grand essay on the death of Nelson. Note the sniper in the rigging of the *Redoubtable*, top right.
Inset: The Death of Nelson, by A. W. Devis. Nelson's body was returned to Britain in a barrel of brandy. An autopsy was carried out and the fatal bullet extracted. The painter attended the autopsy and made drawings which he afterwards referred to in this painting.

taken a hammering. One shot had ripped through her counter, another had holed the stern, and six had penetrated her hull below the water line. Four blasts tore through the main hull above the water line, and at least six shots had hit the yards and masts.

One other fact is known about the *Agamemnon* that day: She first opened fire almost to the instant of 1:15 P.M., the moment that Nelson was mortally wounded by a sniper stationed high in the rigging of *Redoubtable*.

The admiral was taken below deck to the cockpit. He knew he was dying. "They have done for me at last, Hardy," he said, "my backbone is shot through." The bullet had entered his body at the shoulder and, because of its steep angle, passed through the pulmonary artery and lung before smashing through his spine and lodging in the muscle of his back. He was drowning in his own blood.

As he lay in Hardy's arms, the stricken admiral asked to be remembered to Emma and Horatia, but his most pressing thought was still for his ships. He told his flag captain that the fleet and its captured French ships should anchor as soon as possible because a storm was coming. (His old friend Admiral Collingwood, believing differently, would fail to heed the order, but Nelson had been right, as usual. A strong gale blew in, destroying many of the French ships that had been taken as

prizes.) Finally, as his life bled away, Nelson uttered his last words: "Thank God I have done my duty."

He died at 4:30 P.M., with the knowledge that he had won the most glorious victory of his—of any sailor's—career. Fittingly, Vice Admiral Lord Horatio Viscount Nelson, 47 years old, had died at the moment of his greatest triumph.

His body was first taken to Gibraltar, and from there to England, preserved in a cask of brandy. In England, it was transferred to a coffin made from the wood of *L'Orient,* the French flagship that he had taken at the Battle of the Nile.

Britain was torn between the joy of victory and grief at the loss of its greatest hero. "We know not whether we should mourn or rejoice," said the *Times* of London. "The Country has gained the most splendid and decisive victory that has ever graced the naval annals of England, but it has been dearly purchased. The great and gallant NELSON is no more."

Below, top: Nelson's coffin, made from the mainmast of *L'Orient* and presented to Nelson by Captain Benjamin Hallowell following the Battle of the Nile. The decorations include Nelson's crest of arms, his orders of chivalry (including the Star of Bath), and symbols such as Britannia, the British lion, Neptune, and a crocodile to represent the Nile. *Below, bottom: Nelson's Funeral Procession at St. Paul's,* by C. A. Pugin. Not until the funeral of Princess Diana in 1997 was there a match for the national outpouring of grief upon the death of Nelson.

Above, top: The Apotheosis of Lord Nelson, by Scott-Pierre-Nicholas Legrand. Tens of thousands of engravings of this painting were sold in the years following Nelson's death. Bottom: This painting by Pugin shows Nelson's body in state at St. Paul's Cathedral, which was lighted for the first time during the funeral.

that it resembled the bow and stern of the *Victory*. The procession was so long that the Dragoons reached St. Paul's before the last carriages had departed from the admiralty, over a mile and a half away.

Nelson's body was finally laid to rest atop a high bier beneath the great dome of St. Paul's, encased in an elaborate sarcophagus once intended for Cardinal Wolsey. Inlaid in the marble floor in front of the tomb was the inscription: "England Expects That Every Man Will Do His Duty."

DEATH OF THE *AGAMEMNON*

Trafalgar was the last and greatest fleet battle ever fought under sail, and it confirmed then and for over a century more that Britannia did indeed rule the waves. At its height, Britain's empire, forged on the decks of her fighting ships, would encompass a quarter of the earth.

Ironically, however, it was not Trafalgar that turned back a French invasion of England. Napoleon—now Emperor Napoleon I—had simply changed his mind. Two months before the great sea battle, he decided to attack England's allies instead. The troops that had been massed around Boulogne were dispatched toward the Danube to take on the Austrians and Russians at Austerlitz in what would become known as the Battle of the Three Emperors. And, peerless land general that he was, Napoleon won an overwhelming victory. It would be almost a decade before he would meet his

Uncounted thousands jammed the streets and St. Paul's Cathedral for the lavish spectacle of his funeral. It was a scene not to be approached until the funeral of Princess Diana, nearly 200 years later. The cortege began with a troop of Light Dragoons, their hooves muffled by sand that had been spread on the roads; then came 10,000 infantrymen and bands that played Handel's "Dead March" from *Saul*. After them marched 48 men from the *Victory* carrying the ship's ragged Union Jacks and Nelson's ensign.

Finally came the peers and nobles, followed by the Prince of Wales. Behind him was the ornate funeral carriage, decorated so

final defeat at a small Belgian town known as Waterloo.

In the meantime, he still had ships, having had the foresight to keep some of his fleet at Brest. The *Agamemnon* and her sister ships still had work to do.

Following Trafalgar, old Eggs and Bacon limped to Gibraltar with the *Colossus* in tow, taking six days for the 55-mile trip. There she was patched up before rejoining Collingwood, who was blockading Cádiz. She was no longer the slippery ship of her Mediterranean campaigns under Nelson; now she creaked with age and let in so much water that she had to be pumped for long periods twice a day. Despite this, she was part of a squadron that sailed across the Atlantic in search of French ships that had set out from Brest for the West Indies. On February 6, 1806, at the Battle of Santo Domingo, the *Agamemnon* was slow into action, but once there, Berry, together with the *Superb*, concentrated fire on the French flagship *Imperial*, which, together with another enemy warship, was driven ashore, wrecked, and burned. Three more ships were captured. The *Agamemnon* had but one killed and 21 wounded.

On June 29, Berry returned to England, and, on July 8, command of the *Agamemnon* passed to Jonas Rose, who would be her last captain. A man of no extraordinary gifts, Rose was nevertheless a competent officer who had joined the navy as a boy of ten or eleven in 1771 and had spent a lifetime at sea. Command of the famous *Agamemnon*, even decrepit as she was, was an honor for him. In October, she was refitted. She still had one more major campaign before her.

In July 1807, Britain again stood alone (except for Portugal) against Napoleon and his allies in Europe, and the French emperor was again planning an invasion. Britain's vital trade with the Baltics was imperiled, and it appeared that the emperor might use the Danish navy to help take Britain. England sent troops and a fleet to Copenhagen with the ultimatum that the Danes hand over their fleet (to be returned when the hostilities were over), or have it destroyed or taken by force. The Danes refused, and the British fleet of some 40 ships of the line, together with land-based batteries, opened fire on the city. Among the British fleet was the *Agamemnon*. On September 5, Rose wrote in her log:

AM at 6 observed Copenhagen on fire whilst our batteries bombarded the town . . . Copenhagen high steeple burned down . . . PM the fire in Copenhagen apparently increasing . . . After a three-day bombardment the city surrendered. Some 70 vessels were taken and those that were seaworthy were taken to England.

The *Agamemnon* returned to England on November 11, 1807. Less than a month later, she sailed to join the blockade of Lisbon, now in French hands, and then later set off to the waters off the coast of South America, and to her destiny. She would never return to England again.

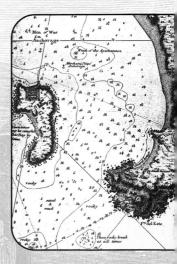

Below: Chart showing area where *Agamemnon* ran aground.

Background: The *Victory's* anchor, on Southsea Beach, in a contemporary engraving from the *London Illustrated News.* Today, it marks the spot where Nelson left England for the final time.

By the time that the *Agamemnon* arrived in Brazil, she and her sister ships were liable to see more use in political missions than on battle assignments. At the end of November, the *Agamemnon* was sailing north out of the Plate after such a mission to Montevideo when she was caught in a fierce Atlantic storm. Lightning shattered her main royal mast, and it and its spars came crashing to the deck. Nobody was hurt, but the damaged ship put back into Maldonado Bay for repairs.

On December 11, she was anchored off the northern tip of Gorriti Island while a new mast was being fitted and rigged. Her launch was being rowed back across the bay, loaded with water casks that had just been filled at the Aguada River. The smallboat was low and heavy in the water—not riding well—when it was hit by a wave that approached broadside from out of the early-morning calm. The launch capsized and sank. Of the men on board, five drowned, all in plain view of their shipmates. Their bodies were recovered, and Captain Rose sailed out of the bay and into the deep waters off Lobos Island to bury them at sea.

The *Agamemnon* returned to Rio de Janeiro on January 16, 1809, and stayed through March 6, the height of the tropical summer. By now, she was little more than a floating wreck. Twenty-eight embattled years had passed since she slid from the stocks at Buckler's Hard. She was sluggish, strained, and leaking badly. Rose knew that his ship should have been retired years ago. In the fierce Brazilian heat he labored with the ship's carpenter to compile a list of the historic vessel's defects. The list was long.

As Rose pondered ways to keep his ship seaworthy, rumors were circulating that back in Europe, a French squadron had evaded the British blockade and had slipped out of the Mediterranean into the Atlantic. The new commander of Britain's Brazil station, Rear Admiral Michael de Courcy, believed the squadron was heading for the River Plate. He assembled a squadron of four ships of the line, a frigate, a brig, and a schooner—the *Foudroyant*, *Elizabeth*, *Bedford*, *Agamemnon*, *Brilliant*, *Mistletoe*, and *Mutine*, respectively—to intercept. They left Rio on May 26, 1809.

On June 3, however, well before the ships reached the Plate, they were hit by a savage *pampero*. Under reduced sail, they battled the wind, but as it worsened, they hove to and waited for the storm to burn itself out. As might be expected, the *Agamemnon* suffered most. Her standing rigging needed adjustment, the pumps were constantly manned, and, to reinforce her planks, her hull was wrapped with hemp hawsers.

On June 15, the ships passed the great rock of Lobos Island, just five miles from Punta del Este and Maldonado Bay. It was late in the day, and de Courcy decided to anchor and wait until morning before going in.

At 5:30 the next morning, the admiral, aboard the *Foudroyant*, signaled the squadron to weigh anchor, and the ships started toward the bay. An hour later, de Courcy flagged the *Bedford* to lead the squadron to anchorage and for the *Agamemnon* to place a buoy to mark a dangerous shoal off Gorriti Island where the HMS *Monarch* had run aground a year before. As she approached the northern entrance to the bay, the *Agamemnon* lowered her cutter and launch to see to the task, then signaled for permission to enter the bay.

The *Bedford* ahead of her, the *Agamemnon* moved down the channel between Gorriti and the shore, her leadsman sounding as she went. Rose proceeded carefully, consulting Spanish and British charts of the area. His ship had been there three times before; he knew the shoals were ill defined and treacherous.

As *Agamemnon* rounded the point of the island, a shout from the leadsman alerted Rose that she was moving into shallows. Trying to keep her bow to the wind, the captain gave the order to let go her best bower anchor, situated on the port bow. Briefly, it held—then pulled loose from the seabed. With a shuddering thud, the *Agamemnon* grounded by the stern, swung, and heeled to starboard. Her ensign lowered, then rose again upside down— the signal of distress.

The other ships sped to her aid, finding her filling rapidly. The sailors did everything possible, but they could not right her. As the other ships tried futilely to help, water continued to rise within her hull, though no one could determine its source. Only after divers went below the water to examine her bottom did the sad irony become clear: this valiant veteran of the line, Nelson's "favorite," had run upon her own anchor; it had dragged beneath her, where the upward fluke fatally holed her hull.

Rose ordered *Agamemnon*'s spanker boom and two of her largest spars to be lowered into the sea in an attempt to support her starboard side. The *Mistletoe* then helped deploy one of the stricken ship's anchors to windward, hoping that, if they drew in on it, it might prevent any further listing. When this failed, Rose ordered his men to save what they could of the vessel's stores, fittings, and accoutrements.

By sunset, the water was above the *Agamemnon*'s lower deck ports, and the next morning it reached toward the maindeck ports as she settled into the mud and sand. The captains, masters, and carpenters of the *Foudroyant*, *Elizabeth*, *Bedford*, and *Mutine* went aboard to determine whether she could be saved. Their opinions were unanimous: she might be refloated, but she could never be made seaworthy again. She should be abandoned.

Below: **Nelson's five commands grouped at anchor at Spithead with their sails loose to dry. From left to right:** *Agamemnon,* *Captain,* *Vanguard,* *Elephant,* **and** *Victory.* **Painted by Nicolas Pocock in 1808, the year before** *Agamemnon* **was lost.**

The rest of the day was spent stripping her of everything usable. By evening, the *Agamemnon* was down to her weather-deck scuppers and was listing even farther to starboard.

The following morning, June 18, was cold, with a northeasterly breeze and leaden skies. Work parties concentrated on removing the ship's fittings and armament. Spars and the topmasts went over the side into waiting boats, as did her cannonades. A team from the *Bedford* set about recovering her anchors.

Shortly before 6 P.M., Rose, his officers, and remaining men prepared to abandon ship. The midwinter darkness was already falling; it had been raining on and off and the exhausted men were damp and cold.

The captain stood on the starboard poop ladder to bid his crew farewell. His voice trembled and faltered as he recalled the *Agamemnon*'s fabled history, "the days and deeds of old with Nelson in the Mediterranean and the glorious victory of Trafalgar." He struggled on for a bit after that, but then his voice gave way altogether and he choked out, "Goodbye Agamemnons, may God bless you Agamemnons—Agamemnons all, goodbye."

Captain and men stood silent for a time. Most of them were weeping, fresh-faced midshipmen and grizzled veterans alike. Then an old boatswain's mate, a man who had served with Nelson, came forward to speak for the crew. "God bless your honor," he started, "wheresoever you may be . . ." But then he, too, started to weep, and after a few more stumbling phrases he stepped back among his shipmates.

Still silent, all of them left the ship and made their way by cutter to the other vessels, or to the emergency shore station on Gorriti Island.

A court-martial was always held following the loss of a Royal Navy ship, and that of Captain Jonas Rose was held August 7, 1809, in the stern cabin of the *Bedford* in Rio. Rose conducted his own defense.

A panel of five captains heard lengthy and repetitive testimony from various officers about anchoring procedures, efforts to refloat the *Agamemnon*, her condition, and attempts to salvage her.

The proceedings were more or less a formality and the verdict came quickly: His Majesty's late ship *Agamemnon* had run aground because of "a bad chart or a sand bank recently thrown up." Captain Rose was not to blame. He and his officers had done their best.

SURVEY OF THE AGAMEMNON

In 1997, four years after we confirmed that the wreck off Gorriti Island was in fact the *Agamemnon*, we were back in Uruguay again, this time with a full survey team. We would investigate the wreck and map the site with an eye toward eventual recovery and preservation. In addition to the archeological work, we were to make two television documentaries. Arriving in January 1997, we had two months to complete the work.

We were thrilled at the prospect of diving on Nelson's *Agamemnon*, obsessed with Nelson and his ship: we thought Nelson, read Nelson, talked Nelson. We analyzed his battles, speculated on his character, and dissected his love life. It was, my wife said, more like a Nelson festival than an archeological operation.

The Uruguayan government, anxious to validate a part of its history through archeology, had generously supplied us with three chauffeured vans, mobile phones, free meals at government-approved restaurants, and five-star accommodations in Montevideo at the old Victoria Plaza, Uruguay's best-known hotel.

It was midsummer, and Punta del Este was awash with the monied classes—the season was in full hedonistic swing. During the morning, the boutiques and sidewalk cafes were the places to be. Wherever there was a gathering, one could usually find a film star or supermodel at its center. In the afternoon, everybody moved to the beaches, in the evening to the restaurants, and after midnight to the nightclubs. It was not the environment for conducting a serious archeological investigation, but we had no choice. To maximize the use of our time, we had to be there when the weather was best. Fortunately, we were able to rent a quiet house several miles from town but still near Maldonado Bay.

Our main diving vessel would be the *Sea Pilgrim*, a boat that Hector and Sergio had acquired since my last visit. We would also work closely with the Coast Guard, which had a much larger boat with better work space.

I made my old friend Bryan Smith supervisor of the *Agamemnon* survey. Bryan had worked with me since my excavation of the 600 B.C. ship off the Tuscan island of Giglio in the early 1980s. He had been on most of our projects since, including the Mahdia wreck. His wife, Ann, was another mainstay of Oxford's marine archeology program. She was put in charge of our documentation—without her our work would count for nothing. When Bryan had to return to England, his place would be taken by another team veteran, Tom Cockrell, who had joined the Giglio campaign

Opposite: Cameraman Mark Silk with Gorritti Island in the background.

Above, top: Sergio Pronczuk, Francis Pope, Hector Bado, Bryan Smith, and Mensun and his wife, Joanna Yellowlees-Bound, pose in their "Lost Ships" wet suits.
Bottom: Aboard *Prefectura*, one of a series of boats seconded to the team by the Uruguayan navy.

in 1982 and risen quickly to become our chief diver. As with Bryan and Ann, he had been with me on projects all over the world.

Bryan, Tom, and I met first thing every morning to discuss plans and methodologies before briefing the team at breakfast. If I was not on board during the day, we spoke on the ship-to-shore, or if I was in Montevideo or elsewhere, we spoke by mobile phone.

Hector, Sergio, Bryan, and I discussed at length how best to map the site, the first step in any project. As a general rule, Bryan and I always favored either grids or a baseline method in which a measured line is stretched longitudinally across the site, and features are mapped from it by taking offset measurements at right angles from the baseline to the object. However, the water's bad visibility and strong currents were factors against these techniques, and such circumstances also ruled out the more sophisticated methods of mapping based on video imaging or still-photogrammetry.

In the end, we decided to use a web of random datum points based on fixed objects within the site itself. Fortunately, there were many large copper-alloy bolts protruding vertically from the wreck. By plotting the position of each of them on paper, we would have a close pattern of reference points from which everything else could be easily and accurately mapped.

On February 9, 1997, we all crowded onto the *Sea Pilgrim* for our first dive to the *Agamemnon*. The wind was from the north at three knots, it was cloudy, and the air temper-

ature was a pleasant 65°F. There were 18 of us (and all our gear) packed into the *Sea Pilgrim*'s aluminum hull that day—far too many for comfort, but everybody was so eager that I did not have the heart to leave anyone behind.

After that day, all dives would be done in relays, with the first wave going out at 7:30 A.M. When they were finished, the next, having been alerted by mobile phone, would be ready at dockside. In this way, everybody but the *Sea Pilgrim*'s skipper would have a break of several hours between dives.

Sergio, Hector, and I were first over the side. We exchanged OK signals among ourselves, then gestured to the timekeeper to let him know that we were ready to begin our dive. He dispatched us with a thumbs-down motion, and we deflated our buoyancy jackets and slowly let ourselves sink beneath the estuary. There was a one-knot easterly current, and we had to struggle in near blackness to stay in contact. The site, however, was just under 10 meters down, so it was not long before we lit on the soft surface of the riverbed.

We were right beside the wreck.

The site was very much as I had remembered it from four years before—a large mound of amorphous ballast blocks, all welded together by corrosion into a solid heap, alive with conger eels and blanketed in mussels. Here and there timbers and planking were visible, along with many keel and bottom-timber bolts. The timbers were mostly free of shells, but the bolts, like the iron concretion of the ballast mound, were packed with living shells.

On my last dive with Hector in 1993, we had hidden two of *Agamemnon*'s sounding leads in holes in the mud—one of them perhaps the very lead in use just before the ship ran aground. I began searching for them. Only one was there; evidently vandals had discovered the wreck.

Before leaving the site, we inflated a small marker buoy, tied it to an iron hoop, and sent it up to the surface. The following day, Bryan replaced its string with heavy cord and moved it to one of the bolts. The cord became not only the descent and ascent line for all dives that followed, but its bolt also became our number-one datum point for the ensuing survey.

During the next four days, 17 more survey points were established, and the laborious work of plotting their relative positions began. Although the wreck was starting to come together on paper, it was still hard to picture the site in the mind's eye. We did not even know which way the ship was pointing, or which end was bow and which was stern. We had the records of her loss from the Public Records Office in London, so we knew supporting archeological data.

Then something happened that helped us make sense of the site. On February 17, we moved into a period of neap tides and clearer water. Almost overnight, our vision improved from a few centimeters to almost eight meters. Although the wreck was in shadow, we could just make out its form from the surface. In dead water I hung neutrally buoyant over it

for more than half an hour, absorbing the site and thinking through its problems, aware that the good conditions would last for no more than another day. After that, we would be poking around in the darkness again.

That evening, back at the house, I talked excitedly about what we had seen with Antonio Lesama, a diver and professional archeologist who had become in many ways the linchpin of our operations at Maldonado Bay. He was also the middleman between us and the Uruguayan archeological authorities under whom we worked. I had given him the almost impossible task of trying to make sense of the ship's timbers, but now, for the first time, we could see the entire assemblage, not just the individual components. The sight confirmed what Antonio, Bryan, and I were beginning to suspect: the ship was lying northeast-southwest and listing to the southeast. This reflected the orientation and list to starboard described in the vessel's logs and the court-martial papers from England.

During the period of good visibility, Bryan had some successful dives. He found what appeared to be the lower part of the ship's pump and what was presumably its sump. This find, together with the forest of bolts that were suddenly visible,

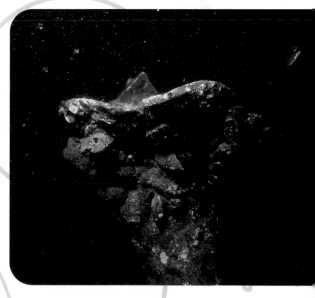

Below: Part of the pump in the lower hull of the *Agamemnon.* According to Jonas Rose, her last captain, by the time she sank, "all the pumps in the Fleet could not have saved her."

allowed him to determine the most likely location of the keel and to identify other features of her construction.

At last, the ship that helped to mold the man who changed the world at Trafalgar was beginning to make sense. Our talk during these days was animated and lasted long into the night, but as fast as it had opened, our portal of visibility closed. In the Stygian blackness, once more we were blind.

The *Agamemnon* was not particularly rich in finds, but we had not expected her to be. Since she had not sunk right away, most of her contents had been salvaged during the course of her abandonment. Nonetheless, we did find an interesting array of ship's fittings and accoutrements.

Among these—including items that were discovered during my 1993 visit—were cannonballs, musket shot, a tap, copper sheathing, hull fastenings, sheaves, coaks, a cylindrical copper jug, and the sounding leads.

We could raise samples for recording,

photography, and drawing, but because we did not have with us any conservation capability, all artifacts were kept wet, then returned to the sea after we had examined and drawn them. To protect them from looters, we buried them at a depot point beside the wreck.

A large bronze pulley wheel was another important find. It represented the very sinews of the ship, and very likely it was from one of the blocks used by Nelson and his crew to haul the *Agamemnon*'s cannon over the rocks and up the slopes for the great sieges of Bastia and Calvi. This wheel was from one of the vessel's largest pulley blocks; it was so heavy I could barely lift it.

Soon after finding the bronze wheel, Joanna found an intact wooden one, a so-called sheave that also served to turn rope within a block. While cleaning it with a paint brush and dental picks, she spotted some markings. Two were the broad arrow denoting British government property, the third said "1797." The date caught my imagination: this was the year of Cape St. Vincent, the battle in which Nelson had taken one Spanish first-rater and used her as a bridge for storming another, the battle that won him knighthood and made him a household name throughout Britain.

These artifacts were evidence of what we already knew: this was indeed *Agamemnon*. Had there been any doubt, however, it was erased by the discovery of the most wonderful and valuable article that I, in all my years of diving, had *ever* seen lifted from the ocean floor.

Below, top and bottom: The bronze pulley wheel found by the team on the wreck. It represents the very sinews of the ship and very likely was from one of the great blocks that were used to haul her cannons up the hills for the siege of Calvi.

Background: Detail from one of the team's technical drawings of the pulley wheel.

Hector found it—a small, unusual object in the sand attached to a leathery tail and ring. Gently he lifted it, shining his light directly at it. It seemed to be a seal of some kind on a short leather strap. As soon as he was back on the surface, he cleaned it gently with his fingers and then held it to the light. The central motif seemed to be a sunburst of some kind. Above it were the capital letters И O S Ɉ Ǝ И . For a second, he was puzzled—until he realized that, quite correctly for a seal, the letters were in reverse. Starting with the last letter first, he spelled out the name: N-E-L-S-O-N.

The main device on the seal was the star of Knights of the Bath, with three crowns at the center representing Britain's three united kingdoms, whose motto was *tria juncta in uno,* "three joined as one." It was awarded to Nelson after his exploits at the Battle of St. Vincent. Commentators of the day had noted the aptness of the motto, seeing an analogy with the way Nelson's flagship was joined to the two Spanish ships she captured. Later, the motto had punning value as a metaphor for the Nelson-Hamilton triangle.

Precious as it was, the seal was also a puzzle: the Battle of St. Vincent was fought in 1797, the year after Nelson left the *Agamemnon.* This seal could not have belonged to him personally. However, there were many commemorative Nelson seals, and where better to have one than on his favorite ship? I knew that Emma Hamilton had sent Jonas Rose a lock of Nelson's hair when Rose was appointed captain of the *Agamemnon.* Maybe she had also sent him the commemorative seal.

It had a strap connected to the corroded metal backing of its stone bezel. On the other end of the strap was a ring with the stubs of two more straps attached. Presumably, these had also been fastened to seals.

It seemed unlikely that its owner would knowingly have left such an item on the *Agamemnon* when she foundered, so why was it there? There were two plausible explanations: First, perhaps it had been stored in a chest in the lower hold, an area quickly flooded when the ship's hull was ruptured; or second, and more likely, it may have been dropped and found its way down into the bilge.

Marvelous as it was, the seal was less important historically than one other *Agamemnon* artifact that we knew lay on the seabed: the cannon that Hector, Sergio, Joanna, and I had first seen in 1993. As the season went on, I became more and more anxious to find it, and I hardly dared define the reason for my eagerness, even to myself. Could it, I wondered, be one of the guns that was actually fired at Trafalgar? And, if so, was it the only gun in the world today known to have been fired there? If the answer to the first question was yes, then so, most likely, was the answer to the second.

The thought had come to me while rereading an account of how Nelson saw the *Agamemnon* approach and exclaimed, "Here comes that damned fool Berry. Now we shall have a fight!" There was also Codrington's remark on the *Agamemnon* "far astern of us, blazing away and wasting her ammunition."

Cannons took a fierce beating from their repeated firing in battles, and they had to be changed every few years for testing. As far as I knew, all the cannons used at Trafal-gar had either been lost from the record, been melted down, or had gone to the sea bottom with ill-fated ships that had never been recovered. However, we knew from the records that our cannon might be a singular exception: At the time of her wreck, eighteen of the *Agamemnon*'s 64 guns had defied salvage. Some of them, then, must still be in the wreckage, and if they had not been changed sometime after the great battle, they had to be Trafalgar guns.

But before we would be able to determine whether this was indeed one of those historic guns, we had to find it.

Everyone on the team was involved in the search at one time or another. I had thought that finding it would be easy—we all remembered it was to one side of the wreck. But which side? Nobody knew. Still, how could we miss such a large chunk of metal? Yet miss it we did, and I was about to conclude that the great gun had either been stolen or buried in mud when one day, quite by chance, during a filming dive for the documentary makers, Hector and I blundered into it. We punched the water in jubilation and hooted our triumph into our mouthpieces.

Now to determine if it was one of Trafalgar's guns.

We knew that after Trafalgar, the *Agamemnon* went for a major refit. During such an overhaul, a ship's guns were frequently exchanged at the Woolwich Arsenal. Since a cannon's life was measured not in years but by the number of its discharges, it seemed to me highly likely that after a firefight like Trafalgar, any ship being refitted would have its guns off-loaded for examination and a fresh complement installed.

Bryan and Ann Smith were returning to England, and the timing was perfect: they could research the records of the Woolwich Arsenal, where every piece of naval artillery for the period was recorded and described by its distinguishing marks and weight.

Early one morning, we received a phone call from Bryan. He had found the records of the *Agamemnon*'s refit, the list of guns she used at Trafalgar and carried with her into the refit, and the list of guns she left with. They were—in every detail—identical. The Trafalgar guns had not been changed, and there had been no more refits.

"Goddamn it, Mensun," Bryan yelled over the phone, "it *is* a Trafalgar gun!"

THE TRAFALGAR CANNON

Our research had demonstrated that the cannon we found on the wreck of the *Agamemnon* had been on board at Trafalgar. And given Captain Codrington's report to the effect that the pugnacious Captain Berry was blasting away in all directions, there could be little doubt that the gun had been fired in anger. Furthermore, research was beginning to con-

firm that this was the only securably identifiable Trafalgar gun in the world. Small wonder that we were all charged with excitement at the find. It was not so much a great archeological discovery—many 24-pounders still survive, and this one would not tell us anything about them that we did not already know—but it was a great historical discovery because of its associations with Nelson and Trafalgar.

But how to bring it up? I knew that it would weigh about three tons, and I knew that this would be a delicate operation. From experience, I also knew that the best and safest way was a straight lift with a crane or winch. But nowhere around Punta del Este was a boat to be found that was right for the job. We could find tugs with enough lifting power to raise the gun to the surface, but none of them had mobile retractable winch arms to bring it on board.

There were, however, a few Uruguayan navy minesweepers that could enter

Below: **President Mario Julio Sanguinetti of Uruguay and Mensun prepare to be filmed for the documentary. Besides being most natural and affable for a politician, Sanguinetti turned out to be a Nelson scholar. He was an invaluable help in all the team's work in the River Plate.**

the bay, as well as the *Sirius*, a naval engineering and diving vessel with a twenty-ton crane used for deploying and inspecting large buoys and anchors.

We contacted our friends in the navy and asked if they would help us with the *Sirius*. They were sympathetic to our problem, but lacked the authority to give the go-ahead. By then, we were nearing the end of our allotted stay in Uruguay, and there was no time to go through channels. The only solution was to go right to the very top.

❧❧

Flying from Punta to Montevideo by helicopter, I met with the president of Uruguay, Mario Julio Sanguinetti, at his office. He was a large, affable man who smiled easily and immediately asked if my team was being cordially received in his country. I assured him that we were. We chatted on, and I knew everything would be fine when, within a few minutes, the president began to show himself something of a Nelson scholar. He talked of films and books about Nelson, and he reminded me that the memory of Nelson lived on in Uruguay—in given names, in street names, even in the name of a sports complex. Somebody—perhaps the president, perhaps an aide—mentioned that the Trafalgar gun would be a wonderful gift from the people of Uruguay to the people of England, perhaps best presented on some suitable state occasion.

We were set. Back in Punta, everybody was much relieved to know that the problem had been solved. Tom Cockrell, who had just arrived from England, set about acquiring the materials necessary to make a large spreader-bar to take the weight of the cannon.

His problem was to distribute the stress of the lift as evenly as possible along the barrel. Underwater, iron migrates to form about itself the crust of corrosion products called concretion. Sometimes the process is so complete that all that is left is a void reflecting the object's original shape. We knew that this would not have happened with the cannon, but we also knew that some migration would have taken place, so the gun would lack the cohesive strength it had when it sank.

Once he had manufactured the bar, Tom laid it beside the cannon. Then, using compressed air, he excavated a tunnel under its great barrel through which he threaded sheathed chain, looping it around the bar at fixed intervals. Now the strains and shocks of lifting would be distributed and absorbed by the bar, which would be connected to the hook of the crane.

Still, despite President Sanguinetti's intervention, there were technical hitches in Montevideo that prevented the *Sirius* from setting out to help us, and time was running out. We had other commitments in Uruguay, and I had settled on March 22 as our last possible date for leaving Punta del Este. By March 20, things looked black indeed. I convened a meeting at a hotel in Punta del Este to mobilize everyone we knew with any connections in high places to start making calls. One of them must have worked, because on March 21 we heard that the *Sirius* would sail overnight to arrive in Punta at breakfast time.

I woke up that night at about 2 A.M. to the sound of wind in the trees. I went to the window. A strong westerly wind was blowing, and I could hear the thunder and see the lightning out over the Plate. Then the rains came. At 5 A.M., they were was still sluicing down. I went out on the veranda to watch the sunrise.

By 7:30, we were all assembled on the quayside. The weather had improved, but there was no sign of the *Sirius*. Maybe she had put in for shelter along the way or had hove to on anchor. There was still time; if she arrived by midday, we would still have all afternoon. Our work would not take long. The cannon was trussed up, ready to go.

We contacted the ship on the Coast Guard's radio. She was not, in fact, far away, but she was stationary and trying to make some repairs. That did not sound good. At 9:30, though, she nosed into port—together with a barge that somebody thought might be needed to take the cannon once it had been lifted.

I greeted the captain, who gave me a perfunctory smile and then explained that there was indeed a serious problem: The *Sirius*'s generator had broken down, and without it they could not power the hydraulic pump that worked the crane and the windlass. They needed spare parts. To drive to Montevideo and back and then install the parts would cancel the day and thus the lift.

To ice the cake, the press and television arrived for a news conference that one of the government ministries had scheduled. Before talking to the reporters, I went with the captain to speak to *Sirius*'s chief engineer. Having worked in the engine room of a ship myself, I recognized the type: reserved, indifferent to authority, irascible with people who did not understand engines—but enormously capable. He would try to make the spare part himself on the lathe in the machine shop.

All morning we waited. Occasionally we heard voices from the engine room, and occasionally an engineer would emerge covered in sweat and oil and wiping his hands on a rag as he went for coffee.

By now, there must have been 400 people, all waiting to go—crews, divers, guests, press, film crews. In addition, a lot of small pleasure boats were gathering. They were all

Above, top to bottom: **Reporters covering the cannon lift from another boat; Mark Silk; divers ready for the lift.**

more confident than we were that a spectacle was in the offing. Even if it were, I was not happy with the carnival atmosphere that seemed to be building. It was incongruous—out of keeping with the cannon, with the *Agamemnon* and all she stood for. But there was nothing to be done about it now.

At 3 P.M., promising noises rose from the engine room, and soon after, the captain informed me that the generator was turning—but only just.

It would have to do.

❧

Within half an hour a whole flotilla was steaming out of port in single file. We were aboard the *Sirius* leading the way; with us were the *Sea Pilgrim*, a barge, a Coast Guard boat that had sometimes been loaned to us for diving, and two large tugs, spilling over with journalists. Behind was a long retinue of motor boats, sailing craft, and anything else that would float.

Tom had gone out earlier and buoyed the site, to mark the position of the gun and a perimeter zone around it, as well as the position of the wreck itself. The last thing I wanted

was for one of the anchors to land on the *Agamemnon*. I told Tom that he would be in charge of all in-water operations, and Bryan, who had just returned from England, would handle all on-deck proceedings. This would leave Hector, Sergio, and me free to address other miscellaneous problems that were sure to arise.

As soon as everything was in position, Tom was dispatched, followed by Hector. While one of them directed the crane's hook, the other slipped it through the ring leading to the spreader bar.

With Bryan giving directions, the crane operator slowly inched the cannon from the seabed. As it broke the water's surface, one of the tugs began to toot. At once, every other boat joined in. The noise was deafening. Everybody was clapping and cheering. Everybody, that is, except Sergio, Bryan, and me. We knew that the difficult and dangerous part—the landing of this great piece of ordnance—was still to come. And we were operating with faulty equipment.

Slowly, the crane retracted and began to turn. I had insisted that we have long tails of rope dangling from each end of the cannon,

x

because I knew that it might go into a spin—a possibility now seeming more probable as the ship did a slow roll in the swell. As it loomed over the deck, the gun slowly started to turn. As it gathered speed, we grabbed the rope ends and were able to guide it onto a bed of hawsers that Bryan had prepared on the deck. I was worried that the shock of contact could crack open the concretion and expose the gun to galloping secondary corrosion, but it landed with a kiss on the ropes and lay there, inert and magnificent.

For a moment, there was silence. Then we all erupted in cheers. Everyone began embracing—all except Bryan, who was standing to one side, scornful of such unseemly display. But on a subsequent TV news broadcast of the event, I would note that he was smiling a broad, toothy, bearded smile that I had never seen before in the more than 15 years I had worked with him on wrecks all over the world.

As daylight began to fade the cacophony seemed to dim with it, and I found myself hearing another din, the distant roar of the last great battle that saw this cannon fire: the beat of sailors' bare feet on the decks as they ran the gun inboard to ram her muzzle full of powder and deadly iron shot, the rumble of her wooden carriage wheels bearing her back to the gunport, the thunder of her firing, the massive rush of recoil. At Trafalgar that roar would have been magnified a thousand-fold as the warring fleets brought all their cannons to bear.

I could see Berry on the *Agamemnon's* decks, a man as fiercely ambitious as his mentor, intent on bringing the massive bulk of the *Santissima Trinidad* under his guns. And I could see Nelson himself on the *Victory*, pacing the quarterdeck, his cool courage inspiring his men to be more than they were, the coolness concealing the complete satisfaction he took in battle, thinking little about death, dreaming of triumph.

Long after Nelson's death, another sailor, Joseph Conrad, wrote this about him: "In a few short years he revolutionized not the strategy or tactics of sea warfare but the very conception of victory itself. He brought heroism into the line of duty."

The oceans of the earth had never seen his like before. They likely never would again. ❑

S ome lost ships exert a gravitational pull as steady as that of a massive planet, attracting and baiting the imagination until there is no choice but to plunge through the fathoms and find it—to touch the wood or

THE DIVE FOR THE *GRAF SPEE*

metal of her shattered remains and to share, for a submerged moment, her fate. I cannot remember a time when I hadn't felt the pull of the German pocket battleship Admiral Graf Spee—from the ship in its grave off Montevideo, but also from its very name, from its fate and that of its remarkable captain. Their roots were my roots, and her graveyard the grand estuary of my austral boyhood; so intertwined were we that I cannot quite say when the itch to dive her first made itself felt. But I can pinpoint the moment of decision, when that lifelong yearning coalesced into an adventure: it was in Oxford on Sunday, November 10, 1996, and it began with the binoculars.

Opposite: **Admiral Graf von Spee, Langsdorff's inspiration and, of course, namesake of the pocket battleship.**

I had just indulged in the one true privilege Oxford confers—besides, of course, our being able to say we are from there. "High table" is a substitute for expense accounts, fine offices, and company cars, and, in social and culinary terms, at least, a fine substitute it is. On that Sunday evening, I had followed custom, drifting from the good food and wine of high table in my college of St Peter's, to the senior common room, where, over coffee and newspapers, we all engaged in the academic equivalent of *sacra conversazione*.

Buried in the columns of the *Times* was a little space filler that riveted my attention. On Thursday, it said, Christie's would be auctioning crests from the Swan Hunter shipbuilders' offices, expected to bring up to £500, and a pair of binoculars, worth an estimated £10,000 to £15,000. The binoculars, according to the maritime expert at Christie's, had a unique provenance: "They belonged to Captain Hans Langsdorff, who commanded the German pocket battleship *Graf Spee*."

By coincidence, my wife, Joanna, has her business roughly opposite Christie's in South Kensington, London, where the sale was to take place, and she was friendly with one of their senior staff. I called Jo. Could she arrange a viewing?

Several days later, among the glass display cases in Christie's large viewing room, I held Captain Langsdorff's binoculars in my hands. They were shiny-black, slightly scuffed. Etched upon one side was the manufacturer's name: Carl Zeiss of Jena. On the other side, a

German imperial eagle brooded over a black swastika. Beneath was engraved: *Kapt. Z. See Langsdorff.*

A naval captain's personalized binoculars were not something to be disposed of—they were the possession of a lifetime, something to be handed down to children. But, according to the authenticating documents, Langsdorff had given his to a German-born electrician in Montevideo who had helped with the repair of *Graf Spee*'s electrical systems. Since the captain had little Uruguayan currency, perhaps the glasses had been payment for services rendered. But more likely, they were the gift of a man who had come to the end and wanted to see his prized possession in the hands of someone he liked and respected. In any event, here they now were, in my hands and, for a moment, I found myself transported back some sixty years to the bridge of the *Graf Spee*.

We hadn't come alone to Christie's on that bleak November day. After talking to Jo, I'd phoned my friend and collaborator, the documentary director Matthew Wortman. "Matt," I said, "we've got to film those binoculars." "What?" he replied incredulously. "Mobilize a film crew for a single day's shoot? Who's going to pay for it?" I kept him talking until at last his resistance crumbled. He had cameramen and sound men who were friends; maybe they would lend him a morning of their time? And so they did.

I could think of only one other man on the planet who would want to hold these

England, 1996

glasses as much: Hector Bado, my diving partner in Montevideo. He was a collector of *Graf Spee* memorabilia. While the binoculars would go at auction for far more than Hector could afford (in the end, they fetched £25,300), somewhere at the back of my head an idea had begun to take shape.

Since I'd first met him, Hector and I had shared a dream: we both wanted to dive the *Graf Spee*. Although the ship lay in only ten meters of water (in fact, until about 1950, the uppermost parts of its bridge could be seen at low moon tides), the dive would be extremely hazardous because of the almost zero visibility, horrendous currents, and a treacherous veil of fishing nets. As well, *Graf Spee* rested in a prohibited area: the Uruguayan navy's live-firing range.

At the time, I was in almost daily contact with Hector and my other friends in Uruguay, as we were preparing for the survey of Lord Nelson's *Agamemnon*, which was situated at the very mouth of the river, only a hundred kilometers east of *Graf Spee*'s remains. When I told him about the binoculars, and suggested to him that now was the time to dive the great ship, he replied: "Mensun, all I have ever wanted to do is touch the *Graf Spee*." It said everything; I myself wanted no more than the same. We decided there and then that we would try.

⌇⌇

Holding Hans Langsdorff's binoculars summoned more than the ghost of his lost ship.

The experience drew ghosts from the earlier world war, the Great War, as well as from my Falklands boyhood. With the glasses to my eyes, I told Matt's watching camera what was on my mind. "If only they could talk; just think what these binoculars have seen. *Exeter* charging in with all guns blazing . . ."

GRAF VON SPEE

Like all Falkland Islanders, I had been weaned on the legendary story of the *Exeter*, *Ajax*, and *Achilles*, and the epic battle they had fought with the *Graf Spee* in December 1939, just outside the mouth of the River Plate. And those stories, in turn, were connected to an earlier conflict that also took place in the South Atlantic, and which involved the eponymous figure of Graf (or Count) Maximilian Johannes Maria Hubertus von Spee, the German admiral whose name graced the modern battleship. It had been Admiral Graf Spee who—if only for a moment—had destroyed the illusion of British invincibility at sea. As with so many of the great sagas of men at war, his story was one of both victory and defeat.

When World War I began, Admiral Graf Spee commanded Germany's prized East Asiatic Squadron, comprising the heavy cruisers *Scharnhorst* and *Gneisenau* and the light cruisers *Leipzig*, *Nürnberg*, and *Emden*. The latter, under the command of Captain Karl von

TYPES OF BRITISH CRUISERS.

H.M.S. Good Hope. 1901.

H.M.S. Kent.

Above, top to bottom: Sir Christopher Cradock and all hands died on HMS *Good Hope* at Coronel when a shell ignited her magazine. Sturdee's HMS *Kent* helped avenge the defeat at Coronel.

Background: HMS *Canopus.* While grounded in Port Stanley, she fired the first shots in the Battle of the Falklands—hitting the *Gneisenau.*

Müller, had left the squadron and become one of the most successful merchant ship raiders in maritime history. In three months, *Emden* sank 23 freighters as well as a Russian light cruiser and a French destroyer. *Emden* had been replaced in von Spee's squadron by the light cruiser *Dresden.* Initially, von Spee's plan had been to attack British shipping in the China Sea; but, with the entry of Japan into the war, he was forced to move his operation to the west coast of South America.

As the admiral's warships prowled among the merchant traffic off Chile, public concern grew in Great Britain. The Pacific had passed into German hands and so, it seemed, had the Channel: U-boats had sunk three British cruisers there in as many months. Winston Churchill, First Lord of the Admiralty, decided to retake the initiative by destroying Germany's Pacific fleet, but did not give the Royal Navy what it needed to do it.

Rear Admiral Sir Christopher Cradock was put in charge of a special South Atlantic squadron comprising the armored cruisers *Good Hope* and *Monmouth,* the light cruiser *Glasgow,* and *Otranto,* a merchant ship fitted out with only a few 4.7-inch guns. (Un-

like in Nelson's time, guns by now were designated by the size of their bore.) Aboard this inadequate fleet, Cradock had a new, untrained, and equally unready crew. To conserve ammunition, they'd had virtually no gunnery practice—indeed, their guns had not been fired since the outbreak of the war. In addition, their armor-piercing ordnance was obsolete; against the armor-clad flanks of *Scharnhorst* and *Gneisenau,* they might as well have been firing Nelsonian cannonballs.

Looking at what Churchill had given him, Cradock saw certain doom, and urgently petitioned Whitehall for bigger, better ships. Churchill relented, but only a little: he sent the battleship *Canopus,* a heavily armed old wheezer with faulty condensers, capable of no more than 12 knots. *Canopus* might serve as a port guard, but it would be no match for the new generation of German dreadnoughts. But when Cradock yet again asked for something better, Churchill must have called his admiral's courage into question, for there were no further requests.

In Port Stanley, Cradock arranged for *Canopus* to have a thorough overhaul and to follow to the Pacific when she was fit. Then he wrote letters of farewell to his family and set off to fight von Spee in the spirit of Hector going off to fight Achilles beneath the walls of Troy.

Cradock's squadron rounded the Horn and traveled almost a thousand miles north along the coast of Chile, finding no sign of their dangerous quarry until the first day of

November 1914. Then, expecting three German ships, they suddenly came upon von Spee's quintet off the coastal town of Coronel, near Concepción.

At 7 P.M., in the gathering darkness of this South American spring, in mounting seas and stiff winds, the squadrons joined in mortal combat. Within 30 minutes, *Good Hope* was ablaze; before the first hour was up, her magazine detonated, killing Cradock and all his men.

Monmouth, meanwhile, was quickly brought to a standstill. Twisted and on fire, she capsized and went under at 9:30. In the heavy seas and darkness, it was impossible for the German ships to lower any boats to save survivors. Everyone on *Monmouth* perished.

"We opened fire at close range," wrote Admiral von Spee's son Otto, who was aboard *Nürnberg*. "It was terrible to have to fire on poor fellows who were no longer able to defend themselves. But their colors were still flying and when we ceased fire for several minutes and they did not strike them, we continued the attack and by our fire caused the vessel to capsize. The ship sank with her colors flying. We were unable to save a single man."

Glasgow, sorely damaged and hopelessly outclassed, beat a retreat south, running for the bottom of South America and the Falklands. *Canopus* met her en route, and together they returned to Port Stanley, where word of the defeat had already arrived by wireless. Now the Germans would almost certainly follow, hoping to acquire this strategically vital station and coaling base. In a state of high tension, the Falklanders evacuated their women, children, and the other noncombatants from Port Stanley to the outlying settlements.

Within a day of learning of the disaster off Coronel, Churchill ordered the sister battle cruisers *Invincible* and *Inflexible* to prepare for sea under the command of Rear Admiral Sir Doveton Sturdee. In addition to the battle cruisers, which carried 11-inch guns, Sturdee was assigned the cruisers *Cornwall*, *Kent*, *Carnarvon*, and *Glasgow*.

Sturdee's fleet reached Port Stanley on December 7 to find *Canopus* waiting—she had been grounded in an area where her big guns commanded the southern approaches as well as the narrow entrance to Port Stanley harbor. Several of the British ships doused their fires so that they could clean boilers and carry out general maintenance; other vessels began coaling. When they had cleaned their boilers, coaled, and resupplied, the six men-of-war would sail for Cape Horn to begin their hunt for von Spee.

The German admiral, however, was much closer than they thought. Since Coronel, he had formulated plans to destroy the naval base and radio station in the Falklands, take the British governor prisoner, and garrison the islands with German reservists. A German governor had already been named, and German nationals living in southern Chile were ready to move in.

During breakfast on the day after Sturdee's arrival, *Canopus* relayed word from a lookout on nearby Sapper's Hill that two men-of-war—a four-funnel and a two-funnel—were approaching Port Stanley. With only *Glasgow* and *Kent* ready for sea, the British forces could not have been less prepared for a fight. They raced to close boilers, reseal engines, and raise steam.

Meanwhile, *Gneisenau* and *Nürnberg* closed on Stanley, believing that they would find—if anything—only the decrepit *Canopus* and damaged *Glasgow*. The German cruisers carried raiding parties ready to storm ashore and occupy the town; the remainder of von Spee's group followed some 15 miles behind.

Canopus greeted the intruders at 9:15 A.M. at a range of 13,500 yards; her first salvo plunged down into the sea some 800 yards from *Gneisenau*. Her second ricocheted across the water and, according to some reports, hit the base of the German ship's after funnel. In the meantime, the other British ships had raised enough steam to begin moving out.

At this point von Spee must have experienced the same frisson felt by Cradock upon seeing the Germans off Coronel—the same cold touch of doom as he realized that the British had him outgunned. The admiral's only chance was to run for cover in the scatter of islands at the western end of the Strait of Magellan. He wheeled his ships about. On *Invincible*, Sturdee signaled a general chase, and under a bright sun, through seas that were calm for those latitudes, von Spee's ships turned southwestward, the predators now the prey.

Sturdee's three leading vessels could manage 25 knots, three knots faster than the Germans' maximum speed. Two hours out of Port Stanley, the British were almost within range. The Germans ran up their flags and took up battle formation, *Gneisenau* and *Nürnberg* in line-ahead on the left, *Scharnhorst* and *Dresden* on the right with *Leipzig* bringing up the rear. Faced with such superior firepower, von Spee's strategy was fatalistically simple: the armored cruisers would engage the British for as long as possible in the hope that the light cruisers would be able to escape. There was no thought of winning this engagement, only of minimizing losses.

Invincible and *Inflexible*, with the *Carnarvon* trailing, attacked *Scharnhorst* and *Gneisenau*, while *Glasgow*, *Cornwall*, and *Kent* went after *Leipzig* and *Nürnberg*. In such battles, the faster ships often dictate the engagement by choosing the range. Although *Scharnhorst*'s prize-winning gunners could straddle and hit *Invincible*, the British ship's thick skin protected her, while her 12-inch guns were capable of ripping *Scharnhorst* open like a can of sardines. Soon the German cruiser was burning from bow to stern.

Signaling *Gneisenau* to escape, von Spee turned his crippled flagship toward the enemy, possibly to try a torpedo attack. But several more 12-inch armor-piercing rounds slammed into her lower works. Her engines stopped. She lay dead in the water, wreathed in smoke and fire. Yet when Sturdee signaled her to surrender, the German ship made no reply. Covered in smoke and with her radio masts shot away, she most likely couldn't see or hear; several of her guns continued to shoot erratically.

Sturdee again opened fire. With her admiral's flag still flying, *Scharnhorst* listed to port—she was so far over, in fact, that her forward turret—still firing—was only eight feet above the water. Slowly, as her bows arced down, her great screws rose from the sea. Then, as she began her final slide, some crewmen jumped, many didn't bother; there were no boats to lower—they had all been shot through with holes. No one survived; those who were not killed by the blasts or sucked under by the sinking ship were numbed to death by the icy waters of the South Atlantic.

The British ships had no time to search for survivors—the battle was still raging. The big twin cruisers and *Carnarvon* turned their fire on *Gneisenau*; standing out of range of the German's six-inchers, they pounded the enemy to pieces with 12-inch shells. *Gneisenau* was blasted open; pigs taken on at Easter Island ran screaming about the burning decks while an escaped goose roamed the chaos, hissing at anybody who came near. All four

funnels were shot away, a direct hit killed everybody in the after turret, another slaughtered all the men shoveling coal in the stokehold, and yet another ripped through the aft medical station, killing 50 who had been previously wounded. The radio station was blown away.

At one point, the British realized that *Gneisenau*'s battle flag had gone and stopped firing. But Captain Maerker had no intention of surrendering—it was just that all of his flags had been shot away. Shortly before 6:00 P.M.—the fight was by then almost eight hours old—he gave the order to abandon ship. His men cheered the Kaiser and the ship, and their captain led them in a verse of "Deutschland, Deutschland uber alles." Then he ordered them over the side.

When *Gneisenau* went down, Maerker was still aboard. The nearest British cruiser was several miles away, too far to do much good for the men in the water. Two hundred were pulled from the freezing sea, but that night a quarter of them still died from wounds and exposure, among them Lieutenant Heinrich von Spee, the younger of the Admiral's two sons serving with the squadron.

While the larger ships blasted away far behind them, *Leipzig*, *Nürnberg*, and *Dresden* ran for the Strait of Magellan,

IN COMMEMORATION
OF THE
BATTLE OF THE FALKLAND ISLANDS
FOUGHT ON THE 8TH DAY OF DECEMBER 1914
IN WHICH THE BRITISH SQUADRON
INVINCIBLE, INFLEXIBLE, CARNARVON,
KENT, CORNWALL, GLASGOW, BRISTOL,
CANOPUS & MACEDONIA
UNDER THE COMMAND OF VICE-ADMIRAL
SIR F. C. DOVETON STURDEE
K.C.B., C.V.O., C.M.G.,
DESTROYED THE GERMAN SQUADRON
UNDER VICE-ADMIRAL GRAF VON SPEE
THEREBY SAVING THIS COLONY
FROM CAPTURE BY THE ENEMY

where they hoped they could lose the British in the maze of inlets and isles off the Chilean coast. But the faster *Cornwall*, *Kent*, and *Glasgow* soon overtook them.

In growing darkness and worsening seas, *Leipzig* took several hits below the waterline. Her ammunition exhausted, she twice discharged torpedoes in the direction of the British searchlights; both attacks failed. There was nothing her crew could do except surrender, else they would face certain death in the frozen wastes of the Atlantic. However, because of the fires that were raging along her decks, the Germans could not strike their battle flag, and the British continued firing. As the Germans labored to launch their only surviving boat, it and all the men around it were literally blown to pieces by a direct hit. Many grabbed anything that would float and jumped into the sea, hoping the wind would carry them to the British and rescue, but the current, which was going in the opposite direction, carried them off into the night. As for *Leipzig*'s Captain Haun, he stayed on deck, smoking cigarettes. *Leipzig*'s flag was still flying at 9:30 P.M., when her stern went up and she began her long plunge to the bottom. Only 18 men survived.

The firing between *Nürnberg* and *Kent*, which had begun several hours earlier, finally ended with the German vessel hammered into submission. Unable to fight on, and hoping to prevent further slaughter, Captain von Schoenberg ordered the battle flag to be struck. He and his crew cheered the Kaiser,

and then the wounded were put into the most seaworthy boat and lowered into the water to await rescue by *Kent*. But in the darkness and building sea, the boat overturned and sank, and many of the wounded drowned. As *Nürnberg* rolled over to starboard, a small group of German sailors could be seen standing on her fantail, waving an ensign. They seemed to be singing.

The lifeboats aboard *Kent* had fared no better than those aboard the German ships, and had to be patched before they could be lowered to pick up any survivors. With the crew working furiously on the repairs, *Kent* eased in among the survivors, throwing ropes, but the men in the water were already too overcome by cold to hold on. Only 12 were rescued, five of whom died. One of them was Lieutenant Otto von Spee, the Admiral's other son and the young man who had so lamented the loss of *Monmouth*'s crew off Coronel.

Dresden escaped, but not for long. Three months later, cornered by *Kent* and *Glasgow* off Mas Afuera in the Juan Fernandez Islands, she blew herself up.

Back in the Falklands, the victors were received with great celebration; Governor Allardyce went on board the flagship to congratulate Sturdee. The day was made a public holiday to be ranked with the monarch's birthday and the anniversary of Trafalgar, and a grand monument was built at what was then the west end of town. The battle represented, after all, the greatest event in Falklands' history, and, every eighth of December since, there has

Port Stanley, 1963

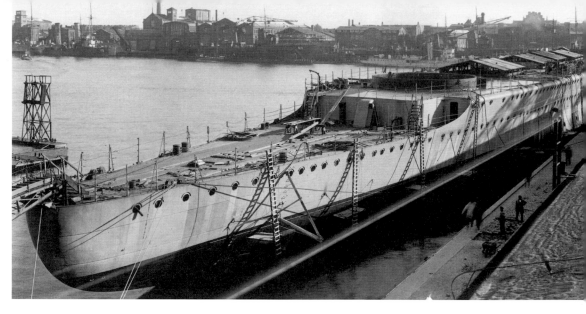

been a parade to mark the occasion, with all attending.

❧

I can remember marching through Port Stanley on December 8, 1963, the implacable westerlies gusting in from Cape Horn and chilling us to the bone. Men and boys, we marched in two columns along the seafront road toward a small hill capped with the white monolith of the monument. As always, Battle of the Falklands Day seemed to signal the beginning of Christmas; already the bunting was up in the window of Ross's, the usual cutout of a reindeer and sleigh had been erected above Hardy's, and a moth-eaten old Santa stood in the West Store.

At the head of the parade, dressed in khaki World War II–style uniforms and carrying Enfield rifles sloped over their right shoulders, came the Falklands Islands' Defense Force. Behind them marched the teenagers of the Boys' Brigade, and, after them, dressed in blue with flat-top sailor hats, paraded the four squads of the Life Boys. The two lads at the front wearing white-topped caps and lanyards were captains, and I—bursting with pride—was one of them. Across the ribbon-band of my sailor's hat were the words "HMS *Exeter*," the name of my squad.

However, through those parades and even today, when one uttered the name of *Exeter*, or *Ajax*, or *Achilles*, one was quickly haunted by those other names: Admiral Graf von Spee and his two sons and the hundreds of others killed at Coronel and in the Battle of the Falklands; and, of course, by the great World War II battleship that bore the Admiral's name and which also closely touched upon the life of the colony. The haunting had begun long before I hefted Captain Langsdorff's binoculars to my eyes in the viewing room at Christie's on that November day in 1996.

THE BIRTH OF *GRAF SPEE*

On August 23, 1932, the Wilhelmshaven Naval Shipyard received orders to build what was then identified only as "pocket battleship C." Although the nameless vessel had been conceived in the dying days of the Weimar Republic, she was the creation of those same post–World War I forces that lifted Adolf Hitler's National Socialists to power just a few months after its construction at Wilhelmshaven had begun.

Above: Graf Spee **under construction at Wilhelmshaven. Innovative technology and a diesel engine made her appear to abide by the limitations of the Versailles Treaty, and all the weight saved went into additional armament.**

Background: **Designer's plans for one of the gun turrets on the pocket battleships.**

Above, top: After World War I, the Treaty of Versailles stripped Germany of her war-fighting capabilities and strictly limited her navy. Here, in 1919, airplane propellers are chopped into firewood. *Bottom:* The Great Hall at Versailles.

Background: Graf Spee under construction at Wilhelmshaven.

Chafing under the constraints of the Treaty of Versailles, which allowed Germany only six heavy ships of no more than 10,000 tons displacement (as well as six light cruisers, twelve destroyers, twelve fast-attack torpedo boats, while absolutely prohibiting submarines), government planners had begun a clandestine program to build a powerful navy. Through deception and some ingenious technological innovations, three 12,000-ton ships were designed to appear to conform to the 10,000-ton restrictions. But they offered speed, range, and weapon power that was somewhere between that of a conventional cruiser and a battleship. Technically, they were heavy cruisers, but this new breed became known as "pocket battleships." They were the *Deutschland, Admiral Scheer,* and the vessel that would become *Admiral Graf Spee.*

In a slip nearby, a new *Scharnhorst* and *Gneisenau,* each displacing 32,000 tons, were aborning. Submarines were being built secretly in Finland and Holland, and German naval architects had already conceived two 45,000-ton superdreadnoughts, *Bismarck* and *Tirpitz.*

The father of this hidden building program, the "Z Plan" as it was called, was Grand Admiral Erich Raeder, commander in chief of the German navy and a keen student of what had gone wrong during World War I. When that conflict began, Germany boasted the second most powerful surface navy in the world; when the smoke from the Battle of the Falklands cleared, the German navy had been swept from the seas. At war's end, the ships that had survived such later battles as Jutland were scuttled by their own crews in Scotland's Scapa Flow.

This time, according to Admiral Raeder, Germany would not attempt to go ship-to-ship against Great Britain. Instead, it would create a fast, offensive force capable of ranging the world's oceans and striking merchant ships either at random or in concert with submarines. His raiders would confuse and disrupt the supply lines and lure away whole posses of fighting ships, leaving convoys vulnerable to submarine and aerial attack. His bandit fleet and wolf packs of U-boats, Raeder believed, would sever the island kingdom's lifelines.

Britain and France cooperated splendidly with Germany's plans. Not only had they been lax in monitoring and enforcing the naval clauses of the Versailles treaty, but they had also entered into agreements with the United States, Japan, and Italy to limit their own naval construction programs—everyone was anxious to avoid the kind of arms race that had crippled the West economically in the years leading up to World War I. At the Washington Naval Conference following the war, it was decided that they would retain their existing battleships and cruisers, but would build no new warships that *exceeded* 10,000 tons displacement. In 1935, the maritime powers further limited the size and fighting capabilities of their navies by restricting the number of 8-inch gun cruisers (such as *Exeter*) that each of the treaty nations might have.

It was ironic that with such cooperation abroad, Raeder found his worst enemy at home. Hitler's understanding of naval strategy was no better than Napoleon's. "Hitler was a land man," the admiral wrote in his autobiography. "He had no real idea of the special peculiarities of naval warfare." Raeder's plan to cut the enemy's supply lines was a bit too abstract for Hitler, who, Raeder said, "felt that the real task of our naval forces, and in particular of our heavy ships, was to engage the enemy; he had no understanding of the indirect effects their operations [would have] on the enemy's war effort."

On the last day of June 1934, the Wilhelmshaven shipyard was teeming with hundreds of spectators. From a flag-draped pulpit beside the towering bow of the new *Panzerschiff's* (panther ship) sleek, 609-foot-long armored body, Admiral Raeder, the architect of the new, still secret German navy, remembered Coronel: "Sunday, November 1, 1914. This date is graven in our hearts forever. For the first time in the history of our Navy, a German Admiral flew his flag far from home in an open sea battle with an adversary of like mettle." Raeder paid generous tribute to "that brave sailor, the British Admiral Cradock . . . who with 1,600 of his ship's company went to

a watery grave." After that tragic victory off Coronel, Raeder told his audience, von Spee had, with typical chivalry, hushed his men's celebrations in Valparaiso.

The new ship was decked out in flags and bunting from one end to the other, with the von Spee coat of arms—quartered diamonds and strutting cockerels—across the edge of her upper bows. Countess Huberta von Spee stepped to the platform to baptize the ship with her lost father's name, sending her seaward with the traditional strike of a champagne bottle. The bottle smashed against the ship's armored prow—but, for a moment, nothing happened. The enormous crowd stood silent. Then, almost imperceptibly, the great ship began to stir, and she began her stately glide into the water.

There had never been a ship like *Graf Spee* and her sisters. Their design was a masterpiece of innovation. To save weight, her plates and frames had been joined by electrical welding rather than bolts, and her structure extensively used aluminum. The tonnage thus saved went into added armor and armament. Moreover, within that sleek hull, the usual bulky steam turbines had been replaced by four two-stroke diesel engines, whose 54,000 horsepower gave her a 15-knot cruising speed and a maximum dash of almost 28 knots. At cruise she had the remarkable range of 10,000 miles.

In addition, the *Graf Spee* was fitted out with a rudimentary radar, called the Dt-Geraet, which was installed in a revolving pil-

lar on the foretop. Intended mainly for range-finding, its sensing field of almost 20 miles also made it useful for navigation and evading other ships. It was such a secret that when *Graf Spee* ventured into port, it was covered in sailcloth. She also carried hydrophones that could hear and locate propeller turns more than 50 miles away.

Two seaplanes extended *Graf Spee*'s field of view. These were originally Heinkel He60s, but in 1939 these were replaced by the new, faster Arado Ar196. Catapulted aloft, the Arado could range several hundred miles before returning for a water landing beside the mother ship. At sea, only one plane was used at a time, with the other stored below deck.

The ship's primary armament comprised six 11-inch (280 mm) guns mounted on rotating mantelets within two turrets installed fore and aft. The guns had been made by the famous Krupp works and represented the very latest in ordnance technology. Each fired a 670-pound projectile; in a single broadside, *Graf Spee* could rain down more than two tons of steel and high explosives on an enemy 15 miles away.

But the pocket battleship also fairly bristled with secondary artillery: eight 5.9-inch (150 mm) quick-loading guns located in single positions down the ship's sides; six 4.1-inch (105 mm) heavy antiaircraft guns; eight 37-mm light antiaircraft guns (both

of which had a continuous stand-by crew); and twelve 20-mm machine guns. She carried eight torpedo tubes, arranged in two groups of four. *Graf Spee* was a steel nettle, and a difficult prey for any ship afloat. Raeder boasted that she could outrun and outmaneuver any bigger ship, and her 11-inch guns could destroy anything capable of overtaking her. He was very nearly right.

On that day in June 1934 when *Admiral Graf Spee* slid into the harbor canal at Wilhelmshaven, the crowd cheered and raised their arms in Nazi salutes, shouting "Heil Hitler." The Reich Chancellor had been scheduled to attend, and many had come more to see their führer than the new ship. But Hitler wasn't there. Not even Raeder could explain his leader's absence, although it must have worried him. He'd never been one of Hitler's inner circle—perhaps the unexplained absence was a deliberate slight, a cautionary message from above.

In fact, Hitler hadn't come because he'd had another, more pressing engagement farther south, near Munich: the arrest and assassination of Ernst Röhm and the senior officers of the SA— the Nazis' Brownshirts. Throughout Germany, any-

Wilhelmshaven, 1934

body who had gotten in Hitler's way was eliminated. The Nazis called it "the crushing of the Röhm revolt"; history knows it as "The Night of the Long Knives."

YOUNG LANGSDORFF

The man whose binoculars had re-awakened my dreams of diving the *Graf Spee* was not her first skipper, but her third. Since her launch and commissioning, the pocket battleship had shown the swastika in Spain—indeed, Generalissimo Francisco Franco had gone on board in the Canary Islands to plead for Hitler's help in the Spanish Civil War. In May 1937, as flagship of the German fleet, *Graf Spee* was an official guest at the Coronation naval review at Spithead, where she almost

foundered on the compliments of those who would soon be hunting her. On October 29, 1938, her third captain took command—44-year-old Sea Captain Hans Wilhelm Langsdorff, a man of average size and build, whose blue eyes and good looks radiated leadership.

In a sense, Langsdorff had been drawn toward *Graf Spee* by the same historical forces that would be tugging on me years later. Born in April 1894 in the Baltic island town of Bergen auf Rügen, he'd grown up in Dusseldorf, the eldest of three children born to Ludwig Langsdorff, a judge of the high court, and his straitlaced Lutheran wife, Elizabeth. As a boy, Hans had been keenly aware of Dusseldorf's great seaman and nobleman, Admiral Graf von Spee, whose castle and estates dotted the fields and forests around the city. Indeed, it was partly his admiration for the admiral and his two lieutenant sons that had led Langsdorff to enter the Imperial Navy in 1912.

When World War I broke out in August 1914, it found him serving as a torpedo officer aboard the small cruiser *Medusa*. While on *Medusa*, he learned of the disaster that had overtaken Admiral von Spee and his two sons off the Falkland Islands.

If their fate, and that of the hundreds of sailors who went down with them, had not taught him compassion, then he learned it in the Battle of Jutland, the only major naval engagement (apart from the Battle of the Falklands) between Britain and Germany during World War I. Aboard *Grosser* when the fight began on May 31, 1916, the young lieu-

Below: **Admiral Erich Raeder (second from left), architect of the German Navy's "Z Plan," who guided the development of the "pocket battleship." He said much later that Hitler didn't see the significance of interdicting enemy shipping; the füehrer "had no real idea of the special peculiarities of naval warfare." At right is Karl Dönitz, regarded by many as the greatest of the German war leaders.**

Background: **Launching of *Graf Spee*.**

Opposite: **Captain Hans Langsdorff.**

tenant saw firsthand the controlled, deadly chaos of modern warfare at sea. Although he would remain a navy man, he thereafter abhorred killing and had little appetite for sinking ships.

The British had dispatched their fleet from Scapa Flow to counter the rumored deployment of the Imperial Navy's main fleet. Scouting forces from both sides had bumped into one another off Jutland, the thumb of land occupied by Denmark. The Germans pulled back, luring the British into pursuit—and into the arms of their main fleet. Heavily damaged in this encounter, the British retreated, this time pursued by the entire German fleet. When both forces turned away, the German fleet sailed right into the main British fleet, and the fight went through the night. In the melee, the *Grosser* exchanged fire with HMS *Bristol*, among others. Years afterward, observers would identify an omen: one of *Bristol*'s young officers was a Mr. Woodhouse, who later captained HMS *Ajax*, the nemesis of the pocket battleship that Langsdorff was to command in the Battle of the River Plate over three decades later.

At Jutland, Britain lost six heavy warships and eight destroyers, while Germany lost six large ships and five destroyers; between them on that spring evening, the two navies sent 8,648 men to their deaths. Hans Langsdorff won an Iron Cross at Jutland, but he also learned the price that men pay for victory at sea, a lesson that later greatly influenced his strategy on *Graf Spee*.

In the late 1920s, as the Weimar Republic tottered and collapsed, Langsdorff was commanding a half flotilla of fast torpedo boats—*Tiger*, *Wolf*, and *Jaguar*—operating out of Wilhelmshaven. He loved the roll and slap of the shallow-draft speedboats under his feet and happily returned to torpedo boats after a spell of staff duty in Berlin. On the first day of 1937, Langsdorff was promoted to the rank of sea captain, and took command of *Graf Spee* almost two years later. Then, at 8 P.M., on Monday, August 21, 1939, he embarked upon the course that would take him—and me—to the waters off Montevideo.

❦

His journey and that of his ship began as the nations of Europe again reached for their cudgels—in ten days, the world would again be at war. *Graf Spee*'s 7,000-ton supply vessel, *Altmark*, had slipped into the night several weeks earlier. *Graf Spee*, re-called from exercises in the North Sea, was quickly outfitted for duty as a raider, the specialty for which she had been designed.

Undetected, she sailed from Wilhelmshaven, out of the Jadebusen and into the North Sea. Under cover of darkness and at full revolutions, she moved northward past Jutland, past the mouth of the Baltic and up the coast of Norway. By August 24th, the day on

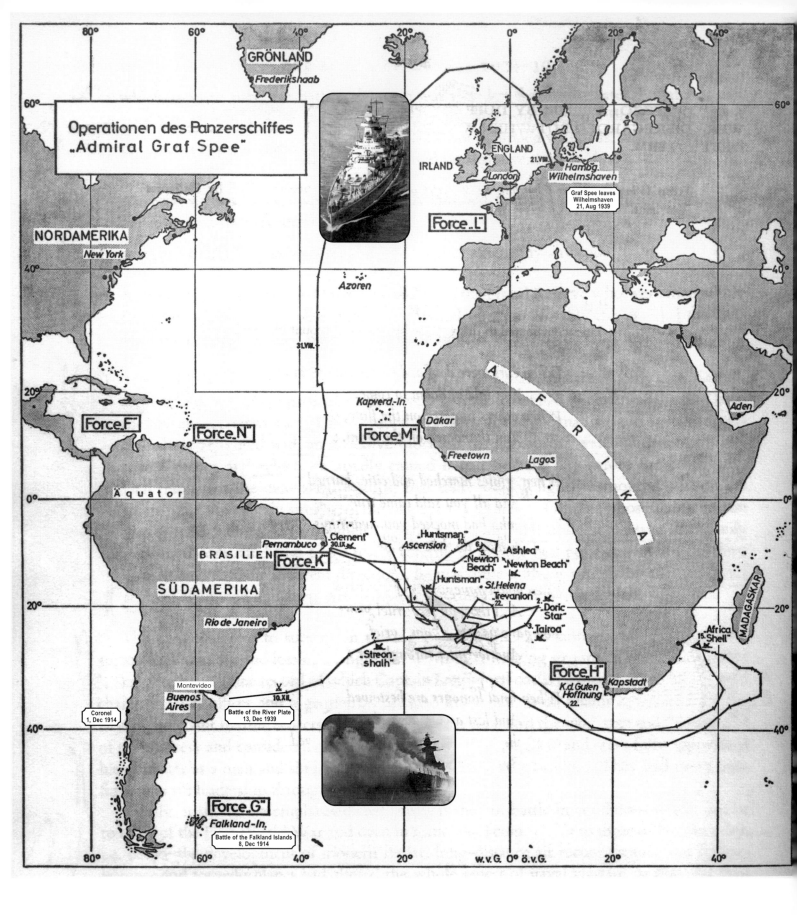

Operationen des Panzerschiffes
„Admiral Graf Spee"

GRÖNLAND
Frederikshaab

NORDAMERIKA
New York

IRLAND
ENGLAND
London
Hambg.
Wilhelmshaven

21.VIII.

Force „L"

Graf Spee leaves
Wilhelmshaven
21, Aug 1939

Azoren

31.VIII.

Force „F"   Force „N"

Kapverd.-In.

Force „M"
Dakar

Aden

Freetown
Lagos

A F R I K A

Äquator

Pernambuco
„Clement"
30.IX.

„Huntsman"
Ascension

„Ashlea"

„Newton
Beach"   „Newton Beach"

10.

6.

B R A S I L I E N   Force „K"

SÜDAMERIKA

„Huntsman"
4.

St.Helena

„Trevanion"
22.

„Doric
Star"   2.

MADAGASKAR

Rio de Janeiro

„Tairoa"   3.

„Africa
Shell"   15.

7.

„Streon-
shalh"

Force „H"

Montevideo

X
10.XII.

*Buenos
Aires*

*K.d.Guten
Hoffnung*
22.

Kapstadt

Coronel
1, Dec 1914

Battle of the River Plate
13, Dec 1939

Force „G"
Falkland-In.

Battle of the Falkland Islands
8, Dec 1914

w.v.G. 0° ö.v.G.

which the British Admiralty signaled the home fleet to proceed to their assigned war stations, she was traversing the Iceland–Faroe Islands gap of the northernmost Atlantic. She then turned south, ever careful to avoid freighter traffic. By the first day of September—the day that Hitler's army invaded Poland, and two days before war was declared—*Graf Spee* and *Altmark* met southwest of the Canary Islands, and the big ship was resupplied. Then *Graf Spee* headed for the Sargasso Sea, the South Atlantic's legendary graveyard of lost ships. There, like a great bird of prey, she folded her wings and waited.

Langsdorff first learned he was at war not from the Seekriegsleitung (Supreme Naval Command) in Berlin, but from a British Admiralty message that had been broadcast from the powerful transmitter at Rugby, which was constantly monitored by *Graf Spee*'s wireless operators. The signal from Rugby was heard at 8 A.M.; 39 minutes later Langsdorff received coded orders from Berlin on his Enigma machine: COMMENCE HOSTILITIES WITH ENGLAND IMMEDIATELY.

"Today is Sunday," Gunnery Officer Lieutenant F. W. Rasenack blithely confided to his diary. "On the deck they are playing shuffleboard, my fishing line for sharks is put out. . . . The Captain has just given us the news of England's declaration of war." Later that afternoon Rasenack learned that he was also at war with France. In the evening, he wrote, "Tropical night. Under a full moon with claret cup and the music of accordions, we sit on deck. Thus the war begins for us while the Army goes into the attack. How far away is our homeland! What are our parents and brothers thinking in this decisive hour? There is something extraordinary about this uncertainty under the starlit tropical sky. We seem far away from earthly things and feel the power of nature and of God."

Then, everyone—the men aboard *Graf Spee*, the opposing nations, the world—waited to see whether Hitler's invasion of Poland would, in fact, trigger a real shooting war. As what came to be known as the Phony War moved into its second week, *Graf Spee* cruised south, into the area west of Ascension and St. Helena, and there, again, she bided her time. Her eager young crew felt frustrated by the inactivity. Why, at this rate, the war would be over before they had experienced action!

Langsdorff knew better. He was one of the very few men on board who understood the black truth at the heart of naval warfare.

≈≈

On September 11, *Graf Spee* rendezvoused with *Altmark* for refueling under the watchful eye of pilot Heinrich Bongardts and his navigator Spiering, who were aloft in the Arado. Twenty-eight minutes into their patrol they spotted distant smoke. Spiering studied the smudge through his binoculars, sure that it was a British cruiser. He didn't think they had been spotted, but he couldn't be sure, and the intruder was just 20 miles from the German raider. Forbidden to break radio

Above: One of *Graf Spee*'s gun turrets.

Opposite: Map, originally from German Naval Command, traces the operational life of *Graf Spee*. From Wilhelmshaven to Montevideo took a total of 118 days.

Sargasso Sea, 1939

The beleaguered *Graf Spee*. In Montevideo harbor, Langsdorff ponders his dilemma: Thousands of miles from home, low on ammunition, badly damaged, cornered by the enemy and hostage to an unsympathetic government.

silence, they headed back to station and flashed a warning on their signal lamp.

The Arado had spotted the cruiser HMS *Cumberland* just in the nick of time. A narrow escape, not because Langsdorff feared a cruiser—*Graf Spee*'s 11-inchers could pulverize any British cruiser—but he didn't want to reveal his position. As well, in any engagement, there was the chance that the antagonist might land a "lucky" shot, and if that happened, *Graf Spee* had nowhere to go to make repairs.

She must remain alone, undetected, a speck of metal floating somewhere in the 62-million-square-mile vastness of the Atlantic and Indian Oceans. As Dudley Pope put it in his excellent account, *The Battle of the River Plate*, a hunter had a circle of vision of only 24 miles diameter, while their quarry could be anywhere in an area more than twice the size of Asia. There was no limit to the amount of havoc a skillful commander could wreak with an instrument like *Graf Spee*, as Langsdorff was shortly to demonstrate.

But, once detected, she would become the prey of Royal Navy ships converging from every corner of the globe; once revealed, Langsdorff knew, his ship was lost. Such fine points, however, would have been wasted on his virgin crew. Hans Ghann, who came to Montevideo as a seaman aboard *Graf Spee* and who lives there today in retirement, put their naïveté into perspective for me: Had they known that the intruder was a British man-of-war, he said, they might have sent a respectful spokesman to one of the officers, asking him to inform Captain Langsdorff of their eagerness to fight. "We had no concept," he told me, "of what hell such a battle might be like." But Langsdorff did, and soon would they all.

For two more weeks, the *Graf Spee* remained in her holding zone. Hans Ghann recalls that the news from Germany was good; clearly, the war was going their way. "Everybody," he said, "seemed to be doing something except us. Gunnery practice went on all the time. Since we could not have been any better, I suspect that much of it was just to keep us busy. We were proud of our ship, we were young and full of war fever and wanted to show what we could do."

On Tuesday, September 26, their waiting finally ended. Admiral Raeder had at last convinced Hitler to unleash the pocket battleships; Langsdorff was ordered to "commence active participation in the trade war." What Raeder did not share with the führer was his certain knowledge that unleashing *Graf Spee* and her sister ship, *Deutschland*, must doom them in the long run: they were vastly outnumbered, vulnerable, and operationally limited. They were only as long-lived as the skill and imagination of their commanders allowed. Langsdorff must have understood this too, although he made no mention of it, not then, not ever.

As *Graf Spee* charted a course for the easternmost corner of Brazil, Langsdorff mustered his crew and stood before them in his white dress uniform with the Iron Cross on his left breast. Another of the *Graf Spee* survivors in Montevideo, Rudolfo Dxierxawa, told me that rumors were flying through the ship; one of them was that they were about to pounce upon an Allied convoy. Langsdorff set them straight, in the kind of brief speech one might expect from such a taciturn and introspective man: their long wait was over; they would begin action as a commerce raider; their primary purpose was not to exchange blows with enemy fighting ships, but to sink merchantmen—Britain's lifeblood. He ended: "Heil Hitler."

"Heil Hitler," they roared back.

The secret of a successful commerce raider was staying always one step ahead of the enemy, both in thought and on the water, in what amounted to a deadly game of bluff and counterbluff. To confuse the enemy, Langsdorff had his crew blank out the ship's name everywhere on her exterior and replace it, in bold Gothic letters, with the name of her sister, *Admiral Scheer*. He even issued *Scheer* ribbon bands for their caps. "We change our name," mused Rasenack, "to worry the British Admiralty."

Then *Graf Spee* went to war.

FIRST KILL

Captain F. C. P. Harris, master of the Booth Line freighter SS *Clement*, was relaxing in his cabin on the last Saturday in September 1939. His 5,050-ton vessel, with 20,000 cases of kerosene in her holds, was pushing through moderate seas off the Brazilian coast, bound for Bahia. The war seemed very distant, although, from time to time, *Clement* would alter course, following the zigzag route that all British merchantmen were urged to take. Suddenly his third officer, H. J. Gill, called on the voice-tube from the bridge: "There's a man o' war at four points off the port bow, coming in fast. I expect that it's the *Ajax* or a Brazilian cruiser."

Captain Harris hurried to the bridge and studied the approaching vessel through his binoculars. "I could see no flags," he later wrote, "only that it was a man o' war. It was about four or five miles off with a huge bow wave, as if he was coming in at thirty knots." He ordered the ensign up and went back to his cabin to change into his white uniform in readiness to greet visitors from a ship that simply had to be HMS *Ajax*. When Harris returned to the bridge, the warship was only a few miles away, and, as he watched, she sent a seaplane into flight. He had been aboard *Ajax* a few weeks earlier, and knew she had a plane.

As the aircraft approached, Harris ordered his crew to reveal *Clement*'s name—it wouldn't do to have *Ajax* thinking she was a German ship. The seaplane zoomed overhead, banked, and came in again. This time it peppered the bridge with machine-gun fire, and then they saw the black cross of Germany under its wings.

"My God," groaned the chief officer, who was also on the bridge. "It's a Jerry." Harris immediately swung the engine-room telegraph to STOP ENGINES. *Clement*, helpless and unarmed, lay dead in the water. The crewmen scrambled to unlash and swing out the boats as the plane swooped again.

"Three or four times more the plane passed over us," wrote Harris, "spraying the boat deck with bullets, although the ship was stopped. The bullets fell around me like hail." In the meantime, *Clement*'s radio operator was transmitting "RRR," a prearranged Morse signal to inform the Admiralty and other ships that they were being attacked by a surface raider.

"Stop. No wireless transmission." It was a warning from the *Clement*'s assailant, but it came too late. Harris knew that his distress call and position had already been picked up by a Brazilian freighter. The ship's confidential papers were weighed down and thrown overboard, and Harris gave the order to abandon ship.

When the crew was in the lifeboats, a German boarding party came over and picked up Harris and the chief engineer, Mr. Bryant, then took them back aboard *Clement*. A pistol-wielding officer from the *Graf Spee* told Bryant to open the sea valves. Bryant, as he would write in his report, thought that the German officer did not have "much idea about it," so he opened the injection valves instead, which would fill the ship's ballast tanks, but not scuttle her.

Harris and Bryant were then taken aboard *Graf Spee* and shown to the bridge. "We met the Captain and ten officers," Harris reported later. "He saluted me and said [in English] 'I am sorry, Captain, I will have to sink your ship. It is war.' Shortly afterwards he said, 'I believe you have destroyed your confidential papers?' I said, 'Yes.' He answered, 'I expected it. That is the usual thing.'" That was the Briton's introduction to Hans Langsdorff.

"They fired a torpedo from the starboard quarter aft from the deck tube at about half a mile range," Harris recalled, "and it passed about fifty feet ahead of the *Clement*. The captain did not seem at all

Below: Doric Star **was part of the 50,000 tons of critical British shipping sunk by** *Graf Spee* **in her short life.**

pleased. . . . Then they fired a second one. It passed about twenty-five feet astern. . . . Then they said, 'We are going to use the guns.' . . . They started with the 6-inch guns and fired about twenty-five rounds. They were not happy with that either—some were going short and some were hitting. Some of the officers could speak English well, and one said, 'If we were farther we would hit, but we are too close!' They gave us cotton wool during the firing to put in our ears."

It was five 11-inch rounds that finally sent the *Clement* down.

Lieutenant Rasenack told me how old Captain Harris and his chief engineer watched their ship rise up perpendicularly before beginning its long plunge to the bottom. Harris had been through it before; as a captain he had lost a ship in World War I to a submarine. As the *Clement* disappeared beneath the water, Rasenack heard him utter, more to himself than anyone in particular: "A damned hard ship!"

Then Langsdorff told the Britons, "If you will give me your word not to attempt any sabotage or espionage, and do exactly as we tell you, you will be left free. Otherwise, I will have to put a guard on you."

The captives promised and shook hands with Langsdorff. Then *Graf Spee*'s executive officer, Walter Kay, took them to his cabin and offered them cigars and red beer while they signed their promise. When they had done so, they received a meal and a glass of rum.

Langsdorff sent a signal to the radio station at Pernambuco, using *Admiral Scheer*'s call sign, DTAR: "Please save the lifeboats of the *Clement*. 0945 S, 3404 W."

The Brazilian station replied, "Thanks. OK. Hasta luego"

As they left the scene of *Clement*'s demise, they saw a ship coming to give help. They had no idea of her nationality; for all they knew, it might well have been British or French, and fair game for a raider. But Langsdorff held to his course. Rasenack told me how, with typical decency, his captain declared he would not take any ship that was going to the rescue of another.

As it happened, Harris and Bryant were aboard *Graf Spee* only briefly. Two hours after sinking *Clement*, the German vessel saw the Greek steamer *Papalemos*, and ordered her to stop to take on the two prisoners. Langsdorff ordered the freighter not to break radio silence for 600 miles, and released her.

I have dwelled at some length on the sinking of ss *Clement*, mainly because it illustrates *Graf Spee*'s modus operandi. First, she would race in at maximum speed, without an identifying flag, at an angle that made it difficult to determine her type and nationality. Second, when several miles from her quarry, she would launch her aircraft, which would strafe the ship if it broke radio silence. (That the Arado fired on *Clement* before she used her radio on this occasion was an aberration.)

But the incident also tells us much about Langsdorff himself, who not only shared

Graf Spee's fate, but whose character looms over the vessel just as Sulla's does over the Mahdia wreck and Nelson's over *Agamemnon*. There are those who argue about Langsdorff's tactical handling of his final battle and his final decisions, but no serious observer has ever questioned his leadership, courage, or integrity. To this day, when you speak to the elderly men who once fought under his command, you find their devotion to the man they call "our captain" remains undimmed by 60 years and their intolerance to any criticism of him quite intact. And, both German and British survivors never tire of reminding one that, on all the merchant ships he sent down, not a single life was lost. He was a better man, one concludes, than he was a servant of his regime.

GRAF SPEE UNLEASHED

After sinking *Clement*, *Graf Spee* headed back into the wastelands of the Atlantic north of St. Helena to await fresh prey. Early on October 5, less than a week after her first kill, *Graf Spee* again sounded action stations. Smoke had been seen on the horizon, and soon the mast and smokestack of a merchant ship hove into view. At maximum revolutions, *Graf Spee* charged in like a wolf upon the fold—but not to sink it. Langsdorff wanted her as an accommodation vessel for prisoners.

The ship was a tramp, SS *Newton Beach*. Carrying a cargo of maize from Cape Town, she sailed under Captain Robinson of South Shields. The *Newton Beach* had been adopted by the Busford St. Senior C.C. School at Haddesdon, Hertfordshire, under the British Ship Adoption Society, a wartime scheme whereby students wrote to the officers and men of a ship, who wrote back about their voyages. It gave the men an interest and it was good for the pupils, who followed the ship's progress on a wall map. But Captain Robinson's final letter was not a very cheerful one.

"Since my last letter was written," he told the students, "many things have happened, first the war and then the sinking of my ship. . . . *Newton Beach* is no more."

Newton Beach's experience was not unlike *Clement*'s—a sudden charge by an unidentified, and then misidentified, warship, a strafing run by the seaplane, the order to abandon ship. The difference was that the freighter was not sunk right away.

The day after acquiring *Newton Beach*, *Graf Spee* encountered *Ashlea*, a merchantman of 4,200 tons carrying a cargo of sugar from Durban to Freetown. After taking off the crew and helping themselves to half of her sweet cargo, the Germans sank *Ashlea* with cartridge charges, so as to conserve shot and torpedoes. A day later, Langsdorff tired of his slow companion. He moved the prisoners to his warship and sent the *Newton Beach* to the bottom, again with cartridge charges.

On October 10, *Graf Spee* spotted her fourth victim, ss *Huntsman*, an 8,200-ton liner with a cargo of tea. By this time, *Graf Spee* had two ships' crews on board, and the prospect of increasing his prisoner population filled Langsdorff with apprehension—quite apart from the inconvenience, there was now a very real risk to security. He decided to keep some of them on *Huntsman* until he had replenished from *Altmark*. After that, he could move the prisoners to his supply ship and send *Huntsman* to the bottom.

Graf Spee and *Altmark* rendezvoused on schedule, west of St. Helena. Heinrich Dau, captain of the auxiliary tanker, was not at all happy to learn that his ship was being turned into a prison. As ferocious a disciplinarian as he was an excellent seaman, Dau had been recalled from retirement at the beginning of the war. He was a difficult man to know, but Commander Diggins, who probably knew him better than most, told me that he was quite vociferous in his dislike of the British because of ill treatment he had received as a prisoner of war in Great Britain during World War I.

Well aware of his feelings, Langsdorff gave strict orders that the prisoners should be treated as humanely as possible and given the same food as his crew. To ensure security, but also to guarantee that his orders were followed, Langsdorff transferred an officer and a guard of eleven men to *Altmark*.

After *Graf Spee* replenished its fuel and stores, *Huntsman* was sunk and then the pocket battleship ghosted to a new operational zone southeast of St. Helena—a vantage point from which Langsdorff could prey upon ships plying the Cape of Good Hope route. Sure enough, on October 22, the Arado spotted ss *Trevanion*, a 5,200-ton steamer bound homeward from Port Pirie with a cargo of concen-

Below: Graf Spee **on tour before the war, in New York harbor. She also impressed the British at the Coronation naval review at Spithead two years before the war.**

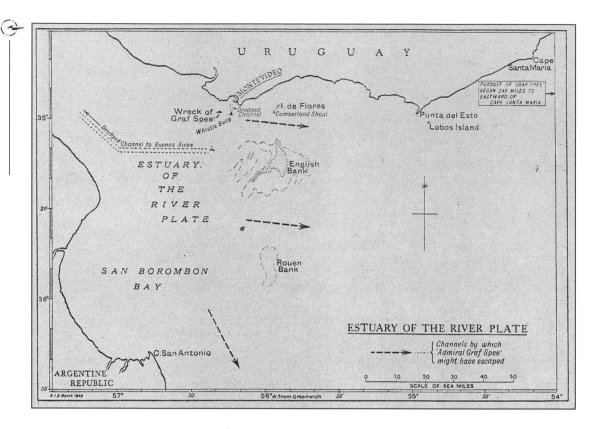

trates. Before being boarded, she managed to transmit a full RRR signal.

Worried that the message might have been picked up, Langsdorff moved *Graf Spee* westward again with all eight of her diesels hammering away at maximum drive—better than 26 knots. Several days later, fearing that things might soon become too hot in the South Atlantic, Langsdorff doubled the Cape of Good Hope and entered the Indian Ocean. It was a feint to draw off his pursuers; once he had created enough confusion he would steal back into the South Atlantic in time for his next rendezvous with *Altmark*.

By November 8, *Graf Spee* was moving north and east toward Madagascar. The only victim in ten days' idling in the Indian Ocean was *Africa Shell*, a 706-ton tanker sailing in ballast. She sent no distress call, and Langsdorff had her scuttled. Among the new batch of prisoners was *Africa Shell*'s skipper, Patrick Dove, who would be at the German captain's side—less as an enemy than an admiring colleague and friend—almost to the end.

Finally, on November 16, *Graf Spee*'s wireless operator picked up the message Langsdorff had been waiting for: an Admiralty warning that his ship was operating in the Indian Ocean. Believing that he had successfully deceived Britain's Admiralty, he headed back toward the South Atlantic, passing through the "roaring forties" well south of the

Cape of Good Hope, where enemy warships at that moment were likely to be converging.

Graf Spee had by now spent weeks at the gallop and was in need of a refit. Marine growth on the lower hull was causing drag, the ship's refrigeration plant was in mechanical decline, and her unexpectedly fragile diesels were badly in need of dockyard maintenance. But Langsdorff was not yet ready to leave the field of battle. He wanted to make a final destructive pass among enemy merchantmen sailing out of the River Plate, then turn for home and a badly needed bit of rest and repair.

By November's end, he had replenished from Altmark and dressed his pocket battleship in an improvised disguise—a faux funnel and a dummy forward 11-inch turret were added, giving the German ship the silhouette of HMS Repulse, which might help her on the long road back to Wilhelmshaven.

On December 2, Langsdorff's lookouts spotted another smear of smoke on the horizon. Doric Star, a Blue Star liner of more than 10,000 tons displacement, was beating her way back to England from New Zealand with a cargo of meat and dairy products. The British vessel was stopped by long-range salvos across her bow, but Langsdorff took his time overtaking her, almost as if he were hoping to stir up a good fight. Doric Star had time to send out a series of distress calls, which were picked up by ss Port Chalmers and relayed to Freetown. Having more or less allowed his presence to be broadcast, Langsdorff quickly

sank the cargo liner and turned Graf Spee southwest, toward La Plata. Radios buzzed with news of a German raider.

The next morning, Langsdorff's crew took up their action stations, waiting for first light to reveal whether or not the horizon was clear. It was not: Tairoa, an 8,000-ton steamer, was en route from Melbourne to Freetown, where she was to join a convoy bound for England. Ironically, Tairoa had come to her present position after hearing Doric Star's distress signal and altering course to avoid the raider. Nevertheless, it was this hapless freighter that put the noose on Graf Spee. While under fire, the Tairoa's wireless operator was able to get off the fateful RRR call; now all knew that the great Panzerschiff was most likely heading westward across the South Atlantic.

On December 6, Graf Spee and Altmark reunited as planned. The raider was refueled, and apart from some officers and wireless operators, the prisoners were transferred to the supply ship. Langsdorff and Dau agreed on a time and place for their next rendezvous —their last, since after that the pocket battleship would be running for Germany.

A day later, Graf Spee chanced upon ss Streonshalh, a steamer of 3,895 tons carrying wheat from Montevideo to Freetown. Her captain put the safety of his crew above duty, and sent no distress signal. His confidential documents, although thrown over the side, were retrieved by the Germans. Streonshalh's papers confirmed the wisdom of stalking the

H.M. SHIPS 'EXETER' & 'AJAX' ALONGSIDE

Plate. On December 10, Langsdorff read, a guarded convoy of four merchantmen would sail from Montevideo. It was too tempting to ignore.

Streonshalh was *Graf Spee*'s ninth victim. In just over two months' hunting, the pocket battleship had sent more than 50,000 tons of British shipping to the bottom. With the war just entering its fourth month, the raider had already destroyed more than four times its weight in enemy vessels. This, its excited crew must have believed, was just the beginning. In fact, it was the end.

Within twenty-four hours of *Clement's* sinking in late September, Whitehall had known a German raider—believed to be *Admiral Scheer*—was prowling the South Atlantic. The First Sea Lord, Admiral Sir Dudley Pound, had immediately convened a meeting in the Upper War Room of the Admiralty to discuss ways of finding and destroying her. Britain's only battle cruisers fast and powerful enough to take on a pocket battleship were HMS *Hood*, *Repulse*, and *Renown*. But even these

vessels, alone, could not be certain of victory. The only way to hunt such a raider was to hunt in packs—in this case, nine groups totalling 23 powerful ships that would be deployed around the world, from Ceylon to the Cape of Good Hope, Dakar to Pernambuco.

The South Atlantic went to Force G, under the command of Commodore Henry Harwood; it comprised HMS *Exeter*, already on the east coast of South America, *Ajax*, then in the Falklands looking for reported German merchantmen off Patagonia, *Cumberland*, refueling in Freetown, and *Achilles*, a sister ship of *Ajax* operated by the New Zealand wing of the Royal Navy and currently on the Pacific coast of South America.

It was the biggest hunt for a single man-of-war in naval history, and it severely drained the resources of Britain's Home and Mediterranean Fleets as well as leaving her convoys vulnerable to U-boat attack. In that, at least, *Graf Spee* had almost immediately accomplished her larger objective. British leaders still remembered how close German submarines had come during World War I to blockading the island nation, and yet they were possibly opening themselves again. But also, as Winston Churchill would note, "we had vivid memories of the depredations of the *Emden*," a much smaller, slower, less well-gunned vessel than the pocket battleship now loose in the South Atlantic.

Langsdorff's ruse of disguising *Graf Spee* as *Admiral Scheer* also achieved its intended deception. In a letter to Pound written twenty-one days after the sinking of *Clement*, Churchill asked, "Are you sure it was *Scheer*, and not a plant, or a fake?"

After the war he wrote, "Our plans to intercept him were foiled by the quickness of his withdrawal. It was by no means clear to the Admiralty whether in fact one raider was on the prowl or two, and exertions were made both in the Indian and Atlantic Oceans. We also thought that the *Spee* was her sister ship, the *Scheer*. The disproportion between the strength of the enemy and the countermeasures forced upon us was vexatious. It recalled to me the anxious weeks before the actions at Coronel and later at the Falkland Islands in December 1914, when we had to be prepared at seven or eight different points in the Pacific and South Atlantic for the arrival of Admiral von Spee with the earlier editions of the *Scharnhorst* and *Gneisenau*. Twenty-five years had passed, but the puzzle was the same."

While *Graf Spee* was chasing *Tairoa* and *Streonshalh* on the western rim of the South Atlantic, Commodore Henry Harwood, still 3,000 miles away, had picked up her scent. Scanning a chart of the southern ocean, Harwood pondered her next likely destination—the Falklands, perhaps? Rio de Janeiro?

Then, in one of those guesses on which the events of war can pivot, the commander of Force G put his finger on the gaping estuary of the River Plate between Uruguay and Argentina. "That," he told his officers, "is where she'll turn up next." No raider, he believed, could resist such easy pickings. He ordered his

available cruisers to converge on the River Plate, to arrive no later than December 12, following with the message that there was to be strict radio silence. He did not wish to scare off the raider.

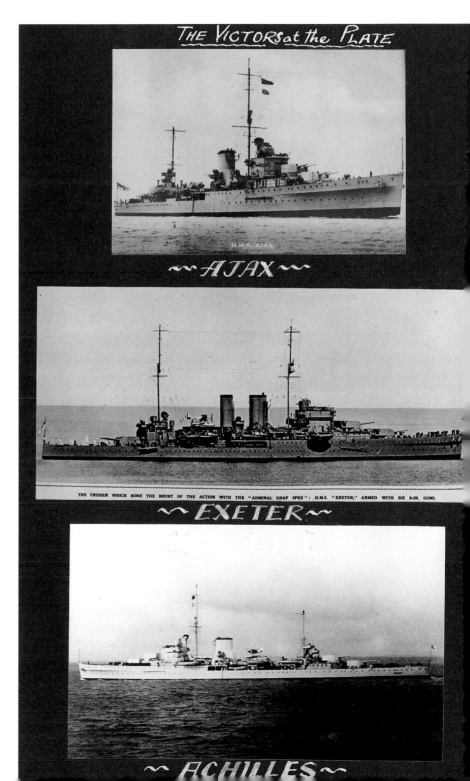

THE VICTORS at the PLATE

H.M.S. AJAX.

~AJAX~

THE CRUISER WHICH BORE THE BRUNT OF THE ACTION WITH THE "ADMIRAL GRAF SPEE": H.M.S. "EXETER," ARMED WITH SIX 8-IN. GUNS.

~EXETER~

~ACHILLES~

Like Cradock in 1914, the 51-year-old British leader knew that he was outclassed and outgunned. *Exeter* and *Cumberland* suffered from the self-imposed, prewar armament limitations and carried nothing larger than eight-inch guns. Although they could send a 250-pound projectile some 27,000 yards, the German pocket battleships could strike from about 30,000 yards—in other words, the British were outranged by almost two miles. The main guns on *Ajax* and *Achilles* were six-inchers. All the British ships were thin-skinned, whereas the seven-inch-thick armor fronting the turrets of the Panzerschiff was almost impenetrable to eight-inch shells.

Harwood's only chance of victory was to have his four cruisers fight together against the pocket battleship and split her fire. Even as a threesome, they would very likely go down beneath the German guns. Harwood

knew, too, that it would be difficult to keep his group together all the time: those tired hunters needed periodic fueling and refitting, and the nearest British base was in the Falklands, a thousand miles away.

On December 12, only three Force G ships were on station off the mouth of the Plate. *Cumberland* was still in Port Stanley, having joined *Exeter* there on the seventh—there had been some apprehension that Langsdorff might try to replicate Admiral von Spee's intended assault of almost exactly a quarter-century before. When the anniversary had passed, *Exeter* sailed for the Plate, but *Cumberland* had to stay behind for a refit.

Just outside the mouth of the Plate, Harwood briefed his captains: "My policy with three cruisers in company versus one pocket battleship: Attack at once by day or night. By day act as two units. First Division (*Ajax* and

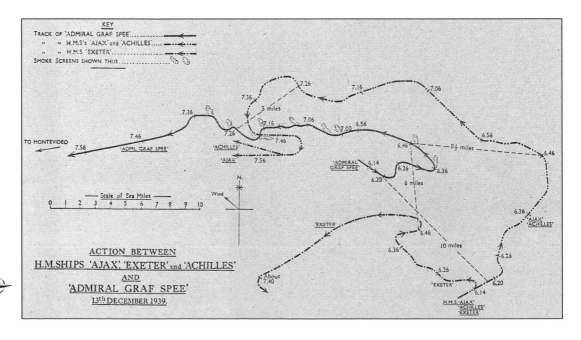

Right: Contemporary newspaper map showing the sequence of the battle.

H.M.S. AJAX VII

Light Cruiser·1935-1949

6,840 Tons ~ 32 (+) Knots ~ 680 Crew (Increased eventually to 840) 2 x 'Seafox' Aircraft

Achilles) and *Exeter* diverged to permit flank marking. First Division will concentrate gunfire. By night ships will normally remain in company in open order."

At first light on December 13, 1939, the trio of British ships were steaming at 14 knots on a zigzag course toward the northeast, about 200 miles east of the Uruguayan coast. Just after 6 A.M., lookouts on *Ajax* reported a puff of smoke to the northwest. Harwood ordered *Exeter* to investigate. Minutes later, *Exeter*'s Captain Bell signaled, "I think it is a pocket battleship," adding immediately, "Enemy in sight."

Force G turned to fight, believing they had at last run down their adversary—the ship that they still believed to be *Admiral Scheer*. As the alarm rattlers sounded and the crew

tumbled out to battle stations, a vermilion flash illuminated the northwestern horizon. The German ship had fired her first salvo.

Against the backdrop of a clear sky, the smoke from the British ships was visible to the lookouts above *Graf Spee*'s fighting top well before their counterparts on *Ajax* saw them. For Kapitän zur See Hans Langsdorff, alone and very far from home, every ship was either predator or prey. He hoped the latter. Perhaps it was the Royal Mail Line's *Highland Monarch*—he had read of her intended departure in a copy of the *Buenos Aires Herald* from the cabin of *Streonshalh*'s chief engineer.

Ordinarily, Langsdorff would have sent out the Arado, but the airplane's fatal design flaw had finally ended her effectiveness. She landed too fast and, in so doing, routinely

River Plate, 1939

cracked her heated cylinders by spraying them with cold water. By then, the spare aircraft's engine had been cannibalized to extinction; both Arados were unusable.

When he had closed to about 17 miles, however, Langsdorff studied the ships through his binoculars—the same scuffed glasses I would hold in my hands at Christie's almost four decades later. He saw three ships in line formation. The last had unusually high masts, giving her a profile as distinctive as *Graf Spee*'s. From his copy of *Jane's Fighting Ships*, Langsdorff knew she was HMS *Exeter*. As the German warship advanced, he saw that the other two vessels were not destroyers, but light cruisers. Although they made it more of an even fight, he still had almost no chance of losing.

But like a lion taking on a pack of hunting dogs, *Graf Spee* was nonetheless vulnerable—a lucky hit could detonate one of her magazines, or take out her electrics, or cause some crippling damage that would render her easy prey for other hunters who, once her position was known, would head full speed for the Plate. Langsdorff may have thought of declining the action, but not for long. Indeed, he may have hoped for this very confrontation, from which *Graf Spee* could go home a naval legend, a ship of heroes.

At 6:17, at a range of 21,000 yards, with his guns well elevated, Langsdorff ordered his main artillery to open fire on *Exeter* —the first salvos seen by the English had been base-fused shells hurled for clearer observa-tion. As the first great white columns of froth boiled up a few hundred yards short of *Exeter*, a second salvo was already screaming toward the British ship, which returned fire at a range of 19,600 yards. Langsdorff drove his ship toward the British. Every three minutes the ships moved a mile closer to one another.

Soon, *Graf Spee*'s fire straddled *Exeter*. Huge gouts of water rose up around her; Langsdorff's gunners had her range. But here, poised for the kill, Langsdorff made what some argue was a tactical error: he retrained his main forward turret and sent a two-ton half-broadside howling toward *Ajax*, which, with *Achilles*, had diverged from the *Exeter* in hope of splitting the Panzerschiff's fire.

Now the two light cruisers opened fire. *Achilles*, crewed by New Zealanders (including some Maoris), trailed *Ajax* by only several thousand feet. Under fire from the smaller ships, *Graf Spee* turned toward the north, presenting a foreshortened target to the light cruisers, and resumed her ballistic focus on *Exeter*, whose crew was about to experi-ence the true bloody horror of naval combat.

The British heavy cruiser had just fired her third salvo when the sea suddenly erupted along her starboard side just forward of midship. Metal splinters sprayed *Exeter*'s decks, killing most of the men on the star-board torpedo tubes and several others; elec-trical power circuits sizzled and died; fires ig-nited. Seconds later, *Graf Spee*'s first direct hit sent a half-ton of spinning steel through the after turret's hatch. The shell then ripped through the sick bay before exiting from the vessel's flank—all without exploding.

By now, the German guns were firing impact-fused shells, one of which disabled *Exeter*'s B turret and killed eight of its crew; sailors lay everywhere, badly wounded and hideously maimed. A marine lost a forearm and had the other arm smashed, yet stayed on deck through the action until he collapsed from shock and loss of blood. It was worse on the bridge, where splinters had killed everybody but Captain Bell and two officers. All wheelhouse communications were down; the ship was out of control and moving to starboard. Bell, himself wounded in the face, reestablished control over the ship from the after conning position, relaying oral steering orders through a chain of men. Slowly, *Exeter* hauled herself back on course and resumed firing from the three still-operational turrets she had.

Despite the punishment she had taken, *Exeter* clung to the raider's tail and began landing shots of her own. One

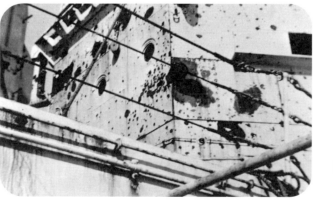

well-placed eight-inch shell hit *Graf Spee*'s control tower, killing a number of officers and vital instrument operators, wrecking the artillery rangefinder, and damaging communications. The main guns could no longer be coordinated by telephone links and began independent fire.

Then *Exeter* absorbed a hit on her anchor sheet that blasted a gaping hole in her side at the waterline; more men were killed and maimed. A fire broke out in the forecastle, threatening to ignite the cordite, nitroglycerine and gun-cloth stored in the forward magazine. An instant later, the ship was staggered as another 11-inch shell slammed into her deck, decimating a firefighting team and littering the deck with more dead and wounded. Bell ordered his starboard torpedo crew to fire, and soon the big silver fish were running at better than 40 knots for *Graf Spee*. But the German ship swung 150 degrees toward *Exeter* and put out a screen of smoke as the torpedoes sped harmlessly past.

Through his chain of men, Bell ordered a sharp turn to starboard, hoping to

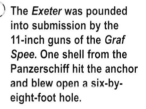

The *Exeter* was pounded into submission by the 11-inch guns of the *Graf Spee*. One shell from the Panzerschiff hit the anchor and blew open a six-by-eight-foot hole.

bring his portside torpedoes to bear. As *Exeter* began the turn, however, three more 11-inch shells rained down upon her. One put A turret out of action; another smashed through the armament office, killing five telegraphists and destroying a four-inch gun; the third tore into the plating of the ship's side, passed through three bulkheads, and then blew a 14-by-16-foot hole in the chief petty officers' quarters. A host of sailors were cut down by a hail of shrapnel; those still alive were choking on the acrid fumes. The cries of the wounded mingled with the hiss of escaping steam as flames crept upon those unable to move to safety.

Exeter was almost destroyed. She was without communications or electrical power, and several fires raged about her decks. She was listing ten degrees to starboard and was taking on water, which put her down at the bow. More than 50 officers and crew were dead, lying in grotesque displays all around the ship. Yet still she fought, firing from Y turret until it was silenced by a short circuit. Only then did Exeter break off the action.

The dazed crew did what it could to patch up the ravaged cruiser, their first task tending to the dead and wounded. Under the hot subtropical sun bodies had already begun to decompose; they were quickly stitched up in hammocks and buried at sea. The survivors, exhausted and filthy from battle, offered prayers, requiescant in pace, and over the side went the dead

But Exeter, while gravely wounded, was not herself dead. She had signaled Ajax: "All turrets out of action. Flooded forward up to No. 14 bulkhead, but can still do 18 knots." Her usefulness in the battle was over; Harwood signaled for her to proceed to the Falklands, a thousand miles away. With luck and good weather, she might make it.

From the bridge of Ajax, a grim-faced signalman contemplated Exeter's destruction. "It looks, Sir," he said to his officer, "as if it is going to be another bloody Coronel."

Meanwhile, the two light cruisers of the First Division had thus far escaped serious damage. Achilles had recovered from a salvo of 11-inch rounds that had blown up along her port side, showering the ship with shrapnel. Six fragments had ripped through the armor of her direct control tower, killing or maiming some of its operators and destroying wireless communications with Ajax. Other fragments sliced through the bridge, wounding Captain Parry and some of his officers.

The twin cruisers closed to within nine miles of Graf Spee, where their primary ordnance at last had teeth—though not necessarily sharp ones. Their turrets pumped three shells a minute at the German raider, registering regular hits, but while some of the six-inch shells found the enemy's vitals, many just ricocheted off its heavy armor into the sea. "We might just as well have been bombarding her with a lot of bloody snowballs," Harwood later recalled. Still, the cruisers used their agility to good effect, harrying the larger vessel like a pair of hounds, all the time careful to keep clear of its claws.

Early in the battle, Graf Spee had abandoned her northerly course and turned west, toward the mouth of the Plate. Then, under cover of smoke, the German swung swiftly back to port; Harwood thought she must be going after the Exeter, which by that point was limping off the field. He drew the First Division closer in an attempt to draw her fire.

The tactic worked, for the pocket battleship swung away from the *Exeter* and turned on *Ajax*, which was immediately straddled by a salvo from the 11-inch guns. Harwood countered with a brace of torpedoes, which ran well until *Graf Spee* sighted them and took evasive action. Then *Ajax* was suddenly staggered, like a boxer caught perfectly, unexpectedly, on the chin: an 11-inch shell came down at a 35-degree angle, ripped through the cabins of Woodhouse, his secretary, and the force commander before smashing through the ammunition lobby of X turret, where it left four mutilated bodies and as many wounded. The shell was then deflected upward into the working chamber below the turret, where it killed two more before ripping through two more bulkheads and exploding in Commodore Harwood's sleeping cabin.

Years later, an *Ajax* veteran told me of how after the battle the commodore had gone below to see what was left of his belongings. "He came up with the remains of his golf bag. It had only two irons in it, the rest was just cinders and ashes and a handle. 'I don't think I'll get a game with this,' he said." The survivor was Ron Clover, and he talked to me about the battle at St. George's Chapel, Chatham, in November 1997, at the unveiling of a plaque commemorating the action. With Clover were two other *Ajax* men, Eric Smith and George Deacon. They told me just how busy they were on that bloody day in the South Atlantic. Smith was in B turret, and had been at Dawn Action Stations until they had been stood down at about 5:30, at which point he went to his cruising station in the four-inch-gun director high above the bridge.

He was only up there for about 15 minutes when the alarm rattlers went off and everybody returned to action stations. "I was quickly back in B turret," he recalled, "but the gun layer had been having a bath and had to rush up as he was, with just a towel around him. He entered the working chamber below the turret from the mess deck and then had to climb up the pipe to get into the turret house. On the way up the pipe, his towel snagged on something and he arrived in the gun stark naked and swearing his head off."

George Deacon, one of the four-inch gunners, remembered the fighting top of *Graf Spee* coming at the British ships like "a block of houses. I always remember its opening salvos at the *Exeter*, great billows of black smoke went up from her guns. It surprised me a little because I was used to our guns which used smokeless cordite as a charge which only left a yellowish haze. But with the *Spee*, great panels of smoke went up from her turrets and, of course, within a few salvos, she had absolutely crippled poor *Exeter* . . . the *Graf Spee* had magnificent gunnery." Deacon has no illusions about the glories of war. He candidly admitted that he went through the entire conflict aboard *Ajax* in "an abject state of terror."

Above: Eric Smith said, years later, how grateful he was to Langsdorff for electing to save his crew and not to leave Montevideo fighting. "If he had done so, many of us Brits, as well as New Zealanders, would also have died."

Above: An eight-inch shell, believed to be from the *Exeter*, recovered during a magnetometer survey. These were the shells feared most by *Graf Spee,* as they could easily penetrate her steel armor.

"I was in A turret," Ron Clover remembered. "We were the only turret that did not take a hit or break down. We had fired so many rounds that the guns were not going back into proper firing position on recoil. Nobody had fired these guns so intensively before. Normally the most you got to practice with was about five rounds, but we had just fired three or four hundred in rapid succession. The ordnance artificer had to get up on top and pour oil onto the recuperator and we had to then push it back into firing position before we could reload."

Indeed, *Ajax* had begun to feel the strain of the running fight. In addition to the difficulties with the guns, the ammunition hoist serving her B turret failed.

At this juncture, too, *Ajax*'s Seafox airplane, launched sometime earlier to transmit spotting information to the ship's gunnery controllers, radioed with a new threat: "Torpedoes approaching; they will pass ahead of you." Harwood ordered a sharp turn to port and the danger slid by.

Clearly, the British ships were losing ground against their thick-skinned adversary. It was just a matter of time before *Graf Spee* turned on them and destroyed first one, then the other. Harwood decided that the time had come to break off, then use the cruisers' superior speed to shadow the raider under cover of darkness. Before they could retire, however, Captain Langsdorff sent *Ajax* a parting shot: straddling 11-inch fire that shredded her main topmast. The twin cruisers fell in some 15 miles

behind *Graf Spee*, *Ajax* on her port quarter, *Achilles* on her right. When they inched any closer, the 11-inch guns swatted them back. Thus the three ships continued westward, toward the Plate.

Langsdorff had not gone in for the kill when *Exeter* lay all but dead in the water, and now he refrained from turning on the two light cruisers shadowing him. They would surely have been easy game, for while their firepower had been cut almost in half, his heavy artillery was still intact. The German captain could have turned on his pursuers, bludgeoned *Ajax* into scrap metal, then turned his entire armament upon a hopelessly overmatched *Achilles*.

Now, as they neared the estuary, *Graf Spee* chanced upon an English steamer, the ss *Shakespeare*. Following his raider's instincts, Langsdorff bore down, intending to blow her apart with a torpedo. He fired a warning shot across *Shakespeare*'s bow and ordered her captain to take to his boats. At the same time, Langsdorff radioed his British shadows: "Please pick up lifeboats of English steamer." He used his ship's true call sign, thus letting the British know that they hadn't been fighting *Admiral Scheer*, but *Admiral Graf Spee* instead.

There was no reply from Harwood, and no cooperation from the freighter—its captain refused to abandon ship. For a time the two ships paused, the lamb against the tiger, and then the tiger turned away. Langsdorff resumed his course toward Montevideo, trailed by the two light cruisers. His action mystified his crew and, no doubt, the men aboard the steamer. Rasenack told me that he thought Langsdorff did not want to antagonize the Uruguayans by sinking a ship so close to their territorial waters. On the other hand, Hans Langsdorff may simply have had his fill of killing—whether men or ships—and wanted no more.

Deep within *Graf Spee*, the prisoners had endured the fight without knowing what was going on above decks. When they first heard the call to general quarters, they had thought it was another merchantman. But there was an urgency in the shouts that they had not heard before, and an officer suddenly appeared: "Gentlemen," he shouted, "I am afraid we must leave you to your own devices today." The doors clanged shut and were locked. Then, as the 11-inch turret above them loosed its thunder, they realized that the Royal Navy had arrived.

Their feelings must have been mixed. They wanted a British victory, but equally they had no desire to be blown apart by their own shells. Although they had been reassured that their compartment was in the safest part of the ship, if the *Graf Spee* went down, they would face a slow death in a steel coffin. "We zig-zagged continually at high speed and heeled over so much that at times I thought we were going to capsize," reported *Ashlea*'s Captain Pottinger in Millington-Drake's account of the battle. "The only view we could get of what was going on was through a small hole in the door through which we could get a running commentary. We could see some men working an ammunition hoist. They all looked very anxious. From what we could tell, things were not going too well with them. The dead were being piled up outside and the stench was awful. We could see men with rubber gloves washing down the corpses with hoses. This may account for the report we used gas. We could also hear and see men being sick all over the place, some probably from fear and others from the gruesome sights around them."

Finally, four or five hours into the *Graf Spee's* westward flight for the River Plate, someone shouted to the prisoners: "Are you all right in there?" They replied that they were, but hungry and thirsty. Half an hour later, the Germans brought them lime water and bread, and, late in the afternoon, more bread and some sausage meat. The galleys, they were told, had been hit.

But damaged galleys were the least of Langsdorff's problems, for *Graf Spee* had absorbed more punishment than the British realized. Some of the six-inch shells had gone straight to her vitals; one had penetrated the starboard quarter, destroyed an ammunition hoist, and cut the electrical supply to the forward 11-inch shell hoists. Another pierced her starboard side and ripped a three-by-six-foot exit wound in her port side just above the waterline, while still a third destroyed one of the four-inch guns and crippled a four-inch ammunition hoist. A 5.9-inch was also blown up, along with its crew.

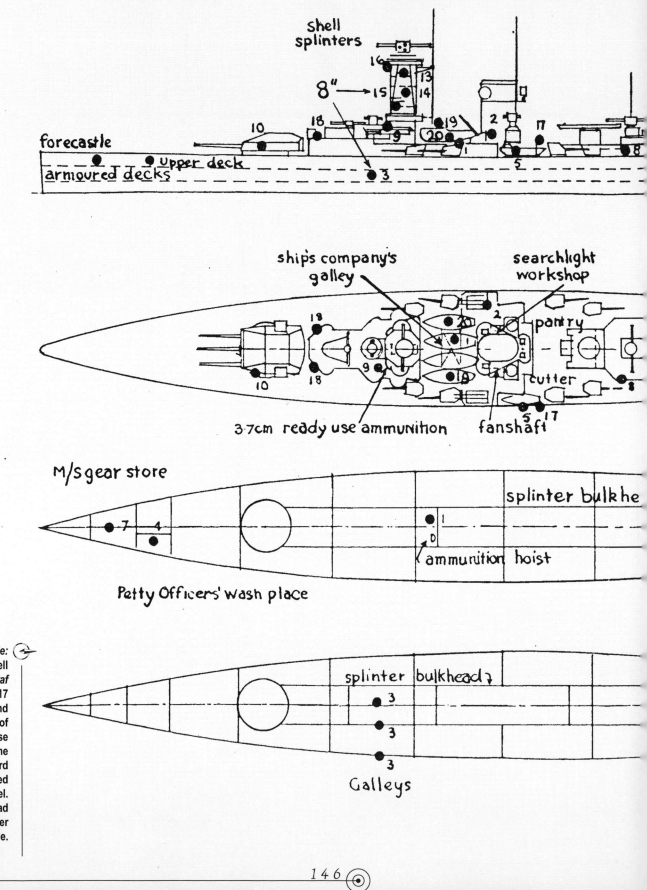

shell
splinters

16

13

8" → 15   14

18   19

forecastle   10   9   20   2   17

upper deck   1   5   8

armoured decks   3

ships company's
galley

searchlight
workshop

18   2

pantry

9

10   18

cutter

3·7cm ready use ammunition   fanshaft   5   17

M/s gear store

splinter bulkhe

7   4

ammunition hoist

Petty Officers' wash place

splinter bulkhead

3

3

3

Galleys

Opposite, top and middle:
A hole left by a 6-inch shell
in the port side of the *Graf
Spee.* The ship was hit 17
times by 6-inch shells and
twice by 8-inch fire. Most of
the 6-inchers did not cause
serious damage, but one
shell wrecked the onboard
refinery that converted
petroleum to diesel fuel.
Bottom: Wounded and dead
on *Graf Spee* soon after
the battle.

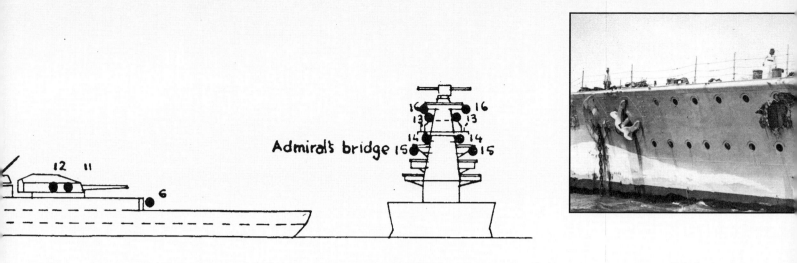

12 11

6

Admiral's bridge 15

16 16
13 13
14 14
15 15

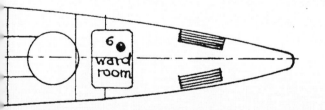

blind shell

6

12 11

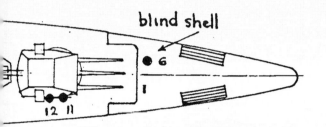

Admiral Graf Spee

Diagram showing hits

6
ward
room

C.P.O.'s mess

6

6

C.P.O.'s cabins

Nᵒˢ 3 & 15 are 8" hits
The remainder are 6"

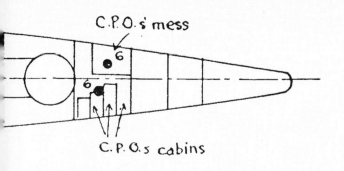

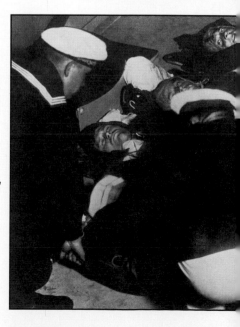

The big rangefinder on *Graf Spee*'s flying bridge took a hit, as did the radar ranging equipment for the guns. Fire also wrecked *Graf Spee*'s cutter and two other boats, the defunct Arado, and Langsdorff's cabin. An eight-inch shell had whined through the bridge without exploding, and there were six leaks below the waterline.

The Germans had also taken casualties: thirty-seven dead and more dying; many more had suffered wounds, including Langsdorff, who had been cut by metal splinters from separate hits.

After receiving the damage reports from various parts of his ship, Langsdorff made his own tour of inspection. When he returned to the bridge, he told his navigator, Jürgen Wattenberg, "We must run for port, the ship is no longer seaworthy."

But where to go—Montevideo or Buenos Aires? Both ports were neutral, but the latter enjoyed a special relationship with Germany. Uruguay, with its avid dislike of authoritarianism, was naturally pro-British. Whether or not Langsdorff was aware of this is difficult to say, but Kurt Diggins, who was at Langsdorff's side on the exposed flying bridge at the summit of the foretop, reminded me that the captain had taken two splinter wounds as well as been knocked to the deck unconscious from the force of a shell blast. When he made the error of going to Uruguay, he must to some extent have been in shock. Another factor that very probably influenced Langsdorff (and which seems to have escaped contemporary and later commentators) was simply that Montevideo was much closer.

THE FIRST REAL-TIME WAR STORY

Thanks to the immediacy of wireless radio, the sea battle had played to a global audience. The German press was proclaiming victory; the *Achilles* was instantly the most famous ship in New Zealand, crewed by champions.

In Montevideo, too, there was great excitement—and no need for radios. Long before the ships came into view, the crump and thuds of gunfire from over the horizon could be heard in Punta del Este, on the northern lip of the River Plate's broad mouth. Late in the afternoon, Captain Fernando J. Fuentes sailed out in the cruiser *Uruguay* to see what was going on in his harbor.

Toward dusk, his lookouts saw *Graf Spee*, still belching fire at her pursuers even as she steamed into Uruguayan territorial waters. As night fell, she occasionally fired blindly into the darkness over her stern, reminding the British to keep their distance. Finally, toward the end of the evening, Langsdorff anchored his ship in the anteport of Montevideo harbor.

Ajax and *Achilles* took up stations in separate channels near the mouth of the 136-mile-wide estuary. They would prove a frail deterrent should the German ship wish to return to the Atlantic, for If she came charging at them out of the darkness, everyone knew

Below: **Kurt Diggins was Langsdorff's main confidant among the officers of *Graf Spee*, and was at the captain's side during most of the battle. After the Plate, he transferred to U-boats.**

that the light cruisers stood no chance. When Harwood informed his crews that, in the event of an encounter with *Graf Spee*, his policy was destruction, someone muttered, "Whose?"

Help, if any, remained far away. *Cumberland* was racing up from the Falklands. Force K, comprising HMS *Ark Royal*, *Renown*, and *Neptune*, was a thousand miles north, off Brazil, and *Dorsetshire* and *Shropshire* were off South Africa, a good five days away.

Unable to bottle up *Graf Spee* by force of arms, Commodore Harwood resorted to guile. He asked the British ambassador, Eugene Millington-Drake—a descendant of the legendary Elizabethan explorer Sir Francis Drake—to "use every possible means" to delay *Graf Spee*'s sailing until reinforcements arrived. Perhaps, he suggested, British merchant ships could be dispatched at suitable intervals: under the international rules of neutrality, *Graf Spee* could not leave port for 24 hours after an Allied merchant ship sailed.

Before daylight, the German minister, Dr. Otto Langmann, boarded the pocket battleship. The stout, pugnacious former pastor peered at the world through a pince-nez perched high on his nose. He had come to rebuke Langsdorff, exhausted and in pain from his wounds, for putting into Montevideo when he might have found more support across the Plate in Argentina.

As Langmann knew, German ministers, German ships, and German politics were not greatly esteemed in Uruguay. Local firms refused to help, and "not a single man nor

Above: Langsdorff, left, sheltering his wounded hand, and Langmann, second from left. When *Graf Spee* berthed in Montevideo, Langmann boarded the ship, and chastised Langsdorff for putting in there instead of German-friendlier Buenos Aires.

screw," Rasenack wrote, was provided by the dockyard. There were, however, a few tradesmen of German origin living in Uruguay who lent their skills, and two German merchantmen in the harbor provided volunteers. Later on that first day, the German naval attaché arrived from Buenos Aires, bringing some civilian technicians to assist in the repairs.

A preliminary survey of the damage indicated that it would take two weeks to ready *Graf Spee* for sea. However, under the Hague

CAPITAN HANS LANGSDORF & CREW IN MONTEVIDEO
14TH DEC. 1939.

Above: Captain Hans Langsdorff—a courageous man, but ultimately a tragic figure who wove his own doom.

Convention of 1907, belligerents' warships could only stay 24 hours in the territorial waters of a neutral power. Extensions could be granted on account of bad weather or for the minimum repairs needed to make a vessel seaworthy, but without an authorized extension, a belligerent ship would be interned after 24 hours.

Langmann requested the extension. The Uruguayan foreign minister, Dr. Alberto Guani, though no admirer of Hitler and a close personal friend of Millington-Drake's, was determined to be fair. He decided that the ship should be surveyed by a Uruguayan technical commission.

Millington-Drake countered with a gambit of his own. *Graf Spee*, he insisted, should not be allowed to stay longer than the 24 hours allotted by the Hague Convention, that it should be forced out. His feigned urgency spun the illusion that the British were ready to take on the pocket battleship—that reinforcements had begun to arrive off Monte-

video. Disinformation fed to the obliging press and radio stations conjured imaginary British squadrons off the Plate; false arrangements were made for the immediate fueling of the *Renown* and *Ark Royal*. Had Langsdorff and Langmann doubted any of this, they would have been convinced when *Graf Spee*'s chief gunnery officer, Paul Ascher, spotted a battleship that he identified as HMS *Renown*. With a speed of 32 knots and an armament of 14-inch guns, she was not a ship that *Graf Spee* could fight.

"Our position is fatal," a dispirited Rasenack confided in his diary. "The nervous tension of the last days has returned. Each one of us sees the fate that awaits him. We are serious and silent. The crew does not give the impression of men after victory. We do not feel as the newspapers over there in Germany describe with large headlines. On the contrary, we feel like men . . . gathering their last strength to fight a lost battle."

At about five o'clock in the afternoon of their first day in port, *Graf Spee*'s British prisoners were released. Some had been onboard for 65 days. "I can see him sitting in the Captain's cabin of the *Graf Spee*," Patrick Dove remembered afterward of Langsdorff, "sipping his whisky (the best Scotch, too!), smoking his cigar, always most formal and military in his bearing." But on that last day on the German vessel, when Dove and *Ashlea*'s Captain Pottinger went to say goodbye, they found their host greatly changed.

"Langsdorff received me in the cabin I had grown to know so well," Dove wrote.

I was shocked at the change in him. For a moment, I could hardly believe that it was the kindly, jocular, supremely confident Captain Langsdorff I had known before. Even his appearance had altered. Splinters had wounded him in the face, and he had shaved off his mustache and beard. His right arm was in a sling. But though his confidence and cheerfulness had both left him, his kindness and chivalry remained unquenched. There was no bitterness in his tone as he greeted me. "Ah, Captain," he said, shaking his head, "I am sorry that you had to be in this action. I am glad that none of you are injured."

Then Langsdorff gave them the hat ribbons of two of his dead. "I would like you and Captain Pottinger to have these."

Dove wrote on:

Twelve hours later my comrades and I filed up onto the quarterdeck to say good-bye to the *Graf Spee*. There, immediately beneath the muzzles of the 11-inch guns, 36 flag-draped coffins lay in two long lines across the deck. Captain Langsdorff, the German Naval Attaché and the German Minister were grouped close to us. The master-at-arms dismissed us. We were free men.

In the evening, as HMS *Cumberland* joined *Ajax* and *Achilles* at the mouth of the estuary, Langsdorff outlined the desperate situation to his officers in the mess. He could not remain in Montevideo, he told them. The ship must not be interned; he would not have *Graf Spee* handed over to the British so that its guns might be used against the German fleet. His intention, he said, was to break out at night.

The next morning, *Graf Spee* buried her dead. A naval band led the sad procession; only a few of the crew and its petty officers accompanied the somber cortege from Montevideo's old quarter to the Northern Cemetery on the outskirts of the city. Among the crowds that lined the way were a number of the British sailors who had been held on *Graf Spee*. Now and then German officers spotted their former prisoners in the throng, went over and shook hands, then walked on.

At the cemetery, Langsdorff, in white uniform, the exhaustion and strain now etched into his features, gave a short oration over the coffins draped in Nazi flags. Then, as the caskets were lowered into the ground, he moved down the line of graves, sprinkling earth into each. At the end of the first row, he lifted his gaze and saw Captain Dove standing there, his arm held in salute. Langsdorff paused, stood to attention, and, looking Dove straight in the eyes, returned the salute.

Finally, Langsdorff stepped back to join the other senior members of the funeral party, and a last salute was then given the lost sailors of *Graf Spee*. Photographs captured the moment and showed it to the world. In these images, everyone extends an arm in the Nazi salute except Langsdorff, whose arm is bent at

the elbow—the salute of the old German navy. And everyone's eyes are on the graves, except Langmann's, who glares disapprovingly at the captain. Editorials pondered the meaning. Was this Langsdorff's way of deliberately and very publicly repudiating Naziism? Perhaps, but as Rasenack wrote to Millington-Drake many years later, the navy was not obliged to give the Nazi salute until June 1943.

Captain Dove left a wreath: TO THE MEMORY OF BRAVE MEN OF THE SEA FROM THEIR COMRADES OF THE BRITISH MERCHANT SERVICE.

It was, wrote Commander Rasenack, "a little gallant chivalry in this war where propaganda kills and tramples on all that is great and noble."

Radio and wire-service journalists converged on Montevideo from around the world to cover what was already known as the Battle of the River Plate. The German press likened the victory to that of von Spee at Coronel and compared Langsdorff to Captain Müller of the *Emden*.

Langsdorff was portrayed as the hero, standing exposed, despite his wounds, at the highest point of the control tower. German propagandists told how the coffins of their brave sailors had been spat upon by the British along the funeral route, a charge that was roundly (and truthfully) denied by the men of the *Graf Spee* itself. That night, Captain Dove talked on radio about life aboard *Graf Spee* and the decent treatment he and his comrades

were accorded by their captors. His views were received with annoyance by the British propagandists, who were anxious to portray all Germans as ruthless monsters.

Now, as time trickled away for the German ship, the reporters gathered in Montevideo, poised to describe to the world the biggest shootout since the O.K. Corral.

On the second day, Langsdorff was informed that the Uruguayan government, acting on the recommendation of its technical commission, would only allow a further stay of 72 hours. In their opinion, this was sufficient to make the vessel seaworthy. The deadline for departure was set at 8 P.M. on Sunday, December 17. Further bad news followed when the lookout added HMS *Ark Royal* (actually still off Brazil) to the ships guarding the Plate, and Uruguayan radio reported the arrival of the French battleship *Dunkerque*. Langsdorff relayed word of these fictional newcomers to Berlin.

Then Millington-Drake dispatched to sea the British merchant ship *Ashworth*, compelling the Germans to remain in port for 24 hours. This narrowed the window between the time it would be *allowed* to depart and the time when it *had* to depart to just one day. The possibility of surprise was slipping away.

"No prospect of breaking out to the open sea and getting through to Germany," Langsdorff reported to Berlin. "If I can fight my way through to Buenos Aires with the ammunition remaining I shall endeavor to do so. As breakthrough might result in the destruction of the *Spee* without the possibility of causing damage to the enemy, request instructions whether to scuttle the ship or to submit to internment." His orders came back: *Graf Spee* must not fall into Allied hands.

Rasenack wrote in his diary: "We know the end that awaits us, but we will not be an easy prey for the foe. It will be a bitter victory for them, for we will defend ourselves to the utmost. Every gun that we put right means more loss for the enemy." As for Langsdorff, Rasenack said, "I know at this moment that every one of our men will follow the Captain blindly, even if he is to take them to their death."

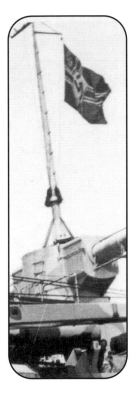

But Langsdorff had other thoughts. That evening, he told some of his sailors that he would fight if he could, but if he could not, he would not let *Graf Spee* become "a target in a shooting match." An engine-room mechanic, Hans Götz, recorded Langsdorff's words in his diary: "'I will not let us be shot to pieces at sea by an overwhelmingly superior force. To me, a thousand young men alive are worth more than a thousand dead heroes.'"

❧❧

The morning of the third day, Saturday, December 16, brought unseasonal drizzle and mist. The crowds that had gathered along the extended waterfront of Montevideo now counted into many thousands. The press, perhaps sensing that there would be no final moment of glory, hinted that Langsdorff was a coward. Later that morning, the beleaguered captain ordered the destruction of all his ship's secret documents, and sent ashore the battle ensigns, the ship's bell, a portrait of Admiral Graf von Spee, and other items of historic interest. They would go home in a diplomatic pouch.

In the late afternoon, Langsdorff convened a meeting of some of his senior officers and the German naval attaché from Buenos Aires to discuss the options. There was a slim chance that *Graf Spee* could make a break for Buenos Aires and, if engaged, that she might even destroy one of the British ships. But she had only 186 11-inch shells left; at most that would allow a firefight of 45 minutes. And

even if she reached Buenos Aires, there was no guarantee that the Argentinians would allow her to stay and refit.

The main problem, though, was the shallow estuary. Every year, the River Plate carries 150 million metric tons of sediment from the hinterlands of South America into the Atlantic. This creates vast, mutating mudbanks that have claimed more vessels than even the ship-hungry Goodwin Sands of the English Channel. The *Graf Spee* drew 22 feet, which meant that she would be almost brushing the estuary bottom in any number of places. If she took a hit below the waterline and drew another foot, she would soon be aground.

Running aground was not the only possible problem presented by the mud, though. The water intakes for *Graf Spee*'s cooling system were situated on her underside; if they sucked up enough mud, they would clog, the engines would overheat, and she would grind to a stop. She would be a sitting duck.

And then, were she able to stay afloat and mobile, she would have to stay within the dredged channel, while the British cruisers, drawing only about 16 feet of water, could range virtually where they wished. The British could attack from several directions and smother *Graf Spee* with fire, as well as attack below the waterline with their torpedoes. There were the aircraft from the *Ark Royal*, too.

If disabled in the river mud, *Graf Spee* wouldn't sink; she might be salvaged by the British and used against the Fatherland.

In any event, such considerations were academic. At 6:00 P.M., SS *Dunster Grange* sailed from Montevideo. Under the 24-hour rule, this meant *Graf Spee*'s departure window had closed to a scant two daylight hours; they must sail then or be interned. The British had not been able to defeat the great ship at sea, but she had been just as deftly neutralized by Millington-Drake's cunning diplomacy.

That night, the rhythms of repair aboard the German vessel subtly changed to bursts of heavy hammering and muffled detonations. It was Rasenack, doing his duty, as usual. With hand grenades and cartridges, he blew up the central fire-control installations, and with hammers his men smashed dials, electronics, and all other essential components necessary for the laying and firing of the guns, whose breech blocks were removed and thrown overboard. "This is the hardest day of my life," he told his diary.

꿍꿍

Sunday dawned calm and cloudless. Three-quarters of a million people crowded Montevideo's seafront to watch the famous German pocket battleship sail to a fiery confrontation with the British warships waiting for her offshore. There was no question of her taking anyone by surprise: her departure time was known to the entire world almost to the minute, partly thanks to a hard-drinking, wisecracking, and world-weary American reporter named Mike Fowler, who had been sent to Uruguay—some said as penance—to record

"Ladies and gentlemen, it is Sunday morning, 10:15 A.M. December 17, the day upon which the time limit given to the *Graf Spee* will expire. To be exact, at 8:00 P.M. local time, she will have to be out of territorial waters or the Uruguayan government will intern her. It is rumored that outside the mouth of the Rio de la Plata there are five, possibly seven British warships waiting for her. . . . We figured that the *Graf Spee* would make a run for it last night during the darkness, but she is still here this morning. Will Captain Langsdorff take the battered vessel out of the haven of the River Plate? Will they make a dash for Buenos Aires, four hours steaming up the channel? Will it be a fight to the death? Nobody knows."—*Mike Fowler, broadcasting from Montevideo*

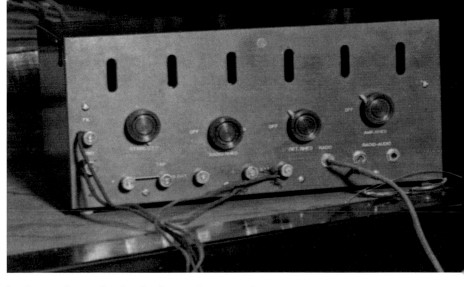

bird sounds, and who had now become the voice of the Battle of the River Plate.

Fowler's broadcasts were live action as never heard before, and the whole world was listening. American President Franklin Roosevelt remained tuned in throughout the diplomatic maneuvering and run-up to Sunday; Churchill listened from the Admiralty War Room (see box above).

Commodore Harwood also kept close to his radio. Forbidden to fly his Seafox within three miles of the coast, Harwood soon found that Fowler was his fastest and most reliable source of information; the broadcasts were transmitted to the United States, then to the BBC, and, seconds later, to the audiences aboard *Ajax*, *Achilles*, and *Cumberland*. It was from Fowler that Harwood learned of *Graf Spee* sailors, documents, and equipment being moved to the 5,000-ton German freighter *Tacoma*, in Montevideo. It was Fowler who told Harwood and the rest of the world at 6:30 P.M. that the pocket battleship had weighed anchor.

By then, at least one British fiction had been exposed: Langmann had learned from his counterpart in Brazil that HMS *Ark Royal* and *Renown*, believed to be waiting in the Plate, were in fact oiling at Rio de Janeiro, two days' away. By then, it made no difference.

As the shadows lengthened over the city, a swastika-emblazoned battle flag was unfurled from *Graf Spee*'s foremast, then another billowed from the mainmast. Slowly the great fighting ship moved forward, alone, as it always had. Without the help of tugs, she nosed out through the gap in the breakwaters. Mon-tevideo and the world watched and listened as the pocket battleship gleamed in the low western sun.

Tacoma followed 15 minutes later, carrying some 900 of the warship's company. Outside the breakwater and out of sight of the crowds, the German sailors were transferred onto the Argentine tugs *Gigante* and *Coloso*, which had come from Buenos Aires to help. Then units of the Uruguayan navy turned *Tacoma* back to port, as she had sailed without authorization.

Graf Spee headed south from the harbor and then, three miles out, swung west near the Whistle Buoy. For a moment, those ashore thought that she was heading for Buenos Aires, but only a few hundred meters further, she moved out of the channel, slowed to a stop, and dropped her anchor. She was just outside the three-mile territorial limit. The crews in the tugs hovered nearby, as the western sky made the calm sea glow like molten steel.

Onboard, the lifts to the turret and the turret itself had been packed with shells and charges. In the middle of it all was a torpedo warhead. Chief Gunnery Officer Ascher and the crew had set the charges, there and in

the engine room. Langsdorff had wanted them on a single circuit that he could activate himself from some point in the control tower—this way he would die in the same instant as his ship. His officers, however, dissuaded him. His job, they urged, would not be over until everyone was safe in Buenos Aires.

Now, aboard *Graf Spee*, the men set the chronometers for 20 minutes. Langsdorff and his last five officers gathered on the quarterdeck; the flags were hauled down. They descended the gangway into the captain's launch, cast off, and moved about a mile away. There they paused to watch.

Ten minutes before the sun touched the horizon, there was a small flash from *Graf Spee*. A few moments later, an explosion in B turret drove a great column of flame high above the mastheads. A giant toadstool of black smoke belched skyward. The Germans who had set the charges waited for A turret to explode, but it never happened. Rasenack soon realized what had gone wrong: the shock from the first explosion, the detonation of a torpedo head in the engine room, had dislocated the circuitry in A turret somewhere between the chronometer, the battery, and the detonator.

It hardly mattered at all. *Graf Spee* had been reduced to a shattered wreck. Blazing from stem to stern, the pocket battleship sank in the water until her decks were awash.

For hours into the night, she burned and burned.

The crowds ashore were stunned into silence by the horrifying vision. Then, after a few seconds, the sound reached them: a roar that tailed off into uneven rumbles, punctuated at intervals by additional bursts as the heat caught the ammunition reserves. It was all very Wagnerian, it was *Götterdämmerung*; the great Teutonic fighting machine convulsed in violence and flame beneath the red spread of the sunset. On the southeastern horizon, the three British cruisers were seen, their searchlights on and their Morse lamps flickering puzzled messages to one another.

"Pilot," Langsdorff commanded, his face grimly expressionless, "enter in the log book: *Graf Spee* put out of service on December 17, 1939, at 2000 hours."

Above, top to bottom: "It was *Götterdämmerung*; the great Teutonic fighting machine convulsed in violence and flame beneath the red spread of the sunset."

Whistle Buoy, 1939

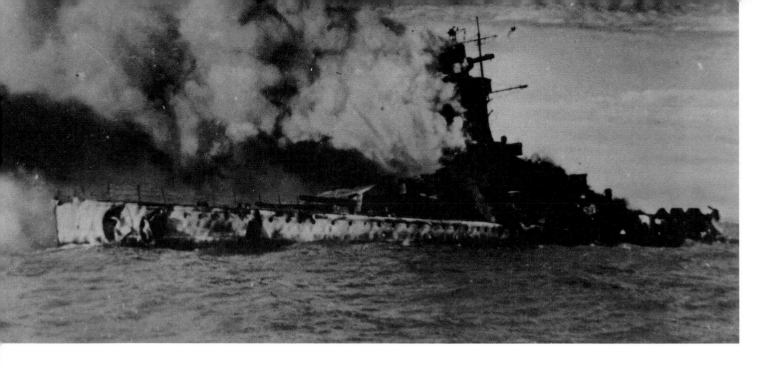

THE SURVEY OF *GRAF SPEE*

We began the dive in February 1997, but I had made a preliminary visit to Montevideo the previous December—only my second visit since the 1960s to my old home. I had come back to discuss the *Agamemnon* project with archeologists from the Ministry of Culture and to prepare for the operational side of the program with my old diving comrades Hector Bado, Sergio Pronczuk, and Carlos Coirolo. But it hadn't been all maritime archeology. I had also brought producer Zev Guber, to lay the groundwork for the arrival of a film crew who were covering my work around the world for a new television series, *Lost Ships*.

When I had lived in Montevideo, home had been the prosperous palm- and eucalyptus-lined suburb of Carrasco, so, naturally, this is where I wanted to be. We checked into the Cottage, a quaint, somewhat faded hotel full of yellowing 1960s airline-travel maps and tourist posters of the Alps. The hotel fronted the river and was within five minutes' walk of all my teenage haunts.

My old house on avenida Arocena, once covered in ivy, had become an English-language school. Just one door away was the old Mascotta, which used to be known as a *boliche*, a kind of saloon and most certainly not a place that was ever frequented by polite society. It had gone a bit respectable; it was no longer the kind of place where you wiped your feet on leaving. But little had really changed. Waiters in white coats still served the regular barflies nursing their Patricia beers, the large mirror behind the bar still advertised Cinzano Punto Rojo, the radio still emitted its drone of accordion laments and Carlos Gardel songs, the walls were still covered with black and yellow pennants from the local-favorite Peñarol football team.

Almost without my realizing it, the old Mascotta became the unofficial headquarters of the operations that followed.

From the start, it had been obvious that we wouldn't be able to dive on *Graf Spee* without help from the Uruguayan navy. We needed their boats and divers, and, besides, the wreck of the great fighting ship was situated in their live-firing practice range. There also remained the possibility of encountering live charges from the unfinished explosions on *Graf Spee*.

Fortunately, both Hector and I had friends who were senior naval officers. My contact was Captain Ricardo Medina, once his country's naval attaché in London. Hector was a close friend of Captain Cabot, head of the navy's diving unit. We went to see them in their offices in the Admiralty building.

The dockside neighborhood that the Admiralty called home was one that I knew well. Countless times as a boy, I had taken the steamer from these docks to Port Stanley, and it had been from here that my family and I had embarked on the Royal Mail ships for trips home to England. Later, when I had finished school, the ship I worked on put into Montevideo every couple of months. Little had changed since then.

But I'd gone there with Hector looking for something in particular, wondering if it had survived the decades. And it was there, just inside the main gate: one of *Graf Spee*'s anchors, still trailing a few fathoms of stud-link chain.

Looking at the anchor that day, Hector and I both thought we should try to retrieve something a bit more imposing. At first, we treated the idea as a bit of a joke, but the thought persisted, however, and in the days that followed, it hardened to keen desire. We wanted to bring up one of *Graf Spee*'s guns.

Inside the Admiralty building, Captain Medina, in full uniform, greeted Hector and me and took us to meet his fellow officers. That day, our friends and colleagues in the Uruguayan navy agreed to help us dive on *Graf Spee*, offering divers, equipment, and boats.

There had been one other person I'd been anxious to see on my December visit: Omar Medina (no relation to Ricardo Medina). A retired ship's captain turned wildlife and environmental campaigner, Omar was the self-appointed keeper of the flame in all matters concerning *Graf Spee*. He had a maritime museum in the genteel suburb of Malvin, and fully half of the displays celebrated the memory of the great ship and its epic last fight. Experts and scholars from around the world came to study his collection.

When I had lived in Uruguay, it was well known that there were quite a few *Graf Spee* survivors still around—most of them were the wounded sailors left behind when the ship sailed for the last time. By the end of the war, many had become enchanted by the country and some had married Uruguayan women. In February 1946, they had been repatriated to Germany on RMS *Highland Monarch* —ironically, the very ship Langsdorff intended to intercept and sink when he reached the Plate—but a significant number had returned, particularly those from the former East Ger-

Below: The *Graf Spee*'s funnel displaced to starboard by the explosion in her engine room. During my first dive I could find no trace of the funnel, but I did find the hole where it had been.

By the time we arrived, about 30 people had gathered. Everybody knew everybody else and chatted in German. The mood was far from solemn; *Graf Spee* reunions, I was told, were generally happy affairs. However, we received frequent and somewhat suspicious glances, especially from a quintet of elderly men—the still-living survivors of the battle.

As I walked along the row of graves, I'd been struck by how young they all were; the sailors all seemed to be in their late teens or early twenties. Here was the grave of Lieutenant Grigat, who had been the first person to spot the British cruisers. After being hurt, he dictated a farewell to his parents and remained conscious until his terrible injury killed him. There was the gravestone of Mattias Pünz, only 17 when he died. What could a 17-year-old ever have known of National Socialism?

many who found that they had no home under the new communist regime.

When I asked Omar Medina whether I might be able to meet some of these men, he said only five or six were still alive, and that they were now very frail. He said that it would be easier if I went with him to the memorial service that was being held in the Northern Cemetery on the anniversary of the battle.

Two days later, on the fifty-seventh anniversary of the battle, we arrived at the Cementerio del Norte. The *Graf Spee* burial area, a tranquil enclosure bordered by a high hedge, lay deep within the cemetery; its graves are marked by simple metal crosses noting only name, position, and dates of birth and death. The three rows of graves, with officers to the fore, faced a large granite boulder inscribed in both German and Spanish. Translated into English, the inscription reads:

> ADMIRAL GRAF SPEE
> IN MEMORY OF THE DEAD
> IN THE BATTLE AT RIO DE LA PLATA
> OFF PUNTA DEL ESTE
> ON DECEMBER 13, 1939

After a call to order, we assembled informally at one end of the hedged enclosure under the hot sun of the early austral summer. A priest opened with a brief prayer, followed by a hymn led by a small church choir. The German ambassador gave an address on sacrifice and remembrance. Finally, a fine baritone stepped forward to sing "Ich hatt' einen Kamerader" (I Had One Friend), a German naval hymn of mourning. It moved me greatly, and none of us joined in until that splendid voice finished the first verse.

After the ceremony, I was introduced to the veterans. The one who impressed me most was Rudulfo Dxierxawa, 78, a bald,

Montevideo, 1997

stocky, kind-faced man with unsteady nerves who had joined *Graf Spee* when he was just 19. He had been an engine-room worker and had just completed his 12 to 4 A.M. shift and was asleep in his bunk when the battle began. He had immediately run to his battle station, up near the bow of the ship. Rudolfo's main memory of the fight had been the hit that cut the gaping hole behind *Graf Spee*'s port bow.

I asked Rudulfo if he had known Mattias Pünz. "No," he said, he hadn't really known Mattias; then he added, rather tentatively, "But I did have a close friend who was killed." Again he paused, and walked to a grave about ten meters away. He studied the metal cross for a moment. "He was my friend." The marker read:

GÜNTHER ARNOLD,
GEFREITER
3.4.20 – 13.12.39

For a time, neither of us spoke. Then the old man fumbled in his jacket and brought out an old passport-type photograph. It was Günther Arnold. He was a good-looking boy; his head was high, the pose stiff and formal. He was no doubt proud of his ship and proud of the dark uniform with the eagle of the German navy. Yet for all that, still just a boy.

Rudolfo held the photo of his friend against the metal cross directly above the name. "He was an only child," he said, still looking at the photograph he had carried with him for fifty-seven years.

It was about two in the afternoon when I left. The others had gone on; I had in-tended to head for the Mascotta, but now I had somewhere else to go. I hailed a taxi: "Cementerio británico."

I had been there only once before, in 1965, taken by my father. I think he wanted to show his 12-year-old son something of the utter waste and futility of war. After the battle, three bodies still wrapped in canvas had washed ashore at Pando, a few miles east of Montevideo. Two of them had come from HMS *Achilles*: Telegraphist F. Stennett and Ordinary Telegraphist N. J. Milburn. The third body had never been identified; his entire face had been shot away and he carried no other clues to his identity. All had been buried under a single headstone. But what I remembered vividly was the overwhelming sense of sadness that I had felt for the unknown third, whose inscription read simply: "Known unto God." Walking between those neat rows, I wondered whether the British embassy had remembered the anniversary with a wreath. It had not.

❧

In February 1997, I arrived back in Uruguay. Although a few was still to arrive, the majority of the team was in place and ready to begin work. I had decided that we would work two sites at the same time; the main team would be on the *Agamemnon* in Maldonado Bay near Punta del Este at the very mouth of the Plate, while a small detachment would remain in Montevideo to concentrate on the survey of the *Graf Spee*. At inter-

Below: The granite memorial in the *Graf Spee* burial plot at Cementerio del Norte, Montevideo.

vals, I would rotate divers and staff so that everybody would have a chance to dive and work on both wrecks.

While the work in Maldonado Bay got off to a running start, the *Graf Spee* survey soon bogged down in logistical and political difficulties. It was not until February 16 that everything was in place and ready to go.

The following day I will never forget. I hadn't slept all night. Every now and again, I went to the window, gazing over a clear view of the inner harbor where, fifty-eight years before, the *Graf Spee* had anchored while Langsdorff, Langmann, Millington-Drake, and Guani circled one another like scorpions in a brandy glass.

Restless, I left the hotel. Directly in front was Plaza Independencia, Montevideo's main square. Diagonally across the square was the beautiful old Palacio Salvo, Uruguay's first skyscraper. It was from a corner balcony on the nineteenth floor that Millington-Drake had watched the *Graf Spee* depart.

Above: Mensun and Gunther Schroeder at the grave of Lieutenant Edgar Grigat, who was fatally wounded while climbing down the ladder from the foretop, where he had been with Captain Langsdorff and Lieutenant Diggins. *Below:* News clip from early 1940.

In the bar at the bottom of the Palacio Salvo, I could see an old man cleaning the counter. Like so many of his generation, he was fascinated by *Graf Spee*. As a child, he had been taken down to the waterfront by his parents to watch the battle. "You cannot imagine," he said, "the astonishment we felt when she blew up. My mother was crying for all the men on board. It was not till later we learned that everyone had been taken off."

～∗～

At nine, Hector and I met up with Captain Cabot at his office in the navy yard beside the docks. Not only was he loaning me much of the equipment I needed, but also he had seconded several of his best divers to the project. Still, a major problem facing us was finding a large seaworthy vessel that could carry the team to and from *Graf Spee*. Here I was helped by Captain Alberto Braeda, the officer in charge of the Port of Montevideo. Thanks to him, the navy had made one of their support ships, *No. 72*, available to us.

By the late morning, we were nosing our way out of harbor, following the exact route along the channel that had been taken

February 9th, 1940   *The War Illustrated*

Here's to the Men Who Beat the 'Graf Spee'!

LUNCHEON WITH 'WINNIE' AT GUILDHALL

AILY TELEGRAPH AND MORNING POST, FRIDAY, FEBRUARY 23

TO-DAY'S NAVAL VICTORY MARCH

WARD NOBLE BETTS DEACON
BRENNAN SWINNEY

INT·1780 THE SAINTES·1782
NDRIA·1801 TRAFALGAR·1805
SEBASTIAN·1813 BALTIC·185·
JUTLAND·1916

THE PLATE 1939

~ And a New Battle Honour ~

Ldg.Sea.
MARJORAM
AB.
Q.O.
GILL

o years' service at sea crowned by the smashing defeat of the " Graf Spee," the " Ajax " docked at Devonport on February 1, 19
r men, standing before those 6-inch guns which they fought with such dash in the running fight of December 13. Full illustrat
ttle in which " Ajax," " Achilles " and " Exeter " covered themselves with glory are given in pp. 526-30, 540-1 and 575 of Volume

O/S DENNIS   AB.   Ldg. SEA.
           LEN PITTMAN   DERBYSHIRE   P.O. COOK
Photos, Central Press, Associated Press and Keystone

Another Photo Call for the Lads ~

O/SEA
COLLIS
MASON   PHILPOT   MICK
                                                    CUNNINGHAM

We stationed *72* several hundred meters downrange from where we thought the wreck was most likely to be, and Hector and three of the navy divers set off in an inflatable. From over the stern they dragged behind them the tender's light anchor; their plan was to follow a search pattern based on ten-meter parallels. It would be only a matter of time before the flukes of the anchor caught on to *Graf Spee*.

by *Graf Spee* on her last voyage. Although the river was in full flood, it was fairly flat.

When we reached the Whistle Buoy, we circled to starboard. By that time we were four miles out and could make out the buoy that, according to the captain, was close to *Graf Spee*. We knew we were in the vicinity of the drowned Panzerschiff, but we did not know her exact position, and the captain had already told us that he would not risk taking *72* anywhere near the wreck, for fear of hitting it. This meant that her sonar would be of no use in helping us locate the exact position. The only way to find her was to go fishing, fishing to hook a battleship.

In the meantime, the dive team gathered at the stern. All expert divers, any lectures on proper procedure would have been insulting. I did, however, remind them of the likelihood of fishing nets. With the fine nylon

Above: George Deacon, who helped the author while he was researching this chapter, and provided access to his personal archive of photos, was with one of the 4-inch gun crews on HMS *Ajax*. "The *Graf Spee* came at us like a block of houses . . . great panels of smoke went up from her turrets . . . *Graf Spee* had magnificent gunnery."

mesh of many modern nets, they would probably not be seen until the diver was already snared. And having been caught in fishing nets off Italy in 1987, I knew well what a danger they posed.

Like test pilots, divers have their own eschatology—part of which is not talking about danger or death. I did not want to be morbid, and I certainly did not want to make anybody nervous, but there were facts we had to face. There would be a lot of sharp, protruding metal down there which, in the darkness, could easily lacerate, entangle, or concuss.

This wreck, in fact, was a killer. More divers had died on *Graf Spee* than any other I knew of in South America. The first had been one of the Royal Navy's top divers. He had been sent down soon after the battle, became entangled, and drowned. He had died while trying to get into the forward 11-inch turret to recover an advanced gyro-firing system that the British did not yet possess. The file that covers this mission is still classified.

⋙ ⋘

At last, Hector spotted a tiny patch of oil on the surface. Since *72* was downriver, the oil had to be coming from another source. After all these years, was *Graf Spee* still leaking oil? They motored over and immediately the small anchor they had been trailing dug into something solid only a few meters below the surface. It had to be *Graf Spee*.

Two of the Uruguayan navy divers suited up and slipped over the side. Within

twenty minutes they were back, one of them brandishing a porthole.

Hector and I had wanted to make our first dives on the *Spee* together, but he was in the tender over the site and I was in *72*. In the interests of time, we decided that he and the third navy diver would go next, and then the tender would come back and take Sergio and me.

Hector was down 45 minutes. Just when I was becoming apprehensive, he and his buddy bobbed up beside the tender. They motored back to *72*.

"Unbelievable," said Hector, grinning from ear to ear, "just awesome." Within seconds, they were out of the tender and Sergio and I and the underwater camera team of Mark Silk and Zena Holloway were in. Hector informed us that the visibility was almost zero and that there were fishing nets toward the stern. "Oh, and watch the current," he added. "It's the worst I have ever experienced."

In my imagination, I had made this journey a thousand times before. Since my father's first story of the battle when I was no older than six, I had been entranced by this great ship and its self-inflicted fate.

Now, here she was, just a few meters below my toes. I was at journey's end.

But it was, in fact, nothing as I had imagined. I had to struggle to pull myself down the buoy-line, which led directly into the eye of the current at an angle of about 40 degrees. The light went out almost as soon as the Plate closed over my head. In my mind's

eye, I had seen myself slicing down through the water, and, as prisms of light played upon the glass of my mask, schools of small exotic fish peeled back to let me through. The reality, however, was disorderly, inelegant, unbeautiful, and dangerous—the kind of diving I hate most.

I could make out the blur of my hand on the rope, but no more. I turned on the light that was attached to one side of my mask; it stabbed about a foot into the darkness. I still could not see anything of the great fighting ship, but I could feel its very presence. If they had not been wet, the hairs on the back of my neck would have been standing on end.

And suddenly, there it was, no more than a dark shadow. Even as I drew to within 18 inches, I had no idea what part of the ship I was looking at. I remembered Hector's words to me over the phone in Oxford: "Mensun, all I have ever wanted is just to touch the *Graf Spee*." I reached out my arm and did just that.

She had worked her way down into the mud. On the day of her death, some of her superstructure had remained above water, but by 1950, it too had been drawn under.

I let go of the rope, grabbed hold of the wreck, and hand over hand moved in what I thought to be a northerly direction, feeling for something, anything, that would give me an idea of where I was. Although I couldn't see any more than a couple of feet of the ship, it made me feel small.

There seemed to be a lot of openings and torn metal—far more than could have been caused by the battle and the later explosions. I knew that two months after the battle, four British undercover agents were sent to Uruguay to recover whatever secret equipment they could. They had traveled on false passports, posing as scrap merchants.

The only one alive today is Ken Purvis, a naval architect, who at the time was working in the "naval construction" division at Whitehall. In Uruguay, his party was met by two other agents, one of whom was the radar specialist Bainbridge Bell, an assistant to the radar pioneer Sir Robert Watson-Watt. Ironically, when Purvis, Bell, and company did their work, the British actually owned *Graf Spee*, having bought her for scrap for under £20,000 from the German government, via a South American intermediary known to Purvis only as "Vegas." Purvis told me that during the secret mission they salvaged and shipped back to England fifty tons' worth of items.

I directed my light into each gap, looking always for conger eels. Although we

Above, top: The Plate provided poor to no visibility on most days. It was not as I had pictured the dive in my mind's eye.
Bottom: A Uruguayan navy diver holds a porthole, one of our first finds on the wreck.

were well within the tidal reaches of the Plate, the water was quite fresh. Too fresh, I hoped, to support such malevolent life forms. Ten years earlier, I had seen what a conger could do to a diver's forearm—his flesh had been shredded to the muscle. When reasonably satisfied that the holes were unoccupied, I reached in and tentatively felt around.

I came upon a particularly large open area full of tubes from which dangled empty lagging clips, and for the first time I knew where I was. These were pipes from the funnel —I was behind the control tower. But the funnel itself, as well as the platform it supported for searchlights and antiaircraft guns, was not there. It must have been salvaged.

Not daring to let go for fear of being swept away, I moved toward what I judged to be the port side of the vessel. Suddenly, I found myself on the edge of a black chasm. Either it was the side of the wreck or a very large hole in her hull. Going into wrecks in minimum visibility makes me nervous: as you move along, feeling apprehensive but itching to know more, you can move into a covered section without knowing it; a wreck can close

over you like a Venus flytrap, and when you try to find your way out, you can't.

I pulled myself over the edge of the precipice and let myself fall feet first. Almost immediately, the current began to fade away and I was in dead water. For the first time in the dive, I began to fin.

I was well into my dive and was becoming concerned that I might not be able to find my way back to the line. If I had to make a dash for the surface in the current overhead, and if the inflatable did not see me, my next stop could be Africa. I headed back up the ship's side and soon was back in the clawing, raging torrent and the twisted metal of the vessel's upper structure. Holding on to the ship, I moved back in the general direction from which I had come. Suddenly, I heard a series of metallic clangs. Worried that Sergio was signaling me for help, I pulled myself toward the sound. I hadn't gone very far when I came upon him hammering the barnacles off what appeared to be the business end of a gun barrel.

It wasn't big enough to be from the vessel's main 11-inch turrets, yet it was too big to be from one of her antiaircraft guns. It had to be one of the barrels from her side armament of 180-mm guns. I stayed with Sergio until we surfaced.

As we motored back to 72, I felt raw and energized. Certainly, it had been a nerve-jangling dive, but it was not as if I had broken the depth barrier or achieved some other death-defying feat. It was purely due to the fact that I had at last been down to *Graf Spee*. I had to admit that there had been no genuine archeological purpose to the dive, that there were no great historical issues to be resolved. The least-selfish claim I could make was that by diving and filming the wreck, we had lifted, for a moment, the veil on a momentous drama that had been forgotten by the world.

My mind went back to Sergio's great gun, and the thought that we had been toying with as we studied *Graf Spee*'s anchor came back: Would it not be wonderful to recover one of her guns? What a memorial it would be!

≈≈≈

Our euphoria was not long-lived. A short time after we reached the bridge of *72*, the radio crackled to life with a priority message from naval command in Montevideo: "Return to port immediately." Just to be sure, it was repeated three times.

Hector and I looked at each other in disbelief. The captain looked at me apologetically and reached for the microphone.

A tanker on its way to Argentina had hit a submerged rock at the entrance to the Plate. Oil was spilling from the ship and was threatening the seal population on the nature reserve of Isla de los Lobos—within sight of where my team was working on Nelson's *Agamemnon*.

The divers vented their disappointment, but the captain gave his orders and *72* returned to Montevideo, where Captain Braeda confirmed that the oil slick was very serious indeed—*72* could be away many days. I could not believe my bad luck—without the help of the navy and their ships, we would not be able to carry out the exploration and survey of the *Spee*. But Braeda was as interested in the *Spee* as any of us; if there was a solution, he would find it. After a few long moments of thought, he said he would let us have a little flat-top powered barge. It was low in the water, had no shelter, and could only be used in dead calm. We could use that, and, in the meantime, he would discuss the situation with his superiors.

The next day, we went out on the barge, but it was patently unsuitable for the task. We needed something bigger and more stable.

Below: **Montevideo harbor, where the drama unfolded. Admiral Raeder: "Hitler was greatly in favor of a breakthrough attempt which he hoped would meet with enemy losses." Langsdorff: "A thousand young men alive are worth more than a thousand dead heroes."**

Above: Oil-soaked seals on Isla de los Lobos, near the *Agamemnon* site. The spill threatened the sea lion population, and the *Graf Spee* dive schedule.

After that, we were given the tugboat *Alejandro Gomez*; of all the vessels we used in our dives on the *Spee*, this was the one most suited to our needs. It was fast, powerful, and agile, and its crew of six became very much part of the team.

Because of the currents and bad visibility, work on *Graf Spee* was very slow indeed. It was, said our cameraman, like trying to understand Wembley Stadium with only a microscope to look through. Nonetheless, a picture of the vessel was slowly beginning to emerge. She was listing heavily to starboard and was fairly deep in the mud, and it seemed to me—for not everybody agreed with this—that her hull was contorted or twisted on its axis. Her upper works had all either collapsed to starboard or, like the funnel, had disappeared altogether.

Her great forward turret was still there, and at least four of her 5.9-inch medium artillery pieces were found. Her great 11-inch after, the so-called B or Bruno turret, was gone completely. This was not surprising, as it had contained one of the charges that had sent the ship to the bottom.

To help us better understand the wreck, we brought in Klein Associates, the leaders in the field of sidescan sonar research. They sent out from the States some of their latest equipment, along with their best operator, Gary Kosak, one of the world's great talents with sidescan sonar. He had already become somewhat famous for his work on two great underwater tragedies, the famous *Ti-tanic* and TWA Flight 800, which exploded over Long Island Sound. Now he was going to use his gear on *Graf Spee*.

Sidescan sonar images are obtained by towing a submerged torpedo-shaped sonar "fish" across the area to be sounded. The fish emits sound pulses—the *pings* familiar from submarine films—whose echoes are relayed to a computer. Because the soundings are angled, each pass provides some overlapping, which the computer can use to construct an image of the seabed—and a three-dimensional view of objects upon it. Using this technology, Gary would give us our first real look at *Graf Spee*.

In his diary, *Graf Spee*'s Hans Götz noted his impression that in her destruction, the stern had been broken off. We ourselves were also beginning to think this, and Gary's scans confirmed it beyond doubt. The stern had been sliced clean off, leaving a gap that you could drive a truck through. Furthermore, it was exactly where the B turret should have been. Clearly, the explosion that had blown a column of fire high into the twilight sky had also blasted downward with equal ferocity, igniting the reserve charges in the ammunition lobby and magazine below the gun.

❧

As we dived, we continued to ponder the possibility of lifting one of *Graf Spee*'s guns, but the resources necessary to do so were lacking. The big breakthrough came from a meeting that I had with the president of Uruguay, Mario Julio Sanguinetti. The purpose of the meeting was ostensibly to discuss the *Agamemnon* and the proposed recovery of the Trafalgar cannon. Our conversation, though, soon drifted to our work on *Graf Spee*. The president was eager to learn what she was like and how much of her was left. As a boy, he also had been taken down to the waterfront to witness her departure and the shootout that all presumed would follow. Would it be possible to recover, in addition, one of her guns? he asked. At last we had it—the presidential seal. With that, I knew it *would* be possible.

We communicated the president's desires to Braeda, Cabot, and Medina. They were pleased, but reminded me that because this was out of their original terms of reference, it would have to be formalized on paper by higher authority.

By that time, I had gone as far as I could on the *Graf Spee* survey without putting the divers at unnecessary risk. Although much time had been lost to bad weather, the work on the *Agamemnon* at Maldonado had been going well and the Trafalgar cannon would soon be ready for lifting. I decided to move the skeleton team in Montevideo up to Maldonado. We had about 10 days left before we had to leave Uruguay. There was a lot to do if we were going to complete the surveys on schedule and lift two large, heavy guns.

Hector gave voice to everyone's question: Which of the *Graf Spee* cannons would we lift? What I really wanted, of course, was A turret, the huge artillery piece that swept the foredeck with its three great 11-inch barrels. The scans had shown that the barrels were still in position and pointing slightly upward. The problem was weight—with all its protective armor, the turret could weigh around a hundred tons.

Even if we could find a crane capable of lifting it at sea, how would we be able to transport and manipulate such a dead weight of metal once ashore? Moreover, the deck and turret were listing to starboard in such a way that a straight lift would have been difficult without the use of explosives. This I was reluctant to do, because, in the words of Commander Rasenack, he had left the turret as "just one big explosive charge."

Before leaving *Graf Spee*, Commander Rasenack had put his ceremonial sword inside the turret, expecting it to be vaporized by the explosion. It was still there, and I briefly entertained the hope of recovering it and returning it to its owner, who was in his eighties and living in a town in Córdoba Province, Argentina. Hector, Sergio, and I had tried to penetrate the turret, but with memories of the Royal Navy diver who had died attempting the same, we

Mensun, Gary Kosak, and Sergio with divers from the Uruguayan navy.

Above, top: Charts of the Plate are never permanent documents—the strong currents and shifting sands make it as much a ship-eater as the Goodwin Sands of the English Channel. *Bottom:* Gary Kosak's side-scan sonar works by towing a "fish," which emits and receives sound signals that give a profile of anything above the level of the seabed.

gave up. If we were going to raise a gun, it had to be a 5.9-inch cannon from her side artillery.

〜〜〜

The next day, I left for Punta del Este in a helicopter of the Uruguayan air force. As we flew along the edge of the Plate, the captain told me that the helicopter was a veteran of the American armed forces and that its logbook showed that it had seen extensive action in Vietnam. Since that was to be my next place of work, I was naturally interested. Swooping in low over Maldonado, I could see our boats at work on both the *Agamemnon* and *Salvador*. Things were clearly going well.

Not so with the bureaucracy in Montevideo, however, where the authorizations for the use of the boats and equipment necessary to raise the *Graf Spee* and *Agamemnon* guns were not being signed. Part of the problem was that it was the holiday season, and key politicians, admirals, and civil servants were on vacation. Every day, Hector and I were on the phone, but progress was glacial.

Even with the president's approval, nobody seemed willing or able to take the first step toward mobilizing the ship we would need on the *Agamemnon* or the lifting barge required for *Graf Spee*. In government, as in the military, careers could be ruined if such projects failed.

We decided to make one last effort. The team split up—some headed for Montevideo and contacted the Admiralty, while we in Punta del Este contacted the ministries of the interior, armed services, culture, and tourism. It worked. By midday the following day, we knew that the navy's dive and engineering ship *Sirius* was preparing to leave; by 5 P.M., we knew also that orders had been given to mobilize the crane barge and three tugs.

That evening, a colleague from Oxford asked why I wasn't smiling, for I had, after all, just been given everything I had asked for. I explained that we had just one day to succeed with each lift. Statistically, there was a two-in-three likelihood of the weather being too troubled to permit such dangerous and delicate recovery work, and there would be no second chances. If we succeeded in lifting both guns, it would be on the order of a minor miracle.

As told in the last chapter, *Sirius* did arrive in Punta del Este and, after some knuckle-biting, we recovered the Trafalgar cannon. We left Bryan Smith and half of the team behind in Punta to complete the work in Maldonado Bay, while the rest of us crammed into the government vans and headed back to

Montevideo, ready to go out the next day to prepare the *Graf Spee* gun for lifting on the following day.

The next day, however, saw the Plate too rough for the *Gomez* to put out. It was a *pampero*, one of the storms that come tearing down from the southern Andes, cross the *pampas*, and whip the great river into a frenzy.

Stuck in port, I arranged a meeting on the crane barge with its master to discuss the lifting of the cannon. Although he knew that I was coming, the barge master was not there when I arrived. Not to worry, I was told —as long as we got off on time, we could discuss the details on the way to the site. In hindsight, I should have been more concerned, but I was not.

Because there was nothing I could do, I went with Omar Medina to meet with some of the *Graf Spee* survivors. Quite by chance, one of the ship's gunners, Günter Schroeder, had just arrived in Uruguay from Germany. He was in his late seventies, and, although very sprightly, this, he said, would be his last visit to his old mates from the River Plate.

We met at the home of Hans Ghann. The house bore plenty of reminders of his Bavarian origins, but there were no pictures of *Graf Spee* or anything else that might remind him of the drama through which he had lived. With Hans, who was in his eighties and very frail, we went on to meet two more of the survivors. The four old men converged shakily on one another, while wives on both sides held back.

With the veterans we went to the set where the filmmakers were reenacting a scene for which they had fabricated a replica of the ship's ensign, with a swastika at center. Like most people, I feel extremely uncomfortable near this symbol, but I was curious to see how these old men would react to it. Clearly they did not share my disgust, and I wondered why.

The more I thought about it, though, the more I felt I understood. They had been boys in 1939, straight from school into the navy. The hideous truths at the center of National Socialism would probably have escaped them. Likewise, for them, the war ended almost before it had started—they left Europe before it had been declared and returned after it was over.

For them, this was not a symbol of Naziism, but their ship's battle flag, the flag they fought under, not so much for Hitler, but for the

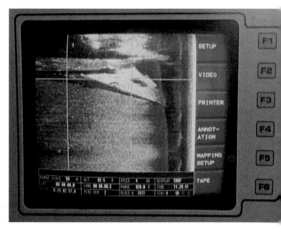

Below and overleaf: The sidescan sonar readouts helped us solve the mystery of *Graf Spee*'s stern—it had been blown several yards away by the explosion of her stern turret.

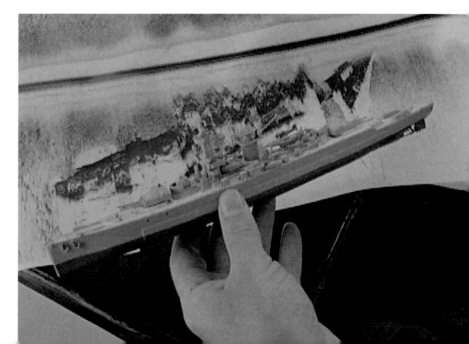

tilla to reach the site, an hour to establish our moorings, 90 minutes to locate and buoy the cannon, two hours to harness and tie it, and, finally, two hours to perform the lift. Braeda explained that the crane barge would have to be on its way by 4:30 P.M. in order to be back in port by dark. It was our absolute deadline, so to make it we had to be under way by 7:00 A.M.

By the early hours of the morning, the storm had blown itself out. At 5:00, I was on the roof of the Victoria Plaza with glasses. The sea was lumpy, but the forecast was good.

An hour later, we were all assembled in the Navy Yard with all our gear. The navy divers were already there, as were a number of senior officers, government VIPs, and press. Our old ship, *72*, was back from clearing up the oil slick on Isla de los Lobos, and the *Gomez* was along, too, with a couple of other boats that I had not seen before to carry the press. The crane and its heavy towing tugs were a couple of kilometers away, down at the far end of the harbor. Any minute now, they would appear. We waited.

And we waited and we waited. The minutes turned into hours. The naval officers were fuming; the divers were tense and irritable. We contacted the barge by radio. Instantly there were raised voices. After a while,

Above: **Mensun and Gary Kosak study the sidescan sonar outputs as the survey boat passes over *Graf Spee*.**

Fatherland, and, perhaps even more to the point, for their captain. The Battle of the River Plate, coming so early in the war, was not for them about hatreds and politics, it was basic mortal combat between professional fighting men. It involved all the classic bromides of men at war: weaponcraft, honor, and raw courage. Speaking to the survivors, from both sides, reveals no real enmity between them then, and certainly none now.

Günter was clearly the fittest and most robust of the old warriors, so I invited him to join us for the recovery—if the weather allowed it to proceed.

❧

That evening, Hector, Sergio, and I met with Captain Cabot and spoke by phone to Braeda. We all recognized that there was a lot to do for just one day: it would take three hours for the crane and the accompanying flo-

one of the officers came over to report. He looked at me apologetically, and said, "The *jefe* of the barge is being a *difficult* man."

Not until late morning did the great lifting barge lumber into view, pulled by two tugs. It was huge. It had been built in Poland and was rated for lifts of more than 100 tons. As it drew near, it gave us a perfunctory little blast of its whistle. That the greeting was not returned said *everything* of the feeling on board our ship.

We were never given any reason for the late departure, but it was the common view that those in charge of the barge simply could not be bothered. One thing was certain—we were now in trouble. We no longer had the luxury of finding Sergio's gun, and, even if we did, there would not be time to harness it properly. We would have to take the most expedient path presented to us.

When we got there, the *Gomez* nosed alongside the barge, and several of us jumped on board. I immediately went to the control room to discuss our problems and the situation in general with the barge master. He immediately made it clear that he didn't much care for the task at hand, didn't like the military, didn't like archeologists (or was it foreigners?), and didn't like being told what to do.

Every second was at a premium. We would have to take the first available gun, sling it, and just hope it came away cleanly and that the cables did not slip. From that moment on, there was no proper consultation; everything was done in whispers, winks, and covert nods.

In addition to the engineering and archeological side of things, I had also to think of the film crews and their needs. If the gun were to come up, it would be an important moment in Uruguayan history, and everybody wanted it recorded on film. There were two camera units on the surface and one underwater. They had to work out their camera positions, moves, and angles; they needed establishing shots, and for every action sequence, there had to be a master take as well as a medium and a wide angle.

All this required coordination with the divers, the navy, the archeologists, and, above all, the crane operator and barge master. The film director, Matthew Wortman, was at the end of a long shoot and he had very little film left. Every frame had to count.

❧

More than anything else in life, I hate foul-ups. In operations of this nature and magnitude, I like everything planned to the tiniest detail: every piece of equipment has to be tested, everything timed to schedule, every move rehearsed and re-rehearsed. But here we were without any real preparation. We had only three hours, and much of that would be taken up with position-fixing and mooring.

Finally, the barge winched itself tight beside the wreck, and the first divers went down. They were navy divers who had been chosen for their familiarity with the wreck.

Below, top: The 150-ton crane barge, whose captain almost aborted the lift at the last second.
Bottom: President Sanguinetti put the resources of the Uruguayan armed forces—including an ex-Vietnam helicopter—at the team's disposal. Without them, the recovery would not have been possible.

But if these divers did not succeed in locating a gun, then Hector, Tom, Sergio, and I would try—if *we* failed, it was over. The crane would have to leave in order to make Montevideo by nightfall.

Just as we were preparing to suit up, the divers suddenly appeared at the top of the buoy line. They had found one of the cannons, but did not know which one it was or even where they were on the wreck. Part of the gun was covered by deformed pieces of collapsed metalwork, but otherwise, the gun itself appeared to be free.

The dive had taken an hour, so we had no choice but to go for the lift and hope that all of the entangled metal pieces would just fall away. I asked them if they could put a secure harness around the gun so that there would be no chance of slippage.

What I feared was the gun emerging from that sea of mud, rising in the air, and then, in plain view of the international press and TV cameras, plunging back into the River Plate, or worse, crashing down on the deck of the barge. As a student, I had worked on the famous *Mary Rose*, and I have never forgotten that awful moment when, as the hull came out of the water, something gave way and the wreck and its lifting cradle fell about two feet. A single bolt had then stood between utter disaster and triumph.

The divers understood my fears, but to securely truss and harness the gun would take at least an hour, on top of the hour needed to perform the actual lift. We didn't have

hours—we barely had minutes. All we could do was wrap the cable, begin the lift, and hope that it held. Because the navy divers were familiar with the gun and its surroundings, I asked if they would complete the job. Without hesitation, they all agreed.

They donned full tanks and again went over the side. After ten minutes or so, they emerged and told us that they were ready to begin slinging the gun.

The great crane cranked to life, cogs meshed, drums turned, cables as thick as a man's wrist went taut, and, slowly at first, there was movement. Then it stopped for the divers to wrestle the cables onto the gun, shackle the ends, and hook it on to the crane.

The crane again began to rumble. It brought in the slack and the lines went rigid as they took the strain of over 30 tons. Cameras clicked, and people began talking in an animated manner. I looked at the faces—everybody else was clearly delighted that something was at last happening. As for me, I felt almost physically sick from anxiety: this was a textbook example of how *not* to raise a gun from a site. Until that gun was safely lying on the deck, I would not relax.

The gun could not have risen by more than a meter or two when suddenly the ca-

Opposite: On the last attempt, the sea crane lifts one of the *Graf Spee*'s 5.9-inch (150 mm), Krupp-made cannon from the River Plate. The delicacy of the huge crane surprised everybody as the great gun softly touched the deck.

Below: Hector Bado celebrates the recovery of the cannon.

ble went limp. Hector and I exchanged glances. I looked across to the three senior naval officers on board; they, too, realized that something had gone wrong. I looked back to the bridge. Through the glass, I could see the barge master shouting into a handset.

Everyone else, though, was acting very much as before, apparently assuming that this was all part of the plan. What plan? I looked at my watch. We had just under half an hour before the barge would have to start preparing for departure. Just time for one more try.

The tender had by then come alongside. Trying not to show any of the concern I was feeling, I sauntered over. The divers said that they had only been able to put a couple of turns around the end of the barrel. Although the gun appeared to be free of the deck, it was not free from the debris that had prevented them from slinging the gun properly.

Perhaps now that the gun had been moved they could do a better job of it, and from their expressions, it was more than obvious that they wanted another go. It had become for them a matter of pride.

The tender flew back to the anchor buoy, and within seconds, the divers were back in the water. Things proceeded as before, and after fifteen minutes, they returned. I studied their faces with binoculars. This time they looked much happier. Again the crane began the lift.

As if on cue, the current almost died away completely, and it could only have been a couple of minutes before a rust-colored, bar-

nacle-encrusted cylinder end rose a few inches out of the water. For a few seconds, I did not realize that I was looking at the muzzle end of the gun's long barrel. I think that all of us had somehow expected it to come up, if not horizontally, then at least breech first.

As more of the gun emerged, others also realized what they were looking at and began to clap. By the time the entire barrel was visible, the boats were honking and everyone was clapping and cheering.

Everyone, that is, except me, for I had just realized that the only thing holding the gun aloft was a slipknot and a couple of turns of cable on a steeply upward-pointing barrel of diminishing diameter. Friction. It was held by friction. At that moment, I wished I had never heard of *Graf Spee*. I wanted to be anywhere but the River Plate. I yearned for the quiet civility of Oxford. The sound of students in the hall. The feeling you get as you slide a wine decanter across an oaken high table.

〰️

I was aware of people patting my back in congratulation. I even registered some of the words and managed a tight smile, but my eyes were all the time on the cable and its turns about the barrel. It seemed to be holding. Then, just as it was suspended over the deck, the whole gun jackknifed with a sickening lurch. Horrorstruck, I waited for the crash—and the sight of the cannon twisted, broken, and deformed upon the deck. There was an audible collective gasp.

But nothing happened. Again, as if possessed of some life of its own, the gun moved. This time, I realized what had happened—the gun's pivot was still functioning. The gun had simply elevated on its pivot.

With consummate skill and precision, the crane operator laid the gun gently upon the deck. If ever the gods had smiled on me, it was that day, that hour, that minute. Everything had been poised for disaster, but it had not come to pass.

While everybody had been focused on the gun, several of the nearby boats had snuck alongside and discharged their passengers onto the crane barge. When the gun touched down, the crew gave up trying to hold the spectators back, and everybody rushed forward, cheering. There, too, was Hector, alongside me with a smile splitting his face. Then, for a second, he became serious. "From this second on we are custodians of the *Graf Spee* legend." I understood. The few survivors of the battle who were left would not be around for much longer. I looked over at Günter, who had actually stood behind one of these Krupp-made masterpieces—maybe this very one—raining three rounds a minute down on the British cruisers. He was in the middle of a group of journalists; overcome by emotion, the tears were pouring down his face—but through them, he was smiling.

Suddenly, the barge master materialized. He was beaming from ear to ear. We shook hands and, in a very Latin way, we embraced. All was forgiven. He, Braeda, Cabot,

Above: Carlos Coirolo and his son study the *Graf Spee* cannon, which has been restored and put on display in a Montevideo park.

the divers, Günter, Hector, Sergio, Carlos, Tom, and I all lined up for photographs. I felt physically and emotionally wrung out—but the day was ours.

THE LAST SHOT

The last shot in the Battle of the River Plate wasn't fired off Montevideo, but upriver, in Buenos Aires, a few days before that melancholy Christmas of 1939. The day after *Graf Spee*'s scuttling, the tugs *Gigante* and *Coloso* had been met in the Argentine capital by small boats carrying friends from the large German community there, who gave the exhausted, famished sailors bread and fresh fruit. But if there was any celebration, it was short-lived, for the next day Langsdorff learned from the German ambassador, Baron von Thermann, that he and his crew would not be considered shipwrecked sailors, as they had requested, and would therefore have to be

CAPTAIN HANS LANGSDORFF

Keystone Pres

(MY OPPINION)
A GOOD. HUMANE MAN.
BUT NOT THE SORT
OF MAN TO COMMAND A WARSHIP

interned. Langsdorff could do nothing further for crew, country, or self.

That evening, he assembled his men for the last time. He told them that, contrary to what some newspapers were saying, he had not lacked the courage to make a final stand against the British, but that such a stand would have killed many, if not all, of them. Then he reminded his men of the sad duties they had performed at the cemetery in Montevideo. They might, he said, have had to do that again. As he left with some of this senior officers, he was approached by journalists. "There is no story tonight," he reportedly told them. "But there will probably be a big one for you in the morning."

Afterward, he joined some of his officers and staff from the German embassy in the senior officers' mess of the arsenal near the North Dock, where they were billeted. According to Lieutenant Dietrich, Langsdorff had been quite at ease until they broke up at about midnight. Back in his room, he lit a cigar and poured himself some of his favorite Scotch whisky. Then he wrote three letters, one to his wife, one to his parents, and one to Baron von Thermann:

> After a long inward struggle, I reached the grave decision to scuttle the pocket-battleship *Graf Spee* in order to prevent her falling into the hands of the enemy. I am convinced that under the circumstances this decision was the only one that I could make after I had taken my ship into

the trap of Montevideo. With the ammunition remaining, any attempt to break out to open and deep water was bound to fail. And yet only in deep water could I have scuttled the ship after having used the remaining ammunition, so preventing her falling into the hands of the enemy.

Rather than expose my ship to the danger, after her fight, of falling into enemy hands, I decided not to fight, but to destroy the equipment and sink the ship. It was clear to me that this decision might be misinterpreted whether intentionally or unwittingly by persons ignorant of my motives as being attributable partly or entirely to personal considerations. Therefore, I decided from the beginning to bear the consequences involved in this decision. A captain with a sense of honor cannot separate his own fate from that of his ship.

I postponed my intentions as long as I was still responsible for the welfare of the crew under my command. After today's decision of the Argentine Government, I can do no more for my ship's company. Neither will I be able to take an active part in the present conflict of my country. Now I can only prove by my death that the fighting services of the Third Reich are ready to die for their flag.

I alone bear the responsibility for scuttling the pocket-battleship *Admiral Graf Spee*. I am happy to pay with my life to prevent any possible reflection on the honor of the flag. I shall meet my fate with firm faith in the cause and the future of the nation and of my Führer.

He signed it "LANGSDORFF, captain, commanding officer of the sunk pocket battleship *Admiral Graf Spee*."

Langsdorff sealed and addressed the letters. Then he unfolded *Graf Spee*'s battle ensign and spread it on the floor beside his bed. Lying on the flag he still hoped to honor, he raised a Mauser pistol to his head and fired. The next morning, Dietrich found his captain's body stretched out on the bloody flag.

Hans Wilhelm Langsdorff was buried the following afternoon, December 21, in the German cemetery of Buenos Aires. His officers and crew were there, shaken and subdued by their loss. Argentine officials also attended, as did the German ambassador. Even *Ashlea*'s Captain Pottinger was there, representing the men who had been held prisoner aboard the *Graf Spee*.

Hans Langsdorff's grave— his final testament read, "A captain with a sense of honor cannot separate his own fate from that of his ship." One of his men said, years later, "A thousand young men owe him their lives."

Buenos Aires, 1939

Above and inset, top: After being patched up in the Falklands, *Exeter* limped back under heavy escort to Plymouth, arriving on February 15, 1940. Winston Churchill, First Lord of the Admiralty, congratulated her ship's company for having fought a battle "in the old style . . . this great action will long be told in song and story."

HANS LANGSDORFF'S LEGACY

Our time in Uruguay was over, but before returning to England, there was something I had to do. Early on the morning following the recovery of the cannon, I took the ferry to Buenos Aires. I was met at the dock by a friend who took me to the German cemetery.

Throughout my time in Uruguay, I had been struggling to understand Langsdorff,

whom the South American papers were that morning calling the "last corsair." At one level, it was fairly simple: his vessel had been the subject of the greatest shiphunt in history, and when it was over, Langsdorff had fought a brief but epic battle that would go down in the annals of naval warfare as the "last broadside." Finding himself trapped and with little prospect of fighting his way to freedom, the captain decided to scuttle his ship rather than risk her falling into the hands of his country's enemy.

But there was more to it than that; for men like Langsdorff, whom Churchill described as a "high-class person" there were other issues at stake—principles and human values that meant more to him than the cause for which he was fighting . . . even more to him than his own life.

In his youth, he had wanted to become a priest. For a man of his integrity and compassion, that might have been the better vocation. But he grew up in Dusseldorf, in the shadow of Admiral Graf von Spee's castle, and so it was perhaps ordained instead that he ended up in the Imperial German Navy, whose officer class had an almost religious devotion to honor, courage, discipline, and chivalry. The virtues of the *ancien régime* might have suited him well in peacetime, but, truly, he was not by nature a fighting man in the tradition of Nelson or Sulla. Apart from a love for the Fatherland, he had little relish for the war in which he found himself.

Certainly he would have had no sympathy for the expansionist views of Hitler, and, indeed, a man of his sensitivity and keen intelligence already may have glimpsed the black corruption at the heart of National Socialism. His consistent refusal to give the Nazi salute can perhaps be seen as evidence of this. Doubtless, he would have been appalled at the way the old credos of his beloved navy were being eroded and perverted by the new political order in Berlin. Indeed, to some of his

British captives, he plainly questioned the war. To Captain Harris of the *Clement*, he said, "I don't want to fight, so what is the use of it all?" What mattered to Langsdorff were human lives, and, in the end, outside of mortal combat, the only life he took was his own.

When I think of Langsdorff's final days, I am struck by the palpable isolation of the man. In those last hours, he must have been the loneliest man in the world. He was thousands of miles from his wife and children and the country he loved, low on ammunition, with a badly damaged ship, cornered by the enemy, and hostage to an unsympathetic government. With little moral support from the German ambassador and even less from Berlin, he was utterly alone.

For him, the world was his ship full of boy-sailors, of whom he had already buried too many. Commander Diggins, who had stood beside Hans Langsdorff throughout the action and was his only confidant, told me that the captain was like a father to him and all the crew. "We loved him and would have followed him anywhere," he told me. Langsdorff knew this, and he also knew that if he took *Graf Spee* out for a fight to the finish, a great many of these boys would die.

Whose possible purpose would be served?

Even if he succeeded in sinking one of the British ships, it would have made little strategic impact on the war. His mission had been to sink the enemy's merchant ships, disrupt its supply lines, and tie up its capital ships, and this he had done, in Churchill's words, with "daring and imagination"—but at the end, that was all over. Now it was a matter of lives. Langsdorff had fought in the Battle of Jutland, the greatest naval battle of World War I; he had seen the carnage and knew that there was no glory in death, just suffering and waste.

Only two years before, he had been shattered by the death of his own son, a child no more than a schoolboy. Grief still ached within him. How could he needlessly inflict that on other parents? His own time might, *must*, be over, but the lives of his young men were still within his gift.

They might not at the time have understood their Captain's situation or appreciated his final act, but later they did. Hans Götz, the engine-room mechanic, wrote that "a thousand young men had to thank him for their lives," while Jürgen Wattenberg said, "Many women and children thank him today for his decision." The same sentiment was expressed by British veterans of the action. Eric Smith, of the *Ajax*, spoke to me of the gratitude he felt to Langsdorff. Many British would have died that day if *Graf Spee* had come out fighting.

Despite all this, for a man of Langsdorff's sense of honor, there was a price to be paid. For having declined battle, and then not having gone down with his ship, there would, he knew, have been whispers of cowardice. Honor—that of his family, his ship, his crew, and the navy—could only be redeemed by his own sacrifice, proof that his final decisions were not those of a coward.

From the invasion of Poland to that final night in his room in Buenos Aires, only 111 days had passed. Standing over his grave, I wondered what he had written in that last letter to the wife and children he would never see again. What, I wondered, was he trying to say by that deliberate act of lying down upon his ship's battle ensign to take his life? Later, back in England, I saw formerly top-secret British government documents on the battle. One of the reports also described the suicide. It mentioned that he had fired two shots. The first had grazed the back of his head. Perhaps his hand was shaking.

MARCH 28, 1997
MADRID, SPAIN

I met up with members of the team in Buenos Aires. We were all booked on a flight to Madrid, where we were to catch a connecting flight to London. Our flight, however, was delayed, and, as a result, we were stuck for twelve hours in Madrid. While walking around the airport, trying to stay awake, I bought a copy of the *Times*. The first thing I saw when I opened it was a large, color photograph of the crane barge lifting the gun. So I came full circle: the adventure of *Graf Spee* had begun with an article in the *Times*; it now ended with an article in the *Times*. ❏

Madrid, 1997

Photo/Illustration Credits

Title page: Frank Boxler (FB). **Copyright page**: courtesy Mensun Bound (MB). **Contents page**: *background*–courtesy Zev Guber Productions/Bibo-TV (ZGP/B); *top*–MB; *second from top*–courtesy Rheinisches Landesmuseum, Bonn, FRG (RL); *third from top*–National Maritime Museum, Greenwich, UK (NMaM); *bottom*–Christie's/MB. 7: MB. 8–9: *all*–MB.

Galley of the Gods

10: *main*–FB; *inset*–RL. 11: Zev Guber Productions (ZGP). 12: *maps*–MB; *bottom*–ZGP. 13: *inset*–UPI/CorbisBettman; *bottom right*–courtesy HarperCollins. 14: *clockwise from top left*–Zena Holloway (ZH); Richard T. Nowitz/Corbis; MB. 15: *background*–MB; *inset*–RL. 16: Richard Hamilton Smith/Corbis. 17: *both*–ZGP/B. 18: ZGP. 19: FB. 20: *left*–RL; *right*–Roger Wood/© Corbis. 21: RL. 22: *all*–RL. 23: ZGP/B. 24: *all*–RL. 25: *statue*–RL; *texture*–MB. 26: *all*–RL. 27: *all*–ZGP/B. 28: *statues*–RL; *texture*–MB. 29: *both*–RL. 30: MB. 31: *both*–ZGP. 32: ZGP/B. 33: MB. 34: *amphorae*–RL; *background*–Austrian Archives/Corbis (AA/C). 35: MB. 36-37: *all*–RL. 38: *background*–RL. 39: *upper right and inset*–ZGP/B; *lower right*–RL. 40-41: *all*–MB. 42-43: *both*–MB. 44: *column*–FB; *texture*–MB. 45: MB. 46: *upper left*–FB; *lower left*–MB. 47: *upper right*–FB; *bottom*–ZH. 48: FB. 49: *upper right*–ZGP/B; *lower right*–MB. 50: *upper left*–MB; *lower left*–ZGP/B. 51: *both*–FB. 52: *both*–FB. 53: *background*–MB; *upper and lower right*–ZH. 54: *background and lower left*–MB; *upper left*–ZH. 55: MB.

Ghost of Trafalgar

56: ZGP. 57: NMaM. 58: *upper left*–Jean-Pierre Banowicz (JPB); *lower left, top and bottom*–MB. 59: Conway's Maritime Press, London, UK (Con). 60: *both*–National Motor Museum, Beaulieu, Hants, UK (NMoM). 61: *both*–ZGP/B. 63: NMoM. 64: Adam Woolfit/Corbis (AW/C). 65: *top*–MB; *bottom*–ZGP/B. 66: MB. 67: *both*–MB. 69: *both*–MB. 70: ZGP. 71: Michael Busselle/Corbis. 72: MB. 73: MB. 74: Geoff Hunt (GH). 75: MB. 76: *top*–ZGP/B; *bottom*–MB. 77: *both*–MB. 78: *top left*–MB; *bottom*–ZGP/B; *background*–NMoM. 79: *upper right*–Corbis-Bettman (C-B); *bottom*–NMaM. 80: *left*–Historical Picture Archives/Corbis (HPA/C); *inset oval*–NMaM. 81: NMaM. 82: *left*–HPA/C; *upper left*–MB; *lower right*–Corbis/Philadelphia Museum of Art. 83: Hulton-Deutsch Collection/Corbis (H-DC/C). 84: *upper left*–MB; *bottom*–C-B. 85: *both*–MB. 86: NMaM. 87: *inset oval*–AA/C. 88: *upper*–HPA/C; *lower*–NMaM. 89: HPA/C. 90-91: NMaM. 92: *main*–MB; *inset*–NMaM. 93: *upper right*–Con; *bottom*–NMaM. 94: *left, top and bottom*–NMaM; *background*–MB. 95: MB. 96: ZGP. 97: NMaM. 98: *left*–GH; *lower right*–ZGP. 99: *top*–ZH; *bottom*–ZGP. 100: *left, top to bottom*–MB, MB, ZGP/B, MB; *background*–MB. 101: MB. 102-103: *all*–MB. 104: *clockwise from top left*–MB, MB, MB, ZGP/B. 105: ZGP. 106: MB. 107: *top to bottom*–ZGP/B, FB, MB. 108: *background*–ZGP; *left to right*–MB, JPB, MB. 109: *counter-clockwise from bottom left*–MB, MB, ZH.

The Dive for the *Graf Spee*

110: The National Archives/Corbis (NA/C). 111: *inset*–Christie's/MB. 113: *inset oval*–WZ-Bilddienst, FRG (WZB); *right*–MB. 114-115: *all*–MB. 116: *all*–MB. 117: *both*–MB. 118: MB. 119: Bibliotek für Zeitgeschichte, Stuttgart, FRG (BfZ). 120: *top left*–H-DC/C; *bottom left*–NA/C; *background*–BfZ. 122: NA/C. 123: *top right*–courtesy George Deacon (GD); *bottom right*–WZB; *lower oval*–ZGP/B. 124: *bottom*–NA/C; *background*–WZB. 125: C-B. 126: *map and upper inset*–GD (modified by Brian Liu); *lower inset*–H-DC/C. 127: GD. 128: *upper left*–GD; *background*–WZB. 130-131: *both*–GD. 132: *top left*–WZB; *background*–National Archives. 133: GD. 134-135: *both*–GD. 136-137: *all*–GD. 138-139: *both*–GD. 140: Christies/MB. 141: *both*–GD. 142-143: *both*–GD. 144: *upper left*–MB; *background*–MB. 146: MB. 147: *top to bottom*–GD, GD, NA/C. 148: MB. 149: GD. 150: *all*–GD. 152: GD. 153: *both*–NA/C. 154: *top left*–GD; *bottom left*–MB. 155: Library of Congress/Corbis. 156: GD. 157: *top to bottom*–GD, GD, H-DC/C, H-DC/C. 158: *both*–GD. 159: H-DC/C. 160-161: ZGP. 162: *top left oval*–ZGP; *bottom*–GD. 163: *all*–GD. 164: ZGP. 165: *top right*–ZGP/B; *lower right*–MB. 166: *upper*–ZGP; *lower*–MB. 167: MB. 168: *left top and bottom*–JPB; *background*–MB. 169: ZH. 170: *upper*–ZH; *lower*–MB. 171: *all*–MB. 172: *all*–ZH. 173: *upper*–MB; *lower*–ZH. 174: *clockwise from top*–JPB, JPB, ZGP, JPB, ZGP, JPB, JPB. 175: JPB. 176-177: *all*–MB. 178: *main*–GD; *background*–MB. 179: MB. 180: *main*–GD; *inset*–H-DC/C. 181: GD. 182: *top*–H-DC/C; *bottom*–GD.